FOR THE FUTURE

For the Future

Poems & essays in honour of
J.H. Prynne
on the occasion
of his 80th Birthday

Edited by
Ian Brinton

Shearsman Books

Published in the United Kingdom in 2016 by
Shearsman Books Ltd
50 Westons Hill Drive
Emersons Green
BRISTOL
BS16 7DF

Shearsman Books Ltd Registered Office
30–31 St. James Place, Mangotsfield, Bristol BS16 9JB
(this address not for correspondence)

ISBN 978-1-84861-490-1
First Edition

Cover image, 'For JHP 1996-2006', copyright © Ian Friend, 2016.
Photograph by Mick Richards.

CONTENTS

A Hand-Out for the Future

Ian Brinton

When the first Bloodaxe edition of the *Poems* of J.H. Prynne appeared in 1999 it was dedicated 'A la mémoire de Bernard Dubourg'. Dubourg had translated quite a few of Prynne's early poems into French, most notably *Poèmes de Cuisine* (1975), *Séquentiel Diurne I, Chansons A La Journée-Lumière* (1975) and *Séquentiel Diurne 2, Lézard de Feu*. These collections were privately printed by Dubourg at Damazan 'sur la presse à main du traducteur'. In 1977 the magazine *Prospice* 7 published some further translations which both poets had worked on, 'Royal Fern', 'The Five Hindrances', 'Cool as a Mountain Stream' and 'Pigment Depôt'. Going on to comment on the art of translation in *Grosseteste Review* 12, 1979, Dubourg suggested that 'To translate is a state, not an act: the state of progression towards a final point already posited. I have often wanted to amend the original; J.H. Prynne has consented once or twice to such corrections: for the rest only dead authors are assailed.' Dubourg concluded his article, a slightly tongue-in-cheek account to which he gave the title 'Some Proposals: To Translate for fancy-readers', with point 20:

> As a provisional ending: to translate is to furnish yourself with the most rash resources of patience, to spend hours on a line of no greater relief than the rest, to jump feet together over another line which exacted from the author—the original— the most finical attention. To translate is in fact to be in on the syllable, and by dint of that, to make sport of the author's own patience. No question of apeing the original: what you do is, you flit.

Writing to Anthony Barnett in November 1975 Prynne highlighted the importance to him of Dubourg's work:

For he is a person of quite extraordinary alertness & finesse, deeply committed to the work of poetry (his own as well as mine); his care for accuracy and for strenuous understanding is quite without parallel. His insights into my texts are more complete than those of any other reader known to me, in any country or from any language. The activity of his mind is strong and completely without evasion—he has given something which approaches dedication to defining the force of my work and to giving a true carriage of it into French. This has involved me in a very great labour of co-operation, still not complete, which I cannot at all begrudge in view of the hugely greater difficulty for him than for me.

In the front of some of the 1999 Bloodaxe copies Prynne had added a hand-written comment addressed 'To each of those friends and promoters of remarkable, precarious and supportive production of books, making the tunes of the age to be heard while out of tune with its jingle, who has assisted some portion of this current bundle to take its place in the passage of years and here in the table of contents, I express my deepest personal thanks; remembering each of you at this moment of somewhat surprised but staunchly grateful retrospection: surprise at the way that slices of text do waymark a life, and gratitude for companionship and adventure along the way.'

When the second, expanded edition of the *Poems* appeared from Bloodaxe in 2005 it bore the dedication 'For Edward Dorn his brilliant luminous shade', words which echoed those the author had inscribed on 14 April, 1999, on the flyleaf of the copy of the earlier edition he had given to the American poet and friend:

Caro Eduardo:
    I have been pining for so long to inscribe this book for you, over the protracted delays & confusions of its production; and now thankfully I can make up this parcel and send it off; thankfully because as I cast many thoughts back over our long-extended friendship and many adventures along the way I am grateful that we have shared so many of the sparks and flights that have provoked our precarious trade in exotic text, and

provided such varied points of vantage from which to squint at the razzle of nearly half a century. Well, nearly. And with the two big empty noughts up front, who knows who may care to read in our anthologies of disorder, and indeed who cares very much anyway; the life of abject slavery to the Muse has its inbuilt compulsions, as well we both know. But as to my perpetual and fundamental regard for your own intrepid practice, you will never fully know how deeply that is rooted in amazement and gratitude constantly renewed and refreshed, as the years stumble onwards and successive outbursts of poetic affront have snapped the bystanders into spasms of white-hot attention. Well, this one at any rate. All the swaps and exploits and swift entertainments make up a caravan which I now remember with profound emotion, and in that spirit I send my fondest salutes and this congealed gamut of text. Published in Australia: how about that?

On 23 April 2015, an auspicious day perhaps for a writer who had written an 86-page monograph on *Sonnet 94*, Bloodaxe produced the third edition of *Poems* which now ran to nearly 700 pages. The dedication at the front simply says 'For the Future' and I found myself thinking, well, that is the direction a teacher would choose.

My enduring respect for the most important teacher I have ever had has been evidenced over the years not least by my determination to give handouts to my pupils. I shall never forget the attention to detail provided in Jeremy Prynne's handouts whether they were Practical Criticism exercises such as 'Ode to Evening' by William Collins, with its introductory comments, or a lengthy series of notes such as were presented to me in November 1969, 'Some Notes on the Outlook and Procedures of the Post-Romantic Mind'.

The Collins exercise in Practical Criticism was headed 'The following "Ode to Evening" appeared in December 1746. Try to account for its very powerful and distinctive excellence; how far does the poise of this language depend on its generality, and specifically upon its personifications? As a secondary issue, develop a comparison between this poem and John Clare's "Syren of sullen moods and fading hues", and with Blake's poems to the four seasons, to the "Evening Star" and to "Morning" (in *Poetical Sketches*, 1783). You might even look forward to Keats' Ode "To Autumn".' As I look back over my copy of this sheet I note with renewed astonishment the wide range of suggested reading that my teacher offered at the supervision following on from the completion of the submitted essay: J.S. Cunningham's *Drafts & Fragments of William Collins*, especially the Ode 'To Simplicity' and 'Ye Genii who in secret state'; *The Life of a Poet, William Collins* by P.L. Carver; an essay on Collins in *From Sensibility to Romanticism* (Hilles & Bloom); *Windows of the Morning: A critical study of William Blake's Poetical Sketches*, 1783 by M.R. Lowery; *An Essay on the History of Civil Society*, 1767, by Adam Ferguson; 'The Language of the Tribe' in Donald Davie's *Purity of Diction in English Verse*; *The Task* by William Cowper; *Colour in Turner* by John Gage; *The Sunset Ship, Poems of J.M.W. Turner*; *Blake and Tradition* by Kathleen Raine; *Caleb Williams* by William Godwin; *The Young Shelley, Genesis of a Radical* by K.N. Cameron; Shelley's essay 'On Life' and poem 'The Triumph of Life'. What had started at 1746 was now being pushed firmly into the nineteenth century.

The twenty-five page handout about the 'Post-Romantic Mind' remains with me as one of the most astonishingly fertile sets of notes I have ever received and I have used aspects of them time and again in my own school-teaching. Divided into fourteen sections they remind me of the style of Erich Auerbach's *Mimesis*: a substantial quotation followed by a commentary. The fourteen begin with the Scottish philosopher Thomas Brown and move on to include, Henry Mayhew, Charles Dickens, Henry James, Matthew Arnold, G.M. Hopkins, J.H. Newman, Walter Pater, John Ruskin, Joseph Conrad, Paul Valéry, W.B. Yeats, Theodore Roethke and J.V. Cunningham. The second section which focuses on Mayhew's 'Rag-and-Bottle Shop' from *London Labour and the London Poor* is a prime example of that pushing forward which a teacher can do.

2.

I was referred to the owner of a marine-store shop, as to a respectable man, keeping a store of the best class. Here the counter, or table, or whatever it is to be called, for it was somewhat nondescript, by an ingenious contrivance could be pushed out into the street, so that in bad weather the goods which were at other times exposed in the street could be drawn inside without trouble. The glass frames of the window were removable, and were placed on one side in the shop, for in the summer an open casement seemed to be preferred. This is one of the remaining old trade customs still seen in London; for previously to the great fire in 1666, and the subsequent rebuilding of the city, shops with open casements, and protected from the weather by overhanging eaves, or by a sloping wooden roof, were general.

The house I visited was an old one, and abounded in closets and recesses. The fire-place, which apparently had been large, was removed, and the space was occupied with a mass of old iron of every kind; all this was destined for the furnace of the iron-founder, wrought iron being preferred for several of the requirements of that trade. A chest or range of very old drawers, with defaced or wornout labels—once a grocer's or a chemist's—was stuffed, in every drawer, with old horse-shoe nails (valuable for steel manufacturers), and horse and donkey shoes; brass knobs; glass stoppers; small bottles (among them a number of the cheap cast "hartshorn bottles"); broken pieces of brass and copper; small tools (such as shoemakers' and harness-makers' awls), punches, gimlets, plane-irons, hammer heads, &c.; odd dominoes, dice, and backgammon-men; lock escutcheons, keys, and the smaller sort of locks, especially padlocks; in fine, any small thing which could be stowed away in such a place.

In one corner of the shop had been thrown, the evening before, a mass of old iron, then just bought. It consisted of a number of screws of different lengths and substance; of broken bars and rails; of the odds and ends of the cogged wheels of machinery, broken up or worn out; of odd-looking spikes, and rings, and links; all heaped together and scarcely distinguishable. These things had all to be assorted; some to be sold for re-use in their then form; the others to be sold that they might be melted and cast into other forms. The floor was intricate with hampers of bottles; heaps of old boots and shoes; old desks and work-boxes; pictures (all modern) with and without frames; waste-paper, the most of it of quarto, and some larger sized, soiled or torn, and strung closely together in weights of from 2 to 7 lbs.; and a fire-proof safe, stuffed with old fringes, tassels, and other upholstery goods, worn and discoloured. The miscellaneous wares were carried out into the street, and ranged by the door-posts as well as in front of the house. In some small outhouses in the yard were piles of old iron and tin pans, and of the broken or separate parts of harness.

Mayhew first began his detailed reports on the conditions of urban life and work in articles published in 1849-50 in the *Morning Chronicle*. It is significant that *The Posthumous Papers of the Pickwick Club* (first issued in monthly parts, London, 1837) came into being as the result of a commission for a humorous text to accompany a projected series of illustrations by the popular comic artist Robert Seymour, and that this commission was offered to Mayhew before Dickens was eventually approached (Edgar Johnson, *Charles Dickens* [London, 1953], Vol. I, p. 115).

Earlier accounts of metropolitan life could not of course overlook the Hogarthian ironies of vigorous and picturesque disorder; but in the first quarter of the century these contrasts are there more simply to be looked at, rather than actually felt to induce serious epistemic or moral confusion. See for example Pierce Egan's *Life in London*, in which the three picaresque men-about-town make a visit to the condemned yard of Newgate Prison; after a few perfunctory observations on the pitiable consequences of social disintegration to be seen there, "the TRIO hastily quitted the gloomy walls of Newgate, once more to join the busy hum and life of society" (p.382). Thackeray, describing his reactions in 1860 to re-reading this passage, comments on the excellence of the plate by the brothers Cruikshank illustrating the Newgate scene, only to continue: "Now we haste away to merrier scenes: to Tattersall's (ah! gracious powers! what a funny fellow that actor was who performed Dicky Green in that scene at the play!); and now we are at a private party..." ("Roundabout Papers—No. VIII. De Juventate," *Cornhill Mag.*, II [1860], p. 510. This sporting and jolly attitude to scenes from town life makes *Pickwich Papers* entirely understandable as part of the nostalgic genre, and makes the portrait of the Marshalsea Prison in *Little Dorrit* (1855-57) only the more astonishingly powerful and unprepared-for.

In the attitudes to town life current in the early nineteenth century, the pattern of eighteenth-century ideas about types of experience and their attendant feelings, as belonging in generally well-defined and distinct categories, helps to insulate the spectator against the sense of pressure exerted by one set of values against another. One kind of incident is full of pathos, the other more distantly comic; no disturbing overlap is forced by the environment unless the subject is willing to entertain the connection. Thus the insatiable curiosity of the hero of William Godwin's novel, *Caleb Williams, or, Things as They Are* (1794) leads him into misery and imprisonment, and Godwin in his descriptions of this stage of Caleb's 'adventures' (Vol. II, Chaps XI-XIV) draws on the evidence of a friend's visit to Newgate, on the *Newgate Calendar* and on *Howard on Prisons* (all cited in footnotes). Caleb's eventual fate is almost a direct outcome of his assumption that an agile theoretic intelligence could carry him without damage through all types and levels of experience—an attitude of which Shelley was later an ardent admirer.

Early connections between the perception of grotesque disorder and profusion as the occasion for humour on the one hand, and for serious moral/liberal concern on the other, are hinted at in E.P. Thompson, "The Political Education of Henry Mayhew," *Victorian Studies*, XI (September, 1967); see esp. pp. 51-52, 60. See also the implicit tension—still unresolved—between George Cruikshank's relaxed and picturesque genre illustrations, and Henry Mayhew's almost Ruskinian hopefulness about the potential dignity of human labour, in their joint production, *1851; Or, The Adventures of Mr and Mrs Sandboys and Family, who Came up to London to Enjoy Themselves and to See the Great Exhibition* (London, [1851])—read for example the opening to Chap. XIII.

The contradictory jumble of perceptual and moral experience in Victorian town life is increasingly the consequence of a literal closeness of one thing—dwelling-house, moral code, specialised cants and styles of speech—to another. The sense of scale and moral perspective secured by the first-generation Romantic artist's image of the self worked out in solitude and recollection is jostled out of the picture, so that what results is often either moral nonsentience (Malthus) or moral vertigo (Ruskin, the Brontës). For Dickens this condition of self and society is underlain by deep and often bitter ironies; on the one hand there is the domestic intimacy of the family huddle, while on the other there are the numerous constrained and distorted forms of life forced on those unable to master the adaptive skills required for minimum self-preservation (compare for example Edgar Johnson's comments on what he calls "Dickens's lifelong preoccupation with prisons" [*Charles Dickens*, Vol. II, pp. 884-885 and ff.]).

The effects of urban crowding at the level of physical fact made their earliest demands for attention as especially problems of public health and sanitation; see the *First Report of the Commissioners for Inquiring into the State of Large Towns and Populous Districts* (London, 1844), esp. such evidence as that given by a private cleansing contractor or 'scavenger', paras. 4537-4713. The consequent mental and moral confusions are also noticed; see, e.g., the evidence of Dr T.S. Smith (paras. 908-1026) for its unexceptional but generous insight into the 'dehumanizing' effects of wretchedly confined living-space.

What this epistemic crowding may have entailed for the imagination, once it became an unalterable component of social consciousness and not just a condition to be observed, is more difficult to determine. But much of the spacious and leisured deployment of experience in Victorian poetry might seem by contrast to regress to a pastoral nostalgia for larger and more amenable distances between things and experiences—where the self could hold its position as the chief axis of the personal life and where the poet could still choose his metaphors rather than have them thrust upon him by the popular press or the idiom of imitative mass-manufacture. Arnold as poet (and often also as social commentator) is very much a case in point here, as for example Thomas Hood's "Miss Kilmansegg and her Precious Leg" (first printed, September-November 1840 in the *New Monthly*) is very distinctively and interestingly not.

The problem is of course much less disabling for the writer of fiction, and the really startling growth in range and power of the novel during the 1840s may in part be a consequence of this. Thus we can trace the early difficulties with visual particularism (brilliantly mimed, for example, in *Martin Chuzzlewit* [1844], Chap. IX) and can follow at least one strand of the logic of objects to its by no means merely erratic conclusion: "The shop seemed to be full of all manner of curious things—but the oddest part of it all was, that whenever she looked hard at any shelf, to make out exactly what it had on it, that particular shelf was always quite empty: though the others round it were crowded as full as they could hold. 'Things flow about so here!' she said at last in a plaintive tone, after she had spent a minute or so in vainly pursuing a large bright thing, that looked sometimes like a doll and sometimes like a work-box, and was always in the shelf next above the one she was looking at" (Lewis Carroll, *Through the Looking-Glass and What Alice Found There* [London, 1872], Chap. V). On this see also William Empson, "Alice in Wonderland: the Child as Swain," in his *Some Versions of Pastoral* (London, 1935); more generally, R.A. Forsyth, "The Victorian Self-Image and the Emergent City Sensibility," *UTQ*, XXXIII (1963); R.A. Forsyth, "The Myth of Nature and the Victorian Compromise of the Imagination," *ELH*, 31 (1964), 213-240; and also *ELH*, 36 (1969), 382-415.

It was a great privilege to be taught by J.H. Prynne and I am sure that I cannot be the only former pupil who still has books which he intends to read at some point before it is too late. The privilege was being challenged by a mind that believed firmly in pressing on 'For the Future'.

Affection

John James

one does not work out of a reaction against but rather out of affection for something

—Barry Flanagan

1

guide my soul to the light from this unwholesome pit
where all is sold for an arm & a leg the stirrup pump
to no avail against the incendiary hail as countless children
hunger for tallow calling from faraway cities while radios
drone on masking the salacious trembling hand to fist
a sardine can almost fast food who wants it now
got no other option the drudgery of minimum wage
or listed in the Sunday supplement bought in the family visit
to the super store with mum & dad & baby buggy large as life
what do they want they do not know until they find the box
American breakfast with green top milk & loads of sugar
shake so nose to the ground the lengthy strap that pulls the dog
so careless like its human chancers show every piercing
& tattoo as yomping down the aisle they go no bended knee
or supplicant incense bow aroma of aftershave will do no
blessing now required as nothing told but enter pin code now
the 4x4 awaits as shriven by the carwash men as cheap as that
a quickie without the smokeless public bar the little town
not quite a capital spot to try for pollination
a double bed can wait

2

             Fruiting bodies vintage
garment by the carpet pile grandpa full of what he's led to believe
some stinking rubbish from the daily junk adorning flaccid
regular the mat falling on us all as the queen lacks semen
popping drones following the soak of neonicotinoid
what good are they well there's munitions
pull up his joggers crossing the road against the red
two fingers to the horn the camera can only lie in shaky grey
by what stretch can this be called an art house cinema
our visions of grown up fillum lacking schedule
would you credit it best to buy your olive oil from Aldi
at least in winter bare flesh concealed from blatant view
dot & carry at the ankle loss of pace in sorry state
wrapt in a shiny body warmer Soviet black felt scarf & woolly bonnet
seeking something good to eat to take home to your kitchen
forlorn sell out of the local to the multiple estate

3

          Bite off the
top of the morning on the high road to the bank no froth
or gain to see the pitiful junky lost to the world beside the path
would you believe it yes it is there tension of neck muscle
can't wait to get back home make fast the door rewind
the dread & disarray of the street to climb the stair
to application love of the creatures seen from the window
at the secrétaire you will continue till you ache the line
will turn & turn again in ascending barometric pressure
before you rest to reconsider what is done a draft
a pattern showing how it's made

4

       Call-sign freedom
of the kitchen taking the bird in hand & spatchcock for the grill
a little pile of carrot slices layered in the pot for Vichy
mortared pepper bursting aroma of the juniper under your nose
man on a roll a glutton for more throw in a soupçon of garlic
pursued as Norah showed you by the glowing range so long ago
toiling in the back of the house away from traffic noise at the front
she's standing on the stair again calling your name faithful as ever
in spite of everything hot on the hob a quick sip of red
a drop to ease the perspiration dripping from your brow
another splash of southern red brought in from Carignan
Napoleonic Guards are marching on back Rod Steiger at their head
a marvellous recreation but the deadly Prussian cavalry in black
infest the possibility stifle the scenario of the struggle
all was lost but now we have to stay alive to get things done
to wish for calm & certitude resist the pelting rain
that drives us to the lee of the house flicker of
painful surrender denied

5

land of the free
TV direction what cost dominant intrusion severed our conversation
broken linkage in the aftermath of 1953 soon to be washing whiter
without blue or so she thought American all over as the hotter prospect
spinning like a running dog & working for the Yankee dollar
removal of hedgerow not recorded in the broken archive
never had it so Macmillan said but why should we always tag along behind
as in a chaingang with mist shrouding the forgotten garden shelter
corrugated pile encased in turf like a charcoal burner bonfire
arms slung over the swaying washing line you play in your bonnet
sheets of glass breaking your volunteer fall in the blink of an eye
take off your socks to feel the pain of shard extraction from your leg
feathered deep in gore a flowing dream of torture worse to come
in Castlereagh heart beating for the ravening constable any old tale will do
then back to your cell would you believe it take it or leave it in your
          own time
one finger one thumb keep talking swear by Almighty God the whole
          shebang
still breathing with a bloody mark on anglo conscience
no further questions asked each man & woman spoken for as beast

6

                    In the curving
surface of the screen the news today a baleful pornographic dance
defies your sofa plump up the cushions skip the ads
the Devil now assails your weary visage
but you say Hail Mary to send him away that's what we do
say no to all his works & pomps deny send back his penetrating gaze
flick the switch tear up the card & cross your legs before the fire
of celebrity eating their way through muck before your faltering hearth
listen to what I say or speak your own sequential prayer
zap each shadowy intrusion & abide the possibility of better times
break off & rearrange your own interior without external guide
that deed of stolen thought it's beaten out of you to cut you down to size
it's take you over time in substitute Weetabix a catch phrase or two
rises in your throat you'd better believe it they want you to swallow it
proceed to eat your Horlicks in the darkened room a spark of light
in the fallen log ash before the power supply gets too expensive
cut down the cost entailed inside the home renew your Senior Railcard
drink deep from history ancient story modern pain unheimlich durance
but for a moment recall all that was not lost in the guarded outlook
of our cherished circle our careful ambience in these four walls
en garde my love a hoard of peace & happiness in time abundant
though worn out by work & visits to the doctor never cost a penny
even when strapped for cash we never lost for thought

7

        All right core rescue
a discount buy one get one free there must be a snag what choice
their sale no goods exchanged sharp elbow mob at the bolted doors
employment some privilege measured by proportional leisure
poor judgement a hazard for the unsuspecting fail to hear the tinkling keys
unwanted stock is what they queue for it's in there ready for the punters
stripped to the limit of a store card an afterthought too late
back at a northern high rise on the forgotten edge of town without a
        prayer
with the digital radio on now chosen over daytime telly the smelly dog
        assents
still us the object of the exercise broadband quicker than ever so watch
        yourself
though remember where you began free nuclear attack advice
that was in advance of the multiple consumer choice of piercing
debase what beauty for a *Hello* colour promo weeping wound
a surplus over youthful skin a guarantee of future anal witness
mastication before expectoration superseded by no legal aid
a cost removed by further difficult decision

8

Entire violation
unnatural condition of the current privation
all in it together club armchairs for some subscription fully paid
but must we succumb what can you do they say
lie down for it under the cosh & boot acceptance
a last defence of '83 now long forgotten the Peoples
March for Jobs Saint Paul what was it you wrote regarding women
Mary Magdelen of Sainte-Baume you'd never credit what has now become

9

Coda: Salut

he appears in my dream
in the glow of his thirtieth year

clad in robes of
blue & gold satin

smiling he approaches
the orchard in winter
sickle in hand

Essay: Discourse on Some Lines from *News of Warring Clans*

Simon Smith

the first shock crisis

& crash

leading to boom & stagflation

a crow-lined tanker fluttered

the tapes/in the chilly air

the funds never ran out

to deploy the oil weapon

NOT the miners but OPEC

this is not the obliteration of napalm but of discourse

& the rhetoric of use

everyday attention

you've paid for

mind

your own business

the first world war

of petrodollars

caught on camera

the queues at the Shell station are cues
to deploy regulars & territorials
to the forecourts

the permanent war footing foreseen
prophet to the profit loss then
gain

& a three-day week

we would file our teeth
into hooks
bodies to which stuff happens

& $12 a barrel the starting point

my loss my coup my loss
their gain

petro-Islam
an entanglement of fire
& a carve up at two minutes to midnight

FOR THE FUTURE

flip Heath to Wilson
& to the Wilson mandate
the dark days of 1974

in the entanglements of crossfire
the singy-songy sections
the pitch is first sung over a drone

the limit of combat
& the Thatcher 'get in'

out of the Woods
& only a step away
from the death squads

the battalions of foot on foot
unfurled the black flag of IS

the first oil shock knock
knock knocks on the second
& the end of the Shah

the scout shouts
in lost dialect, its time
for a war footing

give them their freedom

& they take a lost leader

no sale no return

the pooterish race round the A roads of Essex & Surrey

of lime-green Capris & acid-lemon

Dolomites

what the sales rep wants the sales rep gets

sales like autism

on the face of it

no flight from the overbite

a cup of tea as you await orders

for attack (first phase)

the MIG-21 drifting in clear freezing air

upside down back broken pilot dead

notes are currency

as long as we continue to believe

that that is the case

disbelieve the invasion is happening

paid attention

everything has its place

with networked inundation

increased airflow over

the skin of the airframe

identifies targets

on a range of options

for which there is no answer

no return

or reach for another scotch

the oil tankers glide in their silence

for miles

the ghost ships of 1973

the silent loans of the IMF

between

punk & Yom Kippur

Mirage IIIs & Super Shermans cross three borders

in simultaneous rebuke

a sharp bite down

borders of convenience

expedient lines in the sand

where land re-formats as territory

the mimesis of blood

money & oil

a few seconds out of

synch

exhausted with content

the weekend bigot dips

his shoe in a home steroid

Marines selling ice-cream

out the back of a Humvee

handle

with care

the miners ASLEF & other clans of living tissue

rubbish economic (for which *read* oil) strategy

its threat its treat

The Crass & The Fall

cause to the raising of voice

struck dumb

23.viii.15–1.xi.15

The Garden

D.S. Marriott

1

Those were the best days. In front of us the garden
Seemed tame. Butterflies and bees glided across the greenest land, as if
Recompense for all the solitary years,
Annihilating everything that didn't need a name, screaming Be Saved!

And so it began: a climate for all knowledge, a paradise
Of wondrous inconsequence, colours amorously intertwined.
Then the turning point, and the trees & flowers burst apart,
Falling into fora and flora as if there'd been a cruelty before names.

That was it then, the first day was also the last. This was the place
That nature had brought you, this perilous industriousness.
Like an image in the dream of capital: your own skilful obsolescence…
Unforgiveable that we once walked under giant apple trees.
The sound of innocence, pure and sweet and dependable. But look out
        of the window,
See the vainglorious and rude retreats. Eat, just let me keep this apple.

2

On the first day the garden seemed tamed.
Herbs and flowers, butterflies and bees,
Dying on the short and narrow verges, as if
Complicit in the game. Dying for all of us,
They end their race to the honoured dead,
Only to disappear without trace or consequence.

And there we were: gods speaking to one
Another in signs like discord, dials, or clockwork animals. Feel the rain
Approaching from the other bowers,
Plumes sparkling in the deep mortal climates,
The rush of summer so deeply plush and greenish. But which one,

And what repose will be given us as we step out into the open
From all those dismal years lost in solitude? The best day
Forever deferred to autumn, without proof of its ending,
With dumb unpreparedness, hopeless visitations in the long fields.

Line of What Make or Sort

GAVIN SELERIE

for J.H. Prynne

Here is the mouthway through spirit-walls
set transverse like baffle-plates. A blind tread
by studded doors to a green court.

Bleak-sheen, shards and grains
with a smooth face. Widewhere story
brought to a point, up a spiral
that becomes a candle halo.

In a case of doughty slips you work
from word to idea.

        That disherited
brings weighty strokes from wandering—
burden of the utmost isle in drifty sea.

Water-cords fall on the glass, as inside
a planting pocket asks what throw of terms
will make the leaf in white halves
stand mobile.

        A stretch of free air
closed at the corner, troysome, for those
searching an elixir greatly animal, full of metal.

Memories of hall-joy on island gravel
(no marvel against kind) dart from contemplation
as a spark from burning coals.

This *paradosis* comes over stone to the exit
window, where all is re-verded
to address *trayfoyles and trewloves*
but dispel the mark that ties.

                              For who knocks
a poet is everywhere, nowhere and abroad—
the blanks attest that longer watch.

Fifth from the ground
a book with a register half crossed out
will open the place you sometimes walk.

Orange skies, Mr Lee, Mr Lee
over the flatland

                    a windmill stark by waving reeds

              small boat in sluggish water

        spearshaft tree at the sedge-side,
        keys about to scatter

the aura to speak, centuries in sun-sight
ravelled

                  deal

                      new terms

            (the yen
            to go
            waist deep)

we took they took the gift that is rice paste
over rivets

> can offer to power
> a bulbous steam ball
> with rods flashing

a temple over crushed mulberries

> sinolacquer   turbine switch

a bird finger theory of need

> O missed fellow
> that should be here

> fathom and nail

this humbug strake

> or lightly deflect the barrage

(spring tune to bitter lyric)

Arthur's sword shines on a blazer pocket, his giant
comes a marvel from the east.

No risk assessment for a glowing soul, got to
step right in, what hood is smoking black.

Any tulk you take will say his tub
is crammed with florins, for which read debt record
on a ferris wheel screaming Jesus.

The story has heads unfair, with matted locks
that ask for chicken wages,
a transaction apart the media shower.

But it's too late, as the other said, to drop back
to the straight-on plot, we go like a verb
through sense.

Can't unring the bell or be rid
of ventures. Across space you cleave and clutch
to sideling stir.

Expression comes as we move
in a crinkled passage with each twitch of a silk cord.
By serial wonder it shapes a tale outside
the bound state, gut syllabic.

Acutest self at compass edge, jade under blur of cloud.

Nomads

Elaine Feinstein

We who moved every six months in those days

     from one sabbatical let to the next

found a house in Trumpington we came to love.

     Young poets called unannounced

to sprawl and talk of messy lives   the euphoria

     induced by poetry   and Jeremy Prynne

who sometimes paced the floor there   allowing

     everyone to share Aristeas' vision

of nomadic tribes and the purity of their needs

     we all believed in   at least as he spoke of it,

though along our own time line there would soon be

     tents for us to pack   again and sadly.

'As It Is'

ROD MENGHAM

to J.H.P.

Memory is recast from the ground up
and in your hand is the touch of the proper means.
Being far northerly, we do not open our mouths
in the cold but speak close and inward:
tragedians of labour, resting between roles.

In a momentary slumber, I imagine going to Catford
for its errant springs and anti-Rousseauisms
where night-birds rampage through the undergrowth
of ideals, and R.F. Langley flings his coat on a bush.
The atmosphere is tremulous & wavy
as the mark of a ram's horn snail
on the wall of a Suffolk lean-to.

And I drink to remember the Polish clouds
hallmarked for onward trading.   A purchase is but a purchase
in the hymning of product-placement. But you bring
the invisible into the visible world
and cross out the in- in infinity
to accommodate the living, and pull them out alive.

The 5th essence is the usefulness of the detail
embedded in this foundation stone.

When the stars are inlaid in a vacant strip
of no man's sky, and the fishes swim down
under five crushing fathoms

the bottom of all the land is this stone.

Prynne's Gold-Mine

The Fateful Mark — Enjoying Prynne — Falling off the Trail

MICHAEL HASLAM

In matters of memory I have learned that clarity is no guarantee of veracity, but I do have a clear picture of a sort of brochure, black print on white paper, folded and stapled, a couple of pages of which were of interest to me: a list of the lectures offered by the Cambridge English Faculty, some of which I might care to attend. So I scanned the list and took up a pencil and made my first forceful mark against an item reading "Mr Prynne: Contemporary American Poetry".

I was green and fresh. I was eighteen years old. It was Michaelmas term 1965. I had never heard of this Mr Prynne, but this was my first choice. Why was that? That this wasn't every literature fresher's choice became clear from the fact that none of the half-dozen Petrean freshers (that's Peterhouse, the most unsuitable college of all for my mentality) turned up for this one, so why was it?

A few years before, with West and East in nuclear stand-off, and me at the height of pubertal confusion, the English teachers at my school in Bolton had seen fit to present their pupils with the real stuff of poetry: Blake; Hopkins; Keats; Wordsworth; Eliot; Pound. I was ignited at once, and started making my own versions of poetry, the reading and writing of which became the leading edge of all other study. Sensing this, the teachers, Leavisite Cantabrians, the pair of them, began to prompt me towards English at Cambridge. I could think of no better alternative.

My good teachers were quite up to date. The school, Bolton School, then direct-grant grammar, now Independent, had a reputation in theatre. But their notion of contemporary poetry was very much 'Movement', which I found oddly disappointing, not liberating like Blake, but a part of a general bestiflement oppressing youthful spirits. I had to go extra-curricular, to find what I could at the W.H. Smith's on Newport Street. I found Cummings, and Barker, and Gascoyne, and, supremely, a Penguin Modern Poets featuring Ginsberg, Corso, and Ferlinghetti. This was real fire. I spoke up for it. The teachers tried to dowse the fire. Allen Ginsberg would not do. So I had to go off-piste, with Jack Kerouac, and blues, and jazz, and Easter in Trafalgar Square. I still had a lot to learn. So with the brochure in my hands I wondered what this Mr Prynne might have to show me.

It turned out that he'd just returned from a Poetry Conference in Berkeley, California, armed with tapes of readings and lectures. He started by playing a tape of Allen Ginsberg reading. He invited us to consider it silly, but went on to explain why it might be quite intelligent. I was hooked. I felt vindicated.

In subsequent weeks we heard Charles Olson, Ed Dorn, Gary Snyder, and perhaps some others. We were directed to Don M. Allen's *New American Poetry*. I was not the only one electrified.

A misfit at Peterhouse, I found my social life among a group of friends drawn from various colleges, the core of which was found at Prynne's lectures. A couple of my new friends had already met at the Edinburgh Festival, where poetry, it seems, had been the big thing on the fringe. One had for a friend a poet called Lee Harwood. Another knew a poet called Chris Torrance. Together we discovered certain magazines. And we got to know, to some degree, Andrew Crozier and John James, as well as J.H.P. And there were nets that spread therefrom. I was barely aware that in thinking I'd identified what was *the* contemporary British and American poetry, I'd been recruited by one side in the ongoing, tedious 'poetry wars'.

These wars can't be disentangled from wider 'culture wars', and the 'counter-culture' of the next decade: a revolution that failed, although everything changed. Me and my chums fell in with that. I can't say that Prynne was implicated in it, except as an aloof, amused observer. Take for instance, *Questions for the Time Being*, in *The White Stones*. This could be read as an angry attack on our goings on. I rather read it as a well-meant reproof to the folly of some of his followers. In so far as messages can be drawn from his work, a prime one seems to be that awareness precludes innocence, and that there's no escape from complicity in how things are.

If I were daft enough to feel self-pity for real, rather than as a musical poetic mode, I might claim to have been wounded in the silly wars. 1967 and 1968 deserve their reputations. They enclose the academic year during which, with a friend, I took my tutorials at Caius, with J.H. Prynne, by special request.

I'll repress a digression on how my shy and timid self felt puzzled disappointment with the foibles of various other tutorings, or with a 'Cambridge' tone in general. I think I thought I wanted to encounter Thought, by which I mean, to be in the presence of thinking being thought, and it often wasn't there. There were authorities, or self-confident students, with vast arrays of knowledge, who could refer any notion to its place on a map of universal knowledge, without having to think at all. There were some finely-thought, composed lectures that could be enjoyed, as wrought compositions. What I wanted, direct, was something more like an improvised jazz solo, with or without a set of chords: the music of thought that I took, and take, to be poetry itself. But I found what I wanted, at last, in the Prynne tutorials. At the same time I was cracking up in a hard-to-define distress.

I might mumble or write some barely articulate notion, and this would produce his response, pacing the room, demonstrating the process of thinking thought into language in completely structured, perfectly turned improvised sentences. I'm sure there are other ways of teaching. This way might be seen as showing off. But what is a teacher for but to show you how it's done, in the matter of poetry, and its relation to thinking articulate thought, so you're there in its living presence?

My own cracking up was most evident in the matter of language. I could only present my tutor with broken essays. I'd become highly sensitive to, and suspicious of, the given tones of statement. I could not abide the tone that wraps the conventional student essay. It seemed dishonest from the start, a mendacious template. But I could not concoct an alternative. I'd been moved by novelties of presentation I'd found in D.H. Lawrence, in Charles Olson, in John Cage, but I couldn't emulate them without pretension. I don't know what Prynne thought of my efforts. He responded to thoughts he detected without praise or reproof. It's possible he understood my predicament. I drew my own lesson. I knew what I had to do, for the sake of poem-making. I had to reconstruct my sense of sentence, unenclosed by social notions of tone, to return the metalinguistics of tone to something like music, eschewing if necessary any dabbles in prose till the job was done. It took years.

But more than my essay-style was cracking up. Of my bunch, three had been variously expelled, 'sent down'; one had taken a break; and another refused to sit the final exams, on political grounds. There was only me who took a degree. I went blithely in, despite my confusion, and offered up my broken sentences, indifferent or simply glad at the prospect of soon floating free. I've been told that they gave me a Third, though I never checked. I left Cambridge resolved to not look back. This attests that my resolution must have failed. Poetry kept the strings attached.

Those strings formed a part of a net in which I was either a catch or a knot. This was one way that my brochure pencil-mark proved fateful: I'd been pitched into a clique. The cliques are the scandal of poetry in England. Cliques have thrived on networking since before networking was a word. Some discrete clusters just repulse each other, and it's not entirely a matter of style or political bent. I've met some poets who flare with anger at the mere mention of J.H. Prynne. And my clique tends to disavow anyone adopted by the mainstream press. But I'd found the net in which I could be published. So much for fate.

Another way the mark proved fateful was simply the course of my life. Prynne's not responsible for that. From the canteen by the lecture-halls, before or after those lectures by Prynne, I'd made my friends, and upon graduation I maintained a connection with some of them. I could trace connections through a chain of them to how I came to live where I've lived for nigh-on half a century. And our ethos might explain how I came to drop from one sort of prospective career to another.

Those friends are dispersed. I've just about lost touch with all of them. They abandoned poetry. I stayed with it. Poets arrived in the valley: Paul Buck; Asa Benveniste; Jeff Nuttall; Ulli McCarthy; others—all now dispersed or dead; all somewhere on the same net. The postman brought magazines and books. All the same net. And I was still beset by problems of tone: to turn back from message into music. Prynne's poetry proved some help with that.

Poetry comes out all sorts of ways. It was already clear we were free to be fragmentary. I don't like feeling broken. If the tone of prose is package for its meaning, just as a tone of voice may be, how might I make a polytonal sentence, with chords of contrasting senses? I wanted to make sentences analogise themselves as music, an abstract odd idea but one that I could work with. I went about chasing this idea with no programme but by intuition. Some things in current literature I found inspiring. At the head of this list would be *The White Stones* by J.H. Prynne. Near the top would be *The Veil Poem* by Andrew Crozier. My base I found in a Fulcrum volume entitled *Derivations* by Robert Duncan, a kind of language-users' guide. These were helpful, useful, enjoyable, even thrilling. But reading for this sort of helpfulness and usefulness was just a phase. Thrill and joy remained.

As a teabreak is the blessed point in a factory day, so is the sheer enjoyment of a poem to anything you might feel moved to say, and the natural world goes mental. It's like the space between raucous bells that mark the raucousness's boundaries. That's my maturer view. When I was younger I rather wanted Poetry to woman the barricades like what's-her-name, or take on academic philosophy on its own terms, surpass psychology and accept theology's surrender, and decapitate them all with rhetoric. Now that ambition only remains of use as a partly, if not purely, musical doing.

There was a time when I seem to have wanted Poetry to persuade me of something. It almost did. And I did make mistakes. I have taken declamations by the charismatic Olson as gospel, sensing the mental intensity like pentecostal church, and I believed. For a time I was thinking that Prynne had persuaded me of something. I wonder what that might have been. Surely he's serious. Surely seriousness must mean something. Levity disagrees.

If its tone were the political meaning of a poem, I can hear why some might positively dislike Prynne's poetry. That high Cambridge tone of brittle intelligence is not everyone's choice of tea-break beverage. When the tone is heard musically, I hear brilliance. A test might be, is it possible to simply disagree with what he says. When I was still willing to be persuaded, I found my point of disagreement in a passage of *Die A Millionaire*, in *Kitchen Poems*: a sneer at "some wise and quick-faced historical rat" who would tell us "about the industrial north and its misery". Not long emerged from a childhood choked on coalsmoke, I gagged on that. But the ensuing excursus on coal and economics is absurdly brilliant as the ideal stand-up comic's performance. Even the wrongheadedness is musical.

I've been a follower in so far as I was following his work. I've had the good fortune to be on the list of privileged recipients for almost all of his pamphlets. For years they gave me the clearest sense of pure poetic enjoyment, all the deeper for being wide. Being free of the Universities I was under no pressure to further explain the pleasure to myself. I am only rarely tempted into the traps of prose. The best explanation I found was declared to me by a bright niece of mine. I showed her a couple of pages of maturish Prynne, and she exclaimed: "The words just seem to glow!" That's it, but I don't know why. Could those word-surfaces excite intuition at sight of philological depth? I don't know. I don't mean to be mystical, and I don't think he does either.

The bug I'd caught in Cambridge was an idle amusement at the fashions of high seriousness. It was poetry gave me my perch. Oh! Those tonal follies of prose! But Prynne's poetry is clearly a university product, and much of his reception has been intra-academic, and subject to para-philosophical fashion. Prynne has been well, or not so well, written about. The explanations don't seem to touch my enjoyment. There were a couple of notions I did disagree with. One was that the poet was mounting an attack upon poetic diction. Contrariwise, I'd say, No: He vastly expands the ranges of poetic diction. The glow is the touchstone of what that diction is. Diction is the words in the poem: if they glow, that's poetry. But some old glow words now look so tarnished I fear they won't buff up. Prynne slips some in rather nicely, and recovers their glow. The other notion was that his verse aligned with that which follows the ideal banner of Materialism. The deference to philosophy here seems to invoke the battle between conservative guff and Marxist greed-analysis, a right punch-and-judy show. Jack Spicer discovered in *The Territory is Not The Map*, in *The Heads of the Town Up to the Aether* that a poem can't defeat idealism (Idealism). *Ideal* is the adjectival form of the noun *idea*. As a noun on its own it's inclined to clown. And *ideally* is ideally a mostly useless adverb. The words in a poem are all, ideally, in their ideal forms of material glow.

What I read is no attack on the poetic sweets, but may contain the sugar trade, and include a demand to pay the corner sweetshop what is owed for your shoplifting, even if the gift is free. There might be a warning against blindly parachuting into the jumbles of arcadia. He may illustrate the formidable jumbles of impediment in the struggle for jelly trifles.

Turns seems the right word for the way of times, and mean imagined spirits of how things change. A sign of change was once when Veronica Forrest-Thomson came along with *Poetic Artifice,* a harbinger of the temptations of Theory. I'm glad I was out of Academia for what became of that. Just when I thought I was getting the polytonal sentence together, others started deliberately smashing the sentence up on deranged political grounds. That was a bit disconcerting. And Prynne's poetry changed, not so much under that direct influence, as under the same stars of time as everyone else. The time spirit passes over with a retail bag of tricks.

I just heard on the radio about the California gold-rush, and the Oregon trail, and how many of its followers fell off to death or settlement along the way. One told me he fell off with *High Pink on Chrome.* I liked that pastoral immersed in agricultural chemicals. I liked *News of Warring Clans* as one of the best, and there was much to enjoy thereafter. But towards the very end of last century I found that my enjoyment wasn't guaranteed or warranted. I kept nibbling at the stuff, but was failing to get through it. As the late B.B. King sang, *The Thrill is Gone.*

So just lately I thought I'd try again: read it all, from the beginning. It was very enjoyable, for most of the way. I found it was the rhetorical drive of the earlier work that was carrying me through subsequent decades, until at some point that template dissipates. I didn't get much further. As a sort of hedonist I don't find judging poetry pleasurable. I'm sorry, I seem to want to say, that I don't seem to get the 21st Century music. Perhaps it isn't music at all. So I have fallen off. I have made my settlement with the syntactical sentence, and I shall camp here.

On hearing about the trail I picked up an atlas. I fell off the gold trail I think in the Cascades. Prynne's stake is yet some way ahead. And there he stands mid-stream panning for gold by hand.

'Mixing Memory and Desire':
Eliot and the Subjectile

Michael Grant

There is no Present, no—a present does not exist.

(Mallarmé)

In ignoring drawing as well as nature I had resolved to leave behind those forms, lines, strokes, shadows, colours, and aspects which, just as in modern painting, neither presented anything nor demanded to be united by the consistency of any visual or material law, but rather created, *as if above the paper, a kind of configuration perpetually protesting against the law of the created object.*

(Artaud)

It was one afternoon in the spring of 1964 when I entered, not for the first time, Jeremy Prynne's rooms in Caius Court, and, after receiving the customary hospitable and generous welcome, engaged him on the subject of modern poetry. The poets covered included Williams, Creeley and Olson, all of whom were in the news at the time, as well as the poetry of Yvor Winters. I was particularly keen to hear his views on the writing of J.V. Cunningham, since I had spent the previous year (following Jeremy's advice to me during my final year of studying English with him) in post-graduate study with Cunningham at Brandeis. As the afternoon wore on, the conversation came round to Eliot, and in particular to *Four Quartets*. I remember Jeremy asking me, apropos of nothing that had gone before, 'Don't you think "My words echo/Thus, in your mind" a very arrogant thing for Eliot to have written?' I was at a loss for an answer, and all I could come up with was something along the lines of 'Is not Eliot the poet of impersonality and *disparition élocutoire*? Surely he's not there in the poem in that way'. Jeremy's reply was, if I recall, non-committal, and he left me to think the matter over. Well, it is now over fifty years later, and, though I still have no answer, what follows is in one sense intended as a belated reply. My purpose in writing this piece is to set down some thoughts I have had about writing, with reference to Eliot in particular, and in doing so to engage with some matters that are for me still in 'the process of becoming'.

I want to start with some reflections on what has been called the innermost paradox of the symbolic order, namely its retroactivity. As Austin and Wittgenstein (earlier and later) saw, as well as other now more contemporary figures, language turns in a vicious circle, chasing its own tail. The attempt to step outside language and see it from some meta-linguistic position beyond it simply returns us to an abyss. There is no external point of reference serving as a support for it. In my use of language I act as I do without justification, though that is not say that I am unjustified in what I say and do. I may act blindly, but my judgements form their own support and justification. Language functions as a closed circle which always already presupposes itself (I am referring to some remarks of Žižek's here). It makes no sense to seek the origin of language. Language emerges *ex nihilo*: it is suddenly there, things have meaning, and by a miraculous leap we are in the midst of it, using it. The gap separating the symbolic from the real is impossible to cross, inasmuch as the symbolic, language itself, is the very barrier separating the one from the other. What this leads to is a specific order of causality peculiar to the symbolic, that is, retroactive causality (the example often cited at this point is Freud's discussion of the Wolfman and the operation of deferred action). Ordinary causality runs in a linear fashion, first the cause, then the effect. In the symbolic order, time runs backwards, where what was in the past a meaningless event becomes in the future retroactively significant. This happens not only over the course of many years, as with the Wolfman, but in the course of a single utterance, or speech act, as, I would argue, Austin demonstrated in his account of the internal relation between the illocutionary and locutionary in the speech act. It is also this idea of temporality that informs Eliot's conception of tradition, as presented in 'Tradition and the Individual Talent': the literature of the past and that of the present are shown to be related in ways that are, in effect, operated by and through retroactive temporality.

Perhaps the best known summation of this kind of temporality is given by Lacan, for whom retroaction is inseparable from the constitution of psychoanalytic time (and symbolic time in general). From what I have said already concerning the circularity of language, a paradox would seem to arise, that of the fracturing of a space prior to its constitution, the space of the split between the symbolic order of language and the real, a paradox that in fact points up the inextricable relation between temporal retroaction and the formation of the subject. It is this that finds its expression, for Lacan, in the form of the future anterior. Lacan defines it as follows: 'what is realised in my history is neither the past definite of what I was, since it is no more, nor even the perfect of what has been in what I am, but the future anterior of what I will have been, given what I am in the process of becoming'. I am what I will have been for what I am in the process of becoming. The subject is split between an ever-receding past which is being perpetually redrawn, and the act of becoming turned towards the future, in a movement comparable to that described by the topology of a Moebius strip. This bears on the notion of the real as that which supposedly lies outside language, inaccessible to it. The real is rather to be seen as the effect of the symbolic, an effect of the immanent failure of the symbolic to realise itself, its inability to catch up with itself inasmuch as it is thwarted in itself. The instance of the 'misfire', as discussed by Austin, is to the point here: I make a promise and it fails to come off. As Zizek has it: 'a subject wants to say something, it fails, and this failure *is* the subject—a "subject of the signifier" is literally the result of its failure to become itself. . . .within symbolic space, effect is *a reaction against its cause*, while the cause is a retroactive effect of its cause: the subject produces signifiers which fail, and the subject qua Real is the effect of this failure'.

I have spent time on this because I want to say that what Eliot presents in the opening lines of *Burnt Norton* is at once a statement and enactment of symbolic temporality thus understood:

> Time present and time past
> Are both perhaps present in time future,
> And time future contained in time past.

(In the copy of the poem Eliot signed and gave to Bonamy Dob-rée, now kept in Eliot College, at the University of Kent, 'perhaps' has been bracketed, and a question mark placed in the margin. So: perhaps 'perhaps', and perhaps not. We know Pound's view of Eliot's 'perhapses'—one might elaborate on the basis of their respective attitudes to 'perhaps' what it is that divides Eliot's kind of poetry from the poetry of 'sculpture' that was to become the dominant mode of Anglo-Saxon modernism.) These opening lines at once state a position on time and refer to that stating, refer to that referring. Since this poem is seen generally by the commentators as one in which Eliot engages with Mallarmé, I will try to make the point clearer by citing a sentence from *Les mots anglais* (a phrase discussed by Derrida in *Disseminations*, to which my argument here is indebted), a sentence that reads as follows: 'Lecteur, vous avez sous les yeux ceci, un écrit...'. This confirms the identity of 'ceci' by getting outside of itself to point to itself from the point of view of the other, the reader, who is explicitly addressed by a sentence that seems only to refer to itself. This, of course, is not to get outside language as such, but to have the mark ('ceci') re-marked as itself ("ceci"), by what one exponent of Derrida has called a 'ghostly doubling', whereby 'the mark marks itself as marking, refers to itself referring to itself, only by the fact of separating itself enough from itself to open the gap across which reference is supposed to refer'. The aim of such referring, the referent to which the referring is to refer, is the fact of referring itself. Here, and in other works by Mallarmé, what Derrida points to is mimesis, but mimesis exceeded by mimesis, a second-order mimesis that refers to the act of mimesis effected by the mimesis of the first-order. In the three lines quoted above, the text folds back on itself, as 'time present' becomes 'time past, and both are projected (perhaps) into 'time future, only for 'time future' to be contained in time past. 'Time' here is at once an element or term in the series and that which constitutes, by the action of its sequencing, the series of which it is an element. In effect, 'time' is doing the work in Eliot that 'blanc' and pli' do in Mallarmé. 'Blanc' is to be found in Mallarmé's writing as a theme or pattern of imagery in many of the poems (swan, ice, snow, frost, glacier, white, whiteness, and so on), but it also refers to the gapping or spacing that makes the series possible, something effected by the folding back ('pli') of 'blanc' into the very text it constitutes. As Derrida has it, 'the blank is folded, is (marked by) a fold. It never exposes itself to straight stitching. For the fold is no more of a theme (a signified) than the blank, and if one takes into account the linkages and rifts they propagate in the text, then *nothing* can simply have the value of a theme any more'. This is, first, to emphasise that such writing is a syntax before it is a semantics, and, second, to indicate that opening or spacing between syntax and semantics themselves which is irreducible to syntax and semantics alike. Not only does this draw attention away from the predominantly thematic commentaries Eliot's texts usually receive, but it brings to the fore what Eliot's text itself emphasises, syncategorematic terms, such as 'between', which, like Mallarmé's 'entre', join and separate at the same time, resisting nominalisation, on which thematic readings are dependent.

The lines comprising the first paragraph of the poem were to have formed part of a speech by Becket in *Murder in the Cathedral*, but, according to Eliot, were removed from the play at the producer's suggestion. These lines, when read in their new context, appear in it as a repetition of a past that never took place; that is, though they appear in the poem and form part of the poem's developing context, they could equally have belonged elsewhere. This is to emphasise how inseparable the poem's words are from the differential movement of iterability, something that Eliot's mode of phrasing and his rhythms also bring to the fore, something one might recognise from the fact that many of his lines have entered into and become part of the English language itself. The text seems to be quoting itself, offering itself as something that has always already taken place, elsewhere: 'here preceding, there recalling, in the future, in the past, *under the false appearance of a present*' (to quote Mallarmé). *Burnt Norton* continues:

> If all time is eternally present
> All time is unredeemable.
> What might have been is an abstraction
> Remaining a perpetual possibility
> Only in a world of speculation.
> What might have been and what has been
> Point to one end, which is always present.

Footfalls echo in the memory
Down the passage which we did not take
Towards the door we never opened
Into the rose-garden. My words echo
Thus, in your mind.

I refer back to the first of my two opening quotes, that from Mallarmé: 'There is no Present, no—a present does not exist'. In Eliot's line, what is 'always present' is no sooner present than it has gone, 'always' being no sooner read or spoken than it is replaced by 'present', the very sequencing and spacing of the phrase displacing it from the stability its apparent meaning would seem to claim for it. The presence of the present is relegated to 'the passage which we did not take', only to reach 'the door we never opened'. It would seem that what the poem presents or refers to (and this holds for the whole text, *Four Quartets* itself) as occurring in actual time or reality, is inseparable from the quasi-present of the poem's own taking place. Place is nothing other than the taking place of place. It is only this order of event, this kind of taking place, that is able to 'Point to one end, which is always present'. As for 'My words echo/Thus, in your mind', 'My' is echoed in 'mind', and 'Thus' is also echoed, for example in 'dust on a bowl of rose-leaves', but there is also a usage that is comparable to that of 'ceci' in Mallarmé's sentence from *Les mots anglais*. 'Thus' folds back on itself, doubling and thereby echoing itself "thus". The question of an originating speaker, of whom arrogance may or may not be posited, does not here arise.

I want now to consider the relation between *Burnt Norton* and *The Waste Land*. Many of the commentators have noted that the later poem reflects the structure of the earlier, and one might inquire into what emerges from this patterning. *The Waste Land* is—obviously enough—a poem of fragments, a fact that it notes of itself in the final lines. In this connection, it is crucial to note that the fragment is a favoured romantic figure, the very embodiment of the literary absolute. For the Jena Romantics, the fragment is a form that is at once complete and incomplete, whole and part. It is therefore also important to note that there is a correlation here between the patterns of inclusion and exclusion exhibited by the fragment thus understood and the paradox of the Russell Set, the set of all those sets that do not include themselves, inasmuch as both evince the contradiction of an element that is at once within and without the closure of the totality concerned. One can see that the fragment, as the Schlegels understand it, and the Russell set, both exhibit at the very boundaries of thought and language an structural form of contradiction, a paradoxical topology that for Lacan constitutes the action of the structuring internal to the subject. The fragment, seen in this context, and it is this context that bears on the ordering of *The Waste Land*, manifests itself as a form that embodies interruption within itself, that is, the fragment only *is* a fragment insofar as it fails. It is a genre, if one can call it that, which embodies failure within itself, whose completion is incompletion, and whose incompletion within completion draws attention to that very failure. Adorno describes the Romantic fragment 'as a construction that is not complete but rather progresses onward into the infinite through self-reflection'. The fragment 'mixes memory and desire' inasmuch as its disturbance of the distinction between presence and absence is also the act of disturbing the distinction between inside and outside. Tiresias, old man with wrinkled dugs, neither male nor female, is, one might say, a walking embodiment of the suspension of the transparent relation of signifier to signified, and thus of the sign to a referent reality of which it is presumed to be the mimetic shadow. Just as in Mallarmé's writing the blanks of the page suspend not just meaning but the relations on which meaning depends, so also does the fragmented and interrupted temporality of *The Waste Land* work to the same end, or lack of end.

This leads me to refer to my second quote and suggest that *Burnt Norton* stands towards the fragmented structure of *The Waste Land* in a way that operates to create something similar to what Artaud is evoking: that is, I want to suggest that *Burnt Norton* operates as a text that is '*as if above the paper, a kind of counterfigure perpetually protesting against the law of the created object*'. *Burnt Norton* brings to the fore, as a consequence of the topological structuring of its temporality, that which, though being neither representation nor representable as such, nonetheless brings about, causes to take place, gives place to, representation and meaning. In Artaud's idiom, this is the subjectile. The subjectile is the figure of the between, or as Derrida, in his book on Artaud, puts it: between the beneath and the above, it is at once support and surface... 'the subjectile is irreducible to any stable location or meaning, other than its own surface and support: the word 'subjectile' is a subjectile'. The subjectile haunts the writing of *Burnt Norton* (indeed of *Four Quartets* as a whole, and especially *Dry Salvages*—a much maligned and misunderstood piece of writing) with a performative event that is other than those elements constituting the poem as poem. In other words, the subjectile traduces and betrays the very work it upholds and makes possible: from the point of view of the subjectile, the poetry does not matter. The subjectile is not on the paper, or the page, it is above it (or in the case of Artuad's writingdrawings through and/or under it as well): the subjectile is not an object, nor even an object in motion. It is object *as* motion: it makes possible the act of meaning, even though itself unsupportable by any such act of meaning, being supported by nothing other than itself. The subjectile is that which leaves its mark in leaving the scene of what it will have caused to appear (the workings of the future anterior are a bit like those of one of Eliot's cats). I would also suggest that it is precisely the operations of the subjectile that Eliot's citations of Heraclitus at the poem's beginning aim to alert us to: the second, 'the way up and the way down are the same thing', itself an expression of the *between*, is at once outside the poem and inside it, exemplifying in this undecidability of position that to which it points and which is manifest in the operations of the poetic text, the words 'inside' the poem. The first, 'though the Logos governs everything, most people trust in their own wisdom' (in approximate translation), poses, again like the poem itself, the question of how it is to be read. Who is speaking here, and from where? If a representative of 'most people', then the statement is obviously of uncertain weight, and if from the point of view of the Logos, then who or what is beyond the Logos in order to establish the truth of the statement by the Logos concerning the Logos? A position of undecidability, of self-undermining, similar to that generated by Russell's paradox, applies here, of a sort fundamental to the text of the poem itself. Such a suspension *between* supports meaning, and yet never is that meaning, is never what is directly or indirectly represented. The relation between *Burnt and Norton* and *The Waste Land* is governed, like the two texts themselves, by the temporality of the future anterior.

It will be said that *Four Quartets* is a Christian poem, and that appearance in the poem of the syncategoreme, for example, is a consequence of the basically apophatic theology that Eliot is concerned to express in it. This is to subordinate the poem's language and its displacements to an overriding theme, which might be paraphrased by reference to the writings of St John of the Cross or Juliana of Norwich. The theme of time, and so of eternity, are usually taken up in this connection. But, as I have tried to suggest—no more than suggest— time is to be taken, not only as a theme, but as the supplementary sequencing, spacing or gapping that is a condition for the signifiers that compose the text to have their place in the text at all. 'Time' generates an undecidability on each occasion of its use, inasmuch such refers to the theme at issue and the condition of (im)possibility governing that use. *Time* as the condition of any meaning at all is itself meaningless, not a meaning but that condition of sequencing that I earlier referred to as the excess of syntax over semantics. So what, then, of the pertinence of Christianity to Eliot's poem? I will simply quote Derrida's comments on Mallarmé's Platonism or Hegelianism: 'It is a simulacrum of Platonism or Hegelianism, which is separated from what it simulates only by a barely perceptible veil, about which one can just as well say that it already runs—unnoticed—between Platonism and itself, between Hegelianism and itself. Between Mallarmé's text and itself. It thus not simply false to say that Mallarmé is a Platonist or a Hegelian. But it is above all not true.' Perhaps Eliot has worked in similar fashion, and rethought the Word by investing it with the power of its own disappearance.

I conclude by offering Jeremy Prynne my profoundest good wishes on his eightieth birthday, and to say that the gratitude and respect in which I held him in my days as his student, and, I hope, friend, continue undiminished.

And You Too

ANTHONY BARNETT

"Probably no writer of our time, except possibly Ezra Pound, has had a higher conception of the writer's calling, his obligations to his art and to his reader." So wrote Clarence Brown about Osip Mandelstam. Let us apply that equally to J. H. Prynne, or Jeremy, as some like to familiarize him, as I myself shall do here for the first time in writing, for it may surprise to learn that there never was, apart from the earliest of brief moments, a poet named Jeremy Prynne, only a friend and colleague named Jeremy Prynne. And let us apply that writer's calling as well equally to Paul Celan and to Andrea Zanzotto. Etymologists, philologists, ethicalists, all. Yes, "to his art and to his reader." I refuse to be intimidated by so-called difficulty or those critiques on difficulty, positive or negative, that have infected our academic and popular literary cultures both. I shall not include Jeremy's "Resistance and Difficulty" in that because his essay is a model of clarity. Yes, "to his art and to his reader." Was John Donne ever easy? Even if and when I do not understand. Even if and when I do not like.

It was, therefore, a privilege that Jeremy accepted the proposal of Fiona Allardyce and myself to publish the first collected edition of J. H. Prynne's *Poems*. Would you like to know how that came about? First credit goes to the example of Tim Longville at Grosseteste for gathering in one voluminous volume *The Collected Works* of John Riley, who was no longer with us. It was no use going on printing only our lovely little, though sometimes large, Grosseteste, Ferry, and others, chapbooks. It was time to throw bricks through the windows of book stores and the reviewers of what was supposed to be our high-profile literary and literate cultural press, which today, more than ever, if such is possible, has hardly the faintest idea what it is doing—and I know why—look: these islands may do some things very well but poetry is not one of them. It worked. For one brief moment. Each volume that appeared in the Allardyce, Barnett, Publishers collected series, four followed *Poems*, was noticed at length in that press, and that goes too for my own *The*

Résting Bĕll, if not quite at length, in the *Times Literary Supplement*. Not every volume everywhere but every volume somewhere.

Yes, "to his art and to his reader." A word about the imprint: *Poems* was published by Agneau 2. Perhaps that was a bit silly on its own, though not half as silly as some other publisher names—hush my mouth. But what did it mean? I was editing a tiny little review entitled *Lamb: Standing for Literature, Art, Music, & Baa*, with a penned device, and for the first two issues a masthead, by Fiona Allardyce, depicting a lamb, with a bell, standing, of course. Actually, she drew more of a sheep. Anyway, Agneau 2 was more Lamb. Lamb too. It also sounded like And You Too. And You Too, Dear Reader. And now, Dear Reader, kindly allow a moment's serendipitous amusement to know that Charles Lamb signed a letter from Paris to J. H. Payne "Charlois Agneau *alias* C. Lamb". After *Poems*, Agneau 2 was relegated to its more sensible status as an imprint of Allardyce, Barnett, Publishers. Citationers: for heaven's sake remember the commas and do not give our later imprint Allardyce Book ABP an s. What a life!

At least, it is one. Today, it is an eighty-years life. Congratulations and thank you, Jeremy, for your and your work being an absolutely necessary part, not only of your life, but of ours too.

*

Not done yet. Dearest Ian tells me I have written insufficiently about how *Poems* came to be. Reluctantly, I shall try to recollect the essential facts because I myself cannot bring myself to look back at the newly archived correspondence of old. It is in the past and I must look more to the present. Ian is welcome to delve if he likes.

I began to know Jeremy's poetry around the mid 1960s, while moonlighting from Shell-Mex and BP on the Strand at the New Compton Street department of Better Books off, not on, the Charing Cross Road, next as assistant manager first at the general bookshop of Zwemmer on the Charing Cross Road, then back to Better Books. That section of New Compton Street no longer exists, buried beneath a new block. A curious aside: going up or down one day in the Shell Mex House elevator, *Poetry Chicago* in one hand and the *Melody Maker* in the other, they might have been in the same hand, some fine suited fellow grinned "We don't often see magazines like those in this building." "You won't for much longer because I am leaving in a fortnight's time." Many years later Shell Mex House came to host the headquarters of Penguin Books.

Kitchen Poems appeared. I could hardly make head nor tail of it but patience, or was it persistence, or was it persuasion, eventually, evidently, paid off. I was in Jeremy's presence once around that time, at a gathering in Fulcrum's apartment with, as I remember it, Ed Dorn, Christopher Middleton, Ron Kitaj, Jonathan Williams, unless I am conflating two separate occasions. But I do recall a car lift with Middleton to Dulwich, whereabouts he had a house and Kitaj was renting a house. From the late 1960s for some seven or eight years, for musical and personal reasons, I found myself living first in Denmark, then in Norway (yes, Jeremy Halvard, Norway). Correspondence between us began when I wrote Jeremy asking if I could print 'Of Sanguine Fire', a copy of the typescript of which had been sent to me by Peter Riley, also living in Denmark at that time, in *Canards du siècle présent*, an anthology of new work by fifteen mostly British poets I was putting together. Jeremy said yes. In due course he became a great encourager of my work as revealed in the selection of his letters he graciously allowed to appear many years later in Michael Grant's notionally edited *The Poetry of Anthony Barnett*—not a good title even though there was a reason.

While still in Denmark I had the idea to reprint Jeremy's 'Es Lebe der König', his poem in memory of Paul Celan, which had just appeared in *Brass*, with first translations by Rosmarie Waldrop of Celan's 'Conversation in the Mountains' and 'Answer to a Letter' by Edmond Jabès. Permission to publish the Celan was refused by the professor in whose care Celan's literary estate had been placed. Jeremy volunteered to write a reasoned and heartfelt letter in support of a request for reconsideration, which was not answered. After my move to Norway, I went ahead anyway and the three pieces appeared in a finely printed chapbook as *The Literary Supplement, Writings*, 1. A while later, Gisèle Celan-Lestrange sent a beautiful etching, which is now reproduced in *Snow lit rev*, 1.

To be brief the following years found me mostly back in England. I settled for a while in and around Canterbury. I met Fiona Allardyce who become a lifelong friend. She was restoring the murals in the Cathedral.

We often spoke about poetry. She pasted, I had no idea, a printing on rose-coloured card of my poem "Some Scandal that Has Floated Down from Higher Circles"—Gogol—in the plaster high above in the vault. Wonderful. With Fiona's help the foundations for our poetry bricks were laid. Jeremy's initial response to our invitation for his to be the first was one of caution. He was concerned that the work would be too much to see through. Reassurances of dedication and, indeed, necessity were made and work was began. *Poems* was set on an Exxon Information Systems Qyx, the first intelligent typewriter, with a micro-processor single-line correctable memory, designed to vanquish the IBM Selectric. But Exxon Office Systems, or EOS, was headed for failure, soon to be abandoned by parent ExxonMobil. The Qyx was a potentially interesting machine, with interchangeable cartridge printwheels. The font we chose from the few available, some familiar, others not, was their quixotic Boldface, possibly Garamond-derived but with an undistinguished ampersand and too loose word spacing. The Qyx was unpredictable, its motor would jam, and subsequent collected volumes were set on a reconditioned IBM Composer, electronic memory successor to the Selectric, with its interchangeable golfballs. A second escape from petroleum. The Qyx could have done better in another respect too. Unlike the IBM, it was not equipped with typographer quotation marks or apostrophe. I typed, cut out, and pasted heaven knows how many commas onto the paper printing plates in place of typewriter-style marks. The title *Poems* was letraset in Cloister, which seemed appropriate. Despite all the proofing in the world we could not do away with an errata slip, typed out at the last moment in Jeremy's office. Most shocking was "suprise". I think the print-run was four hundred hardbound and one thousand paperbound copies. And then there were *Poems* … was *Poems*? … were *Poems*?

What happened to the Allardyce, Barnett, Publishers collected series after the editing of the fifth volume, Veronica Forrest-Thomson's *Collected Poems and Translations*, for which, far from incidentally, Jeremy provided a copy of a key authorial typescript, was frightful but it is another story, involving resistance and difficulty. Here we are concerned only with the gestation of the Allardyce, Barnett, Publishers original collected edition of J. H. Prynne's Agneau 2 *Poems*. It was a task. It was a pleasure. From the opening "The whole thing it is, the difficult" to the closing "you say stuff it."

      Happy Anniversary, Jeremy,
         Fiona and Anthony

Looking at/Looking for
J.H. Prynne's 'Stone Lake'

Harry Gilonis

The poem I will be writing about below is nearly-unique among
J.H. Prynne's poems, in that even the dedicated reader may well not
recognise the title, it being not given in English in any of its various
publications[1]. The poem, written in Chinese, was originally published
as a folded sheet, around five-and-a-half inches wide by nine high—a
little narrower and a bit taller than A5. The front cover bears the imprint
details ('POETICAL HISTORIES No 22 / CAMBRIDGE / 1992'),
plus five large and three smaller Chinese characters, reproduced from
the author's own brushwork, these being, although the Anglophone
reader is nowhere told this, the title [in pinyin transliteration *Jie ban
mi Shi Hu*] and an authorial name [pronounced, approximately, 'Pu
Ling En']. The back cover is blank save for, at the foot, in small print,
an English-language publisher's colophon, which identifies the work as
"© by J. H. Prynne 1992". This is the sole English-language authorial
identification, appearing to be the publisher's concern rather than that
of the poet. All in all, Chinese characters predominate numerically over
words by a ratio of 4:3, and occupy a far higher proportion of the
visual field. When opened out, the inside of the sheet repeats the title
of the poem and the author's name to either side of a thirty-character
poem; this spread, the heart of the publication, is *entirely* in brush-
drawn Chinese characters.

I wanted to open by emphasising the appearance of the physical
object, because in it what an Occidental will see as Oriental very much
predominates; not least because so much of the text is hand-written
(brush-drawn) rather than printed. Prynne has set down his thoughts
on Chinese calligraphy in the context of discussing *contemporary*
Chinese literary production, so we may take his words as untinged by
reverence for museum-mummified antique exemplars:

This language of the written character is painted on to the paper, abstracted from the world-surface, whatever now is the more abbreviated practice. Its iconic deployment by stroke play and contexture makes a traffic with the eye worked by a different ground-plan. There is lexical transference and collocation, but also the sense of the occasion ramifies within the stroke-field itself: not by symbolism or imitation or assigned convention but by homologies intricately linked to the affective diagrams of social consciousness and activity.[2]

Further, our publication continues to be unusual *beneath* the calligraphy; the paper itself is atypical, unbleached, off-white. This, combined with Prynne's personal seal-imprint—placed on each copy, in the canonical cinnabar-coloured ink—produces an object wholly unlike any mass-market poetry publication, and not much like most small-press material (though it obviously shares the format and high production values with other Poetical Histories publications). This powerful and estranging effect is much inhibited when the poem appears within the larger Prynne collections: reduced to a quarter of its original size, restricted to a single page, with a Westernised numeral at the foot of the page and English text opposite. It seems much less assertive, more of a forlorn interloper than in its initial publication.

What *isn't* immediately evident is that, despite the aura of antiquity surrounding Prynne's brush text, the poem itself is written using, where applicable, the modernised/simplified Chinese characters (*jianhuazi*) that Prynne would have learned, as a regular visitor to the People's Republic of China. These easier-to-master characters were employed to increase mass literacy; their use is the 'abbreviated practice' he refers to above. Some characters in traditional Chinese have not changed under these 'reforms'; and, contrariwise, some of the simpler 'modern' forms have been used for centuries, in cursive rather than printed contexts. So the situation is a complex one, and I don't propose to dwell on it here, save to note that, had Prynne's poem somehow fallen into the hands of a Tu Fu or a Li Po, a Wang Chen or Meng Hao-jan, it might have posed some difficulties.

There is one other feature possibly worthy of remark. Chinese verse is often printed with its versions of a comma-*cum*-semi-colon-*cum*-

colon, the *dunhao* (，'pause mark') and a full stop, the *juhao* (。'sentence mark'). These often appear at the ends of alternate lines of traditional verse, marking a shift in focus and then a stronger pause at a couplet-end. Both are entirely missing from Prynne's text, making it look, perhaps, more modernist than traditional visually. This isn't a definitive marker of a text's positioning, but arguably says something about authorial stance; compare, say, Mallarmé's mid-career abandonment of punctuation, or Stefan George's decision to write German without capitalising nouns.

•

Turning now to the text, what we meet is first of all the title, written in standard Chinese fashion, reading from top to bottom: *Jie ban mi Shi Hu*[3]. Chinese poem-titles are every bit as varied as those in English, running a gamut from Li Shang-yin's 'Untitled' to Tu Fu's 'Many people come to visit and bring wine after I fell off my horse, drunk'. Prynne's title sits in the middle ground. Its first two characters, as well as having individual meanings, also make up a 'binome' (Chinese *lianmianzi*), that is, a composite word with a linked but different meaning—as, e,g, "slow-coach" in English. Here 结 [*jie (jyē)*], 'connect', together with 伴 [*ban (bàn)*], 'friend(s)', 'companion(s)', means 'go with somebody'[4]. The middle character, 觅 [*mi (mì)*] means 'seek', 'look for'. The last two characters, 石 [*shi (shr)*], 'stone', and 湖 [*hu (hú)*], 'lake', combine to give a place-name in Jiangsu province, on the outskirts of the eastern city of Suzhou. Prynne was teaching an English Literature course at the University there in 1991, when this poem was written[5].

Suzhou is a city in the Yangtse delta, not far from a very large, shallow lake, 'Taihu' (Tai Lake), which covers some 850 square miles; the old imperial 'Grand Canal' also passes nearby. Although there had been some small-scale industrialisation—electronics and factories— the city was in the early '90s largely unmodernised[6]. Its style has been characterised as 'small bridges, flowing water, white-washed walls and black tiles'. These buildings are interspersed with gardens, both ornamental and agriculturally productive—alluvial sediment from the Yangtse is very fertile, and high-ish average temperatures give a nine-month growing season. There were also, then, a large number of pig-farms. Historically Suzhou was the capital of the state of Wu, and it is said that in the course of an early squabble with the neighbouring state of Yue that that the latter dug a channel through low hills in order to attack Wu, and that this channel became 'Shi-hu', Stone-Lake. More probably it is a now-separated outlier of the larger Tai Lake. Both are very shallow, with stony bottoms (from which Stone Lake takes its name). The lake has famous temples nearby, and a prominent range of low, forested hills to its west, and has been a refuge for the aesthetically-minded for centuries; it is still a centre of tourism, and nowadays easily reached by buses from the city centre.

The poem proper has, like the title, five characters per line; here they are to be read from right to left, and from top to bottom—from top right, then, to bottom left. Such exact regularity in line-length is common in Chinese poetry, though not obligatory; however, it doesn't in itself suffice as a genre-marker, and it is hard to assign Prynne's poem to one formal category. Five-syllable lines go back a long way, at least 1,500 years, and are usually divided into two categories; 'old style' and 'regulated'. The 'Stone Lake' poem has, as we shall see, structural elements in common with both the earlier and the (far more complex) latter, later, mode; but that employs solely 4- or 8-line forms, making our poem *potentially* heterodox[7].

A language composed of monosyllables has different prosodic quandaries to face than Western languages do, and Chinese verse trad-itionally deploys what has been called 'semantic rhythm'.[8] The first two characters of a pentasyllabic line invariably form a logical unit, and the remaining three are divided either '2 + 1' or '1 + 2', which introduces a pleasing variety, and one which can be combined with other variables to produce complex formal structures. Set against these, however, can be an intriguing readerly freedom, pretty much unique to Chinese poetry. Here is J.H. Prynne explicating the matter:

> A complicating factor in the discussion of uncertainty and indeterminateness in poetic texts and their interpretation is the notorious perception that in Chinese traditional poetry the kinds of inherent ambiguity at all levels, in meaning and grammatical structure, have always been consistently high and also very distinctive as features of how such poetry gains its

effects and sets special tasks for the sophisticated reader. [...]
The perceived absence of Western-style sentence morphology,
including subject-predicate determination and inflectional
governance constructions, is commonly held to constitute
Chinese lyrical poems as fundamentally more indeterminate
and ambiguous than any of their non-oriental counterparts.
But of course such conventionally nuanced features are, in
native context, expressive of interpretation-choices much more
than they are obstacles to comprehension: ambiguity as poised
indecision in construal and the multiple possibilities of only
part-resolved implicature, especially in such aspects as number
and tense structures and person-forms in verb systems, are or
were a way of life for such text-practice and its adept readers.[9]

It would I think be fair to say that there are often conventions guiding
reading-decisions, so there has rarely if ever been *completely* free play
for readers of poetry in Chinese to get ludic—and that the extent to
which this option is taken up varies between poet and poet and era
and era.[10] However there is clearly more structurally-inbuilt latitude
than is *possible* (not just *common*) in most Western poetics, especially
comparably 'classical' ones. Hence the possibilities for greater 'creative
reading' need to be born in mind in reading the 'Stone Lake' poem
(although it is relatively restrained in its implicit deployment of such).

A good example proffers itself with the first two characters of the
poem proper: 上 [*shang* (*sháng*), 'ascending'], and 桥 [*qiao* (*chyào*)],
'bridge'. I've used the participle 'ascending' in order *not* to make
a decision Prynne's text is *not* making: his poem does *not* say "we
ascended", *nor* "we ascend", *nor* "we will ascend"—nor, indeed, does it
specify "we" (although that is a reasonable interpretation-choice, given
the opening of the title, and it would, I think, go against the grain
to read "I" or "he/she" or "they" here). The important thing is that
the poem has set us in motion, and given us a place. When Marco
Polo visited Suzhou he said there were at least 6,000 bridges; three-
quarters of a millennium later, in the 1980s, there were around 300
still extant. It applies particularly to the flatter east of Stone Lake, but
the land on all sides of it is still criss-crossed with a regular lattice of
small canals, all of them traversed at regular intervals by a grid of small

intersecting roads. It is said that Suzhou has 'water and land in parallel, and river and street as neighbours', and at a rough count there are at least 30 bridges on the lake, and another 25 or so with a clear view of it. Several of the bridges are of some antiquity (though often much-reconstructed), and one in particular, the Xingchun bridge, is a major tourist destination because of a curious one-night-a-year phenomenon when a summer full moon can be seen reflected under each of its nine arches. (I mention this last fact because it might help show why bridges would be particularly foregrounded in a visitor's consciousness; nothing in Prynne's poem suggests that it is set after dark, nor that 'his' bridge is of any particular cultural significance.) The median character, 推 [*tui* (*twei*)] means 'pushing'; again, we do not know singular or plural, male or female. What is being pushed is given by the semantically-paired 古 [*gu* (*gǔ*)], 'old', 'ancient', and 載 [*zai* (*dzǎi*)], '(loaded) vehicle(s)'[11]— perhaps a wheeled cart (Birgitta Johansson's reading)? Perhaps a bicycle with panniers? (To employ synecdoche, that near-relation of metonymy, to say "wheels" might be simplest.)

Regulated verse is traditionally structured in a fourfold movement: a beginning (*qi*); a continuation/elaboration (*cheng*); a turn (*zhuan*) and a conclusion (*he*). Given that regulated verse invariably uses 4 or 8 lines, it is easy to see how these will subdivide into single lines or couplets; in a 6-line poem it isn't so easy. However, we can see clearly that the second line offers a continuation, in that we are still on the bridge (桥 *chyào*). This repeat is a slight solecism in a Chinese poem of this length; the character is half of a pairing, qualified with 头 [*tou* (*tóu*)], 'top', 'high'. In the rest of the line the semantic rhythm switches to '2+1': another repeat (古 *gǔ*, 'old'), is paired with 景 [*jing* (*jǐng*)], 'scenery'; these are then set into place by 看 [*kan* (*kān*)], 'looking at', 'seeing', 'observing'. As before, there is no indication of person or gender; nor of tense or mood.

Line three is a continuing development: it opens with another binome: 青 [*qing* (*chīng*)], 'green-blue', and 苔 [*tai* (*tái*)], 'moss', combine to mean, rather reductively, 'moss'. However, the phrase is a most suggestive one; it occurs in what is probably, for Western readers, the most famous single Chinese poem, Wang Wei's T'ang dynasty quatrain *Lu Chai* ('Deer Park'). A whole book has been written on its assorted translations;[12] even a novice at Chinese poetry—which

Prynne is not—would know the poem and the phrase. (Indeed, for those who've looked further afield, it has a longer poetic history; I've found it in poems centuries before and centuries after Wang Wei.[13]) Its use here is—perhaps—a tiny gesture towards the common practice of allusion in Chinese poetry, the re-use of vocabulary from previous or contemporary writers. It might be thought of as a form of metonymy; with the advantage that—in contrast to the highly-mannered terminology of earlier court poetry like the *New Songs from a Jade Terrace*, which can verge on private language—this is public, and need not trouble the reader who fails to spot the reference.[14] Sometimes green moss is just green moss; and the everyday reading of it, and a literary one, will be the same.[15]

It has been suggested to me that there is a possible subtler associative play occurring here: there is an <u>exact</u> homophone of our poem's *qing* (*ching*), which character visibly combines the 'water' radical 氵 to the left of the 青 present in our poem to produce 清. This *qing*, which is <u>absent</u> from Prynne's poem, means 'clear', 'pure' or 'clean'; in the circumstances of the poem's watery milieu might a second visually <u>and</u> aurally similar *qing* have lurked at the edges of authorial consciousness? Vocabulary choice is complex and not always rationalised.

The third line concludes '1 + 2': 遮 [*zhe* (*jĕ*)], 'covering', refers to 荒 [*huang* (*hwăng*)], 'abandoned', plus 苑 [*yuan* (*ywàn*)], 'garden(s)'. It is up to us, not knowing the precise vantage-point in the real world, to decide if there is one garden, or several, or many; Suzhou has a tradition of both small-scale agriculture and large-scale ornamental gardens. (It seems to me unlikely that Prynne is thinking of the famous 'Gardens of Suzhou', written about by landscape historians around the world in a multitude of languages;[16] these are all arranged around the historic centre of the city, away to the north-east of Stone Lake.)

The fourth line begins with the necessary pairing, 伴 [*ban* (*bàn*)], the second character in our poem's title: 'companion(s)', 'friend(s)'; plus 友 [*you* (*yŭ*)], 'with'. The next three characters are 谈 [*tan* (*tán*)], 'talking'; 心 [*xin* (*syīn*)], 'heart(s)', 'mind(s)'; and 意 [*yi* (*yì*)], 'intent' (which itself suggestively contains *syīn*). The last two appear also as the last two characters in the penultimate line of a very famous early Chinese poem, the third of the 'Nineteen Old Poems', well-known before that time but (partially) re-anthologised in the *New Songs from a Jade Terrace*;[17] this is another instance of an allusion which doesn't wear its heart, or mind, on its sleeve. I am unclear on the semantic subdivision of the three final characters in Prynne's line; "talking-with-my-heart/our-hearts" or "my/our heart(s) intent" are equally syntactically possible. (Heart-intent would work better for a feature the Chinese text *gestures at* rather than fully sustaining: syntactic 'parallelism', which I do not propose to go into here.)

Perhaps fittingly the line might seem to have an uncertain developmental status; it isn't immediately clear whether our protagonists are talking on this crowded bridge, holding up the traffic as tourists do; or if they have moved on elsewhere. However, there is a solution to this analytic quandary. From the earliest times Chinese poetry has employed what Zong-Qi Cai calls a "bipartite structural block", being "two lines of natural description [*jing*] and two or more lines of emotional expression [*qing*], brought together purely on an analogical-associational basis".[18] Given the absence of any non-subjective reference in line 4, it is evident that we've made this transition. Prynne's problematic decision to write a 6-line poem means that this entirely correct structural move takes place *within* a couplet, as traditionally defined; which is profoundly heterodox! (This is assuredly an even more radical *zhuan*-turn than could have been anticipated...)

Line 5 offers, as it were, a *cheng* continuation/elaboration, *post-turn*; in Western terms, the development of the second subject of a sonata, or the continuing movement after the *volta* of a sonnet. Given the humid climate of Suzhou[19], it might come as no surprise that the opening pairing is 雨 [*yu* (*yŭ*), 'rainy', and 天 [*tian* (*tyān*)], 'day(s)'/'sky/skies'. The rest of the line reads 杯 [*bei* (*bēi*)], 'cup(s)'; 香 [*xiang* (*syāng*)], 'fragrant'; and—depending on how one pronounces the character 叶 [*ye*]—either *yè* (meaning 'leaf/leaves') or *syé* (meaning 'harmony', 'be harmonious')—though there are arcane complications I will relegate to an end-note.[20] As with the previous line, this leaves the semantic rhythm, 1+2 or 2+1, unclear. While the leaves need not be tea-leaves— bamboo-leaves are fragrant in the rain—it is hard to resist the reading of a refreshing cuppa, exemplifying the harmony of English and Chinese cultures... in the last analysis I'd plump for *yè*, 'leaves', and read them as tea-leaves to boot, because the Lake Tai region is famous for growing a very highly-rated, strongly-scented green tea, *biluochun*.[21] Its original name, *xiasharenxiang*, ends with *xiang* (香), 'fragrant', the penultimate character in this line of our poem. What would be more natural than Prynne's party companionably sharing a famous local brew?

As the final line opens we should logically be moving to the conclusion (*he*), and the opening pairing confirms that: 久 [*jiu* (*jyoŭ*)], 'late', and 回 [*hui* (*hwei*)], 'returning', which we might better Anglicise as "returning late". The close of the line has the 1+2 rhythm: 享 [***xiang*** (*syăng*)], 'enjoying', qualifying *syīn* (心), 'heart(s)', 'mind(s)'—repeated from line 4—and 间 [*jian* (*jyān*)], 'in'. It seems pleasingly unclear whether all the party are returning, after a long day, with pleasure in it; or whether Prynne alone, rather later, is returning solo in happily reflective mood.

•

This, of course, is where there is supposed to be A Conclusion, which Sums Up Definitively; but, *equally*, of course, neither the openness of Chinese poetic syntax, which as we have seen allows (some) variant re-reading of the same text *ad libitum*, nor Prynne's own poetic practice—which Ryan Dobran characterised as invoking "the inbetweenness of multiple sense-constitution"[22]—really suggest that such a rhetorical move would be appropriate, even were it possible. As the above juxtaposition suggests, despite radically different features and origins, despite a broadly traditional mode in Prynne's Chinese poem as against the radical modernism evident in his English poetry, there is in the final analysis a gratifying concordance of operating procedures, a foregrounding of what art criticism calls the 'beholder's share'; which suggests that my best place is to step back and let you, gentle reader, get on with it.[23] As Prynne puts it,[24] 'no translation will exhaust its originals, though it may tire them out'.

Notes

[1] Titled only in Chinese [结伴觅石湖] in its first and second publications [from Peter Riley's Poetical Histories imprint (1992, repr. 2004)], the title is given in unaccented *pinyin* transliteration, 'Jie ban mi Shi Hu', in all 3 editions of Prynne's *Poems* in which it appears (1992, 2005, 2015), in each instance on

page 380. (See www.aprileye.co.uk/histories.html in re the first publication.) There was also a magazine reprint, in *Notus* issue 12 (spring 1993)—which I have not seen. It apparently subtitled the Chinese text as 'Poem on Stone Lake', a *gloss* on the poem rather than an accurate translation of its title. The only published English titles that I've seen are: (1), Birgitta Johansson's 'In Search of the Stone Lake with a Companion' in her *The Engineering of Being: An Ontological Approach to J.H. Prynne* (Umeå, 1997), in footnote 65, pp. 190f.; her version draws on versions by several Chinese speakers and a gloss in Peter Riley's papers [now in Cambridge University Library]; (2), Li Zhimin's 'Going Together to Seek for Stone Lake', in his 'Four Different Ways of looking at J. H. Prynne's Chinese Poem—A Harmony of English and Chinese Cultures' (in *QUID* 7a [2001], pp. 14-18) and (3), a character-gloss by Peter McCarey's un-named Chinese teacher (!), in his essay 'Squink: Reading J.H. Prynne', in *PN Review* 205 [Vol. 38 no. 5 (May-June 2012)], collected as 'Squink' in his *Find an Angel and Pick a Fight* (Geneva, 2013), footnote 1, p. 201.

The character-by-character gloss referred to is said by Johansson to be by Prynne, whereas Peter Riley recollects it as circulating, unofficially, shortly after the first publication of the fascicle. As its authorial status is uncertain it would seem ill-advised to rely on it more heavily for exegetical purposes than any other anonymous gloss.

The other *illisible* Prynne poem is that written in runes, "ᛒ ᛒ ᛒ..." (*Poems*, p. 244 in all recent editions), glossed by Peter Manson in *Quid* 17, a previous Prynne *Festschrift* [2006], and also by Justin Katko in *If A Then B* no. 1 (August 2010).

[2] J.H. Prynne, 'Afterword' to the 1994 special 7th issue of *Parataxis*, 'ORIGINAL: Chinese Language-Poetry Group' (pp. 121-124, here p. 122); reprinted online in *Jacket* 20 (December 2002), at http://jacketmagazine. com/20/pt-chinese.html#pry-pro . Prynne discusses classical calligraphy in 'The *Night Vigil* of Shen Shou'—see *SNOW* lit rev 2 (autumn 2013-spring 2014), at p. 102.

[3] The Cambridge University Library catalogue record prefers all lower-case save for an initial capital, which fails to signal that the last two characters make up a proper name. Given that the first two characters are also a composite 'binome', a case could be made for writing the title as *Jieban mi Shihu*.

[4] I supply throughout (*in italics within round brackets*) the 'Yale' transliterations, which follow a system developed during the Second World War to help Americans communicate more easily with their Chinese allies. They are obviously rough-and-ready, but to my mind give a better sense than *pinyin*, developed by Romanian sinologists and ultimately best left to Romanian Sinologists. I have added accentuation from *pinyin*, as this gives information about the spoken

tones. A horizontal macron denotes the first (flat, or high level) tone; an acute accent the second (rising, or high-rising) tone). The third tone (falling-rising, or low) has an accent with no everyday English name, variously called a *caron*, *háček* or *breve*. The fourth (falling or high-falling) tone is represented by a grave accent; the fifth (neutral) tone is unmarked.

[5] Birgitta Johansson reports, in *The Engineering of Being*, p. 15, that Prynne was in China for 6 months in 1991. (I should say here that I have not found her Heidegger-inflected reading of our poem—*op. cit.*, pp. 190-192—particularly helpful or convincing.)

[6] Suzhou was heftily redeveloped in the mid-to-late '90s, winning an international award for the sensitivity with which this was done. Overseas journalistic accounts stressed that, for example, pig-farmers were amply recompensed when forced to relocate because manure was contaminating Stone Lake. Suzhou, even viewed *post hoc*, might escape some of the criticisms of redevelopment conducted with no eye to social justice which Prynne sets out in his 'Brief Note on "Harmony" in Architecture' delivered at a conference in China in 2006 and subsequently published in *Quid* 18 (2007).

[7] The unorthodox form of the 'Stone Lake' poem (and the complete absence of the tonal patterning essential to 'regulated' verse) mitigate against seeing the poem as properly 'regulated'. If pressed I would probably settle for considering the 'Stone Lake' poem as an example of reformed *yüeh-fu*, the loose category into which examples of 6-line pentasyllabic verse are placed in the most famous Chinese poetry anthology, the *Tang-shi T'an-pai Shou* ('Three Hundred T'ang Poems'). There is, however, an important other categorial contender to consider. Prynne has great admiration for an earlier (6th century) anthology, entirely comprising 'old-style' writing, the *Yü T'ai Hsin Yung* ('New Songs from a Jade Terrace'). 'China Figures', his lengthy review of Anne Birrell's 1983 English translation of the *New Songs*, was reprinted as a 'Postscript' when the book was paperbacked as a Penguin Classic in 1986. Prynne writes fascinatingly about metonymy in this earlier Chinese poetry, emphasising that the *New Songs* reconfigure the standard Western mental model of Chinese poetics. The *New Songs* also include a considerable number of 5-character, 6-line poems. However, I see no deployment of metonymy in the 'Stone Lake' poem, whose flavour seems to me much closer to the standard T'ang lyric exemplified by the *Tang-shi*. Anne Birrell's 47 pages of 'Notes' gloss quite exhaustively metonymic figures she has identified in the *New Songs*; I have been unable to find any shared figures, or even any non-trivial overlap of vocabulary between the *New Songs* and the 'Stone Lake' poem. Indeed, Prynne would seem to distance the core *New Songs* poetic from that embodied in the 'Stone Lake' poem: "The tendency towards a deliberately metonymic

system is [...] explicitly opposed to landscape poetry, if by that is meant the unmediated associative contemplation of natural objects and perspectives through a heightened personal perception" ['China Figures', in Anne Birrell, *New Songs from a Jade Terrace* (Harmondsworth, 1986), pp. 363-392, here p. 374]. Any totalising dichotomy read into the above would be an exaggeration; there is metonymic allusion a-plenty in T'ang lyric (as Prynne points out in 'China Figures', with regard to Pound's translation of Li Po's "Jewel Stairs' Grievance" in *Cathay*—an observation I owe to Dominic Lash's excellent thesis, in part on metonymy in Prynne, findable at http://bura.brunel.ac.uk/bitstream/2438/4668/9/FulltextThesis.pdf).

(Prynne has some suggestive and less 'public' remarks about the *New Songs* poetics in a 1983 letter, contemporary with his initial review, subsequently published in *SNOW lit rev,* issue 1 [spring 2013], pp. 73-77, specifically pp. 73-74.)

[8] I take the term from Zong-Qi Cai's *How to Read Chinese Poetry* (New York, 2008), pp. 103-104 (see also pp. 385-387).

[9] Prynne gave a keynote speech at a conference in Shijiazhuang in Hebei province, China in 2008, which was published, with apparatus appropriate to a print instantiation, as 'Difficulties in the Translation of 'Difficult" Poems' in *Cambridge Literary Review* Vol. 1 no. 3 (Easter, 2010). I cite here endnote 8 on p. 163; Prynne gives a small bibliography of relevant authorities in this endnote. The piece is findable online at www.cambridgeliteraryreview.org/wp-content/uploads/PrynneCLR3.pdf

[10] The Sinologist A.C. Graham (whom Prynne rightly admires) is splendidly precise as to when this option arose, suggesting that in China it would be plausible to trace the beginnings of the development to poems which Tu Fu was writing in 766 AD (whereas English poetry "begins to concentrate on multiple meanings during the late sixteenth century")—see Graham, *Poems of the Late T'ang* (Harmondsworth, Middx., 1977), p. 20. Arthur Waley's favourite poet, Po Chü-I, was born in 772 AD, two years after Tu Fu's death; his decision to write in a very clear and unambiguous manner would seem to be personal (and inspired by *yüeh-fu,* interestingly) rather than reflecting any *Zeitgeist.* Prynne considers the extent to which these pluralising poetic options were a total mode at any given period (as against the alternative mode of allusion-heavy, metonymic 'court poetry') both in his 1983 review/postscript 'China Figures' (in Birrell, *op. cit.*), and in his 1987-91 lecture 'Image and Figure in Twentieth-Century English Translation of Chinese Poetry' findable online at http://babylon.acad.cai.cam.ac.uk/students/study/english/chinese/imaglect.pdf

[11] I should mention that the previously-published English-language translations of our poem read this phrase radically differently. Johansson has "I pushed" (which obviously imposes decisions of number and tense), whilst Li Zhimin, in his 'Four Different Ways of looking at J. H. Prynne's Chinese Poem', reads *zai* more usefully imprecisely as 'push'. This has lexicographical mandate*, but he goes on to suggest that Prynne wrote a phrase varyingly translatable (by Li) as "to push open ancient ages", "push open the ancient", "to push ancientness" or "to push open the ancient ages". I think this radically unlikely!

[*Mathews' Chinese-English Dictionary gives "To load; to contain; to carry" as the primary meaning for *Tsai* [M6653], and gives as the fourth reading "A year".]

Li Zhimin's 'J.H. Prynne's Poetry and its Relations to Chinese Poetics' (in [ed] Ian Brinton, *A Manner of Utterance*, pp. 51-58) refers only *en passant* to the 'Stone Lake' poem; an opportunity unfortunately missed.

[12] Eliot Weinberger, *Nineteen Ways of Looking at Wang Wei* (Kingston, RI, 1987). I have, without undue effort, found a dozen more translations, and have indeed added another 7 stones to the poetic cairn in my *Wheel River* (London: Contraband, 2015).

[13] "Green moss" also appears in the poetry of Fan Ch'eng-ta (1126-93), a poet who famously lived by Stone Lake and wrote about it repeatedly. I've found no convincing signs of direct allusion to his poetry in Prynne's poem, which is a pity, given that Fan is the first poet in China to present the lives of the rural poor sympathetically *and* with close attention to the actual detail of their lives—that is to say, *unsentimentally*. Arguably the 'Stone Lake' poem would share with this part of Fan's work a general category-description, *tianyuan* or 'fields-and-gardens' poetry, which deals with nature humanised or cultivated, not in its 'raw' state.

[14] The Sinologist Arthur Cooper refers to "latent association", wherein there is an "assumption of free-will on the part of the reader to activate or not to activate such assocations", guided by considerations outside the poem - see his *Li Po and Tu Fu* (Harmondsworth, Middx., 1973), pp. 52-53. This obviously fits well with a poetics of concision (or metonymy), in that one utterance can do two jobs.

[15] Li Po writes—using a different character for 'green'—"Where Hsieh Ling-yün walked is buried in emerald mosses" (my translation); Paula Versano glosses the line as "an unambiguous reminder of the pastness of the past" (in Cai, *op. cit.*, p. 233). It is unambiguous enough not to need to be literary.

[16] The paradigm-shifting book is Craig Clunas, *Fruitful Sites* (Durham, NC: 1996), which I can thoroughly recommend for its revolutionary re-insertion

of economics into Chinese garden history, a move as welcome as G.E.M. de Sainte-Croix's equivalent scrutiny of Roman country estates. The English landscape garden awaits its Clunas.

[17] The (pentasyllabic) 'Nineteen Old Poems' were probably written in the Later Han dynasty (25-220 AD), though, as their title suggests, they purport to be older (see Cai, *op. cit.*, p. 103). The 3rd poem, 'Green, green grows the cypress on the hilltop', is not one of the 6 re-presented in the *New Songs*; it can be found in Cai, *op. cit.*, p. 106.

[18] Cai, *op. cit.*, p. 8; see also pp. 43, 112-113. There is intriguing light shed on this twin focus in Prynne's polemical 'No Universal Plan for a Good Life'*, in which, having spoken of the necessity for political consciousness and commitment, he refers to the need for "the silence of inward thought, and feeling not directed towards an object" which will "pose always the question, whether the self can be sufficient in its own truth. The life of plants and landforms, almost silent and local to their own accident of position, echoes this question in their solitary and companionable forms of being."

[*Prynne's piece is the only English-language contribution to a Nepali anthology, *Sahitya Ra Jeevan Darshan* ['A Collection of the Expressions'], edited by Rajan Prasad Pokharel (Kathmandu, 2010); available via https://dl.dropboxusercontent.com/u/16002249/images/prynneinnepali.pdf]

For some similarly polemical suggestions as to possible *political* implications of Chinese poetics, see my talk on 'Chiu Chin (1875-1907) and Chinese/revolutionary poetics', delivered at the May 2012 Poetry and Revolution International Conference in London; published in *Tripwire* issue 9 (2015), and findable online at www.bbk.ac.uk/cprc/events/Poetry_and_Revolution

[19] From Prynne's 'Afterword' to the *Parataxis* special issue on the ORIGINAL Chinese poetry group, we know that he "met the kernel pair of the ORIGINAL collective near to the banks of the Imperial canal in the eastern city of Suzhou, during the summer of 1991" (*op. cit.*, p. 121). Suzhou has its annual rainy season from mid-June to mid-July, which would fit with the rain in our poem… In an improvised talk in 2011 Prynne referred to the group including "Che Qian-zi and Zhou Ya-ping and others" [published as 'Introduction to Prynne's Poems in Chinese' in *The Cambridge Quarterly* [Vol. 41 no. 1 (March 2012), pp. 197-202 and 204-206, here p. 201; findable online at http://camqtly.oxfordjournals.org/content/41/1/197.full.pdf+html] Might one or both of these poets be the 'friend(s)' of our poem? (Alas, the Imperial Canal passes to the east of Suzhou, and Stone Lake is to its west.)

[20] The two candidates have two character-forms; one, pronounced *syè*, 'harmony' (Mathews M2633), appears solely as it does in Prynne's poem, 叶. The other, pronounced *yè*, 'leaf/leaves', can appear as 叶, but also very differently: 葉 (Mathews M7319). The advantage to reading *yè*, 'leaf/leaves', is that it arguably provides a rhyme—according to the *very* arcane rules of Chinese rhyming—with the final character of line 4. (Or so one Sinologist I spoke to thought could be the case.) This is *highly* unorthodox, as rhyme is almost invariably supposed to be contained within a couplet; and in any case, another Sinologist saw no rhymes there, but thought lines 2, 3 and 6 all rhymed, which is *equally* impermissible. Prynne himself has disavowed the presence of rhyme in the 'Stone Lake' poem, in an interview published in Chinese in *Yangcheng Wanbao* ['Yangcheng Evening News'] on 20 July 2012:

> "They said 'it doesn't rhyme!'. I explained that I knew it didn't rhyme, because I had a small [Chinese] vocabulary. They still said 'it doesn't rhyme!'. So I didn't write a second poem."
> [My translation, from www.ycwb.com/ePaper/ycwb/html/2012-07/20/content_1444348.htm]

Did they mean that it didn't rhyme *properly*? Or that it didn't rhyme *at all*?

The counter-advantage to reading *syé*, 'harmony', *if* it was read as meaning "being-harmonious", is that this would allow 'parallelism' with *kan*, 'watching', in line 2. Chinese poetic parallelism is a complex business, and it seems clear Prynne has *not* employed it rigorously; but, then, the 'Stone Lake' poem lacks other necessary features of 'regulated' verse. For what it's worth, Li Zhimin, in his article in *QUID* 7a, reads "leaves" in all four of his readings. I say 'for what it's worth' because Li himself feels clear that the poem can be read in any of the four possible directions with equal effect; not only are some of his proffered versions chaotic—"years view the garden's wishes among leaves"?—but it seems to me that to carry out this programme he has to ignore essential features of Chinese prosody, in three instances wilfully disregarding the evident semantic rhythms established in the fourth reading—which the layout suggests—and also requiring in two instances five-line poems with 6 characters to a line, as far as I know entirely unprecedented. Given the extent to which my reading shows Prynne doing his best to deploy traditional poetics, I find this approach very implausible. (Prynne, however, has not publicly disavowed it, to my knowledge.)

[21] Apparently the *Cha Shuo*, a famous 'tea encyclopaedia', rated *biluochun* as the best green tea in China. (Johansson's translation concurs in seeing the leaves as those of tea.)

---

[22] In his 'Introduction' to *Glossator* volume 2, 'On the Poems of J.H. Prynne', (2010), p. 3. Simon Jarvis comes nearer to the Chinese model when he says of Prynne's later work that "[t]he words themselves are not always the difficulty so much as the fact that their syntactical status remains uncertain" ['The Incommunicable Silhouette...', published online in *Jacket* 24 (November 2003), findable at http://jacketmagazine.com/24/jarvis-tis.html

[23] The dictionary definitions provided in my text collate from print dictionaries (Mathews' and Oxford) as well as online ones, specifically:

Chinese Text Project: http://ctext.org/dictionary.pl?if=en
Collins: http://dictionary.reverso.net/chinese-english
Zhendic: http://wengu.tartarie.com/wg/zhendic.php

The first of these also provides the 'Tang reconstruction' of a character's rhyme-sounds. As these are *very* distant from contemporary soundings, they are only relevant for a scholarly and retrospective notion of "rhyme", and thus only matter here for end-of-line characters. I supply those reconstructions here, with 'traditional' formations of the characters where necessary (in round brackets), *almost* all derived via www.chinese-tools.com/tools/converter-simptrad.html

5	载(載)	*tzài / *tzǎi / dzhài / tzài
10	看	*kan / kán
15	苑	*qiuǎn
20	意	qià
25 [*tradit.*]	叶	*lap / *l[a]p
25 [*simplif.*]	(葉)	*iɛp
30	间(間)	*gɛn

Readers are now (arguably...) equipped to produce their own translations of the *Jie ban* poem; I for one would welcome seeing any versions anyone wanted to forward via the publisher.

[24] 'Afterword' in *Parataxis* 7, *op. cit.*, p. 123.

••

My thanks to (amongst others) Ian for the invitation, Peter for a helpful chat, Michel and Louis for friendly assistance, and to John and Bridget for comments on an earlier draft; obviously I propose to hug my mistakes zealously to myself and not share them with anyone else.

A Bash in the Tunnel

Ian Friend & Richard Humphreys

Picture The Morpeth Arms, Millbank, London, near the Tate Gallery, sometime in the early 1980s. I can't be more specific than that, because escaping the Tate, as somewhat errant but nonetheless conscientious curators, Ian Friend and I would drink so much in those days that hours, days and weeks became, and remain, a blur scented with cigarette smoke and the distinct aroma of bitter-drenched pub floorboards. I seem to remember we spoke about many things but strangely I recall nothing much which would pass for supposed intellectual conversation; just shapes, smells, sounds and the realisation that this was a friendship forged on common ground, shared loves and interests, and all conducted in a sense of mutual trust. It often began relatively early, say at midday, when a huge beard followed by a hand mimicking the rapid downing of a pint would appear around my office door. "Fancy a bash in the tunnel?" he would ask. The invitation was always accompanied by a literary reference, in this case the title of a short story by Flann O'Brien about a man who would habitually drink himself into a stupor in a railway carriage parked in a tunnel in Dublin.

We would talk about something serious like football or poetry and occasionally art, Friend sucking in the beer froth from that great jungle of hair over his face. I have listened to him enthuse about the poetic genius of Neruda, O'Hara, Olson and many others and thought I'd also better show willing, so I told him about J. H. Prynne and about his amazingly difficult and peculiar poetry. Ian ordered more drinks. It was sometime towards the end of another ridiculous lunch hour, which re-enacted in current institutionally temperate days would probably have resulted in our employment being terminated.

I have never understood Prynne's poetry in the way one might understand Larkin or even Donne, for whom some prose translation is usually more or less possible. Prynne offers lyric intensity, specialist languages of high finance, research science, digital communication, tabloid wordplay—all orchestrated in memorably unusual prosody as if a Cambridge college librarian had been possessed and started speaking in tongues. Brave and clever people write about Prynne's poetry and cast some light on this fluctuating screen, but in doing so inevitably cast more shadows. So, I won't say too much about the poetry, except that I am totally engaged by the weird range of references, the obvious formal brilliance, subtle music and heart-tugging feelings these poems generate when read intently, breaking through to some entirely undiscovered worlds and uncovering at times a quirky sense of humour.

Friend, on the scent as ever, went off to Duck Soup, a small esoteric bookshop run by Nick Kimberley, conveniently near The Enterprise, a pub in Holborn, which was renowned for the quality of its India Pale Ale, and acquired every available volume of Prynne's poetry and read it all repeatedly. Friend had a habit of writing to poets he admired and Prynne responded to some of his observations, and his desire to visualise, in an allusive manner, some work in relation to the poetry. This did not surprise me as Prynne has previously stated his preference for references other than those of the critical and literary establishment.

Friend left the UK for Australia in 1985 to teach at the Victorian College of the Arts, Melbourne. He has lived in Brisbane for the past 17 years. We have met on each of his subsequent return visits to England, and once also in Australia. The conversation invariably turns to Prynne, with whom he has maintained a correspondence for over 30 years, but they have still never met.

The particular suite of poems that has resonated with Friend, and engendered a significant, and ongoing, body of work, is the volume titled *The Oval Window*. From a scientific and medical point of view the oval window (fenestra ovalis) is a membrane aperture in the middle ear, in which location are millions of delicate calcite crystals which transform sound into neural signals, thus allowing us, on a basic level, the faculty of hearing and speech. The crystals also react to gravitational change and play a crucial role in balance. It is an almost sacred site of our inner space where extraordinary things happen or have their origins.

Friend has found a unique visual language to interpret and re-enact this world. The techniques of the observer, scientific and imaginative, which are suggested are those of the microscopist, the x-ray technician, the ear specialist and the visionary psychoanalyst. The search is in part for the aberrant cell as it turns, lighting up the rupturing space. Or perhaps for the light at the end of the tunnel, the supposed joyous moment of near death experience. The collective title of these works is *Joy at Death Itself*, an ongoing series, some of which have been up to 15 years in progress.

There is also embedded here an understanding of a broader historical and cultural context. Friend's work has a deep sense of relationship not only to modernism but also to the Renaissance, a broad arc which can be defined by the writings of Adrian Stokes whom Friend has studied avidly. He has the Stokesian sense of the imaginative and cultural richness of the aesthetic impulse and its many interlocking affinities.

The poet Laurie Duggan wrote a perceptive essay on Friend's work for a 2002 exhibition at Brisbane City Gallery. He wrote of the ubiquitous white ovals as floating gateways between the interior and exterior of the body, drawing on the clues from Prynne's poems. Duggan also states that the forms "vary greatly in definition, multiplied like cells that could represent growth in benign or malign (cancerous) forms". The *Joy at Death Itself* works celebrate this paradox.

Duggan's words provoke thoughts which I can still feel nervous about, although I don't think I fear them. My first wife, Cat, died at the age of 51 from a rare sarcoma in 2001 after a five-month illness. When someone close to you dies, everything changes. I told Ian and he was understandably shocked. He was someone who understood this reticent and richly unusual woman in a typically intuitive way. He gave me one of the *Joy at Death Itself* works in Cat's memory and this now hangs as part of the Sidney Sussex College collection in Cambridge University.

Everything I can understand about Prynne's poems in *The Oval Window* and in Friend's response to them, is about sensing the limits of self-understanding, the points at which we can no longer think but move into some quite different experience of ourselves, standing on the edge of the abyss. Cancer cells are strange. They can develop or disappear depending on things that may not just be biochemical. When they get a grip they change everything, inside and outside, effecting a metamorphosis.

Something I dimly recall from our long lunch hours is the discussion of the ever-present sense of something dark and imminent. Not another pint of Guinness, but that feeling that one's life has a shape which is just perceptible, eyes shut, as a poetics of inner space, a dance of changing forms. And the conversation would possibly have then moved on from Prynne and embraced Gaston Bachelard and *The Poetics of Space*, and other, vitally important, shared concerns about Chelsea FC and Wolverhampton Wanderers FC and how they would fare on the coming weekend.

2003
(edited and revised
by Richard Humphreys
and Ian Friend 2015)

I Staircase, Gonville and Caius

John Wilkinson

My memory has always been poor because I grew up without relatives to occupy my mind. But if I evoke a place, actors start returning, and instead of remembering them, I recognise them and their ways. This short evocation is a way of approaching through a room someone whose poetry occupies me.

The room was white panelled, although little wall-space was visible, and looked out onto the sixteenth century Gate of Honour leading from Senate House Passage to Caius Court, Gonville & Caius College, Cambridge—the finest of Cambridge's formal gates, hexagonal and with a suite of sundials about the top. As usual with rooms at Cambridge colleges, it was entered through double doors, a closed outer door signifying the occupant's absence. This occupant rarely arrived until the early afternoon, and sometimes a few minutes late for appointments then, bounding up narrow stairs from the dank approach passage below.

But if the room were occupied, the inner door would be flung open and students, one or half a dozen, would be gathering themselves out of the sofa and chairs to leave. "Sit down, sit down" and a gesture of welcome towards a chair. A few pleasantries before the supervision. The occupant paced the room, talking in complex and complete periods, plucking books from shelves. The effect was more generous than soliloquy implies, with pauses for my assent, with its back-tracking, re-considering, and further expatiation; I was admitted to a dialectical process where for all my inadequacies, I had conferred on me the part of a silent but equal disputant. This could be worrying, since to follow, let alone accompany the occupant, was a dizzyingly strenuous adventure. Nonetheless I understood that I would never be tricked, checked on, or made to feel ashamed. I felt held to account only when a book was pressed on me as vitally important, and would spend anxious hours turning phrases in my head which might show I wasn't hopelessly unworthy of the precious text. Eventually I found that so indefatigable was the occupant's dialectical habit of mind, that should I demur at his valuation, my demurral would be seized upon and returned to me with an instantly-spun rationale that allowed me to feel vindicated.

Bestowal of books was unreserved and included rare, irreplaceable volumes. I know the occupant lost countless books in this way, through spontaneously lending them, but this risk never tempered his impulse. The room was filled with books, a commonplace statement which met its fullest material expression here. Every possible wall was lined to the ceiling with bookshelves, packed, double-ranked, overlaid. There were further bookcases, such as the small low case whose top shelf held the German works of Paul Celan. To the left of the door on entering was a long low table piled with recent acquisitions. Below a small window was a cheapish LP deck which in the evenings would often play records of early music. This was not a room that looked out, but a room that drew in.

The occupant's character was apparent in the room's extreme combination of hospitality and secrecy. Most Cambridge rooms felt either like offices or private living rooms. From the middle of the evening this room was open to all comers, through the small hours of the morning and often through dawn. Students and local poets would smoke, roll joints, and drink at the tenant's expense, talking in their clusters or clustering around Ed Dorn or Barbara Guest or another visitor. Hospitality was the occupant's most notable personal quality too, in such collective openness and in what he made artistically and intellectually available to me as an individual. Then there were his astonishing letters, screeds of several pages' length sent to undergraduates whose writing he felt showed promise, as well as his extensive and international literary correspondents. Only when I received such letters did I feel inadequate, struggling to interpret a commentary so much more eloquent than my poems. As poets' correspondence from the last century starts to be published, it is reassuring to see a George Oppen struggling too. Such letters may have been written as much for posterity as for the recipient, but only generosity could explain the occupant's presence at countless undergraduate poetry readings, or his inviting large groups of students back to his room afterwards, acting as a perfect butler.

What of the secrecy? This was a chamber of deeper enclosures. A large wooden desk contained the telephone in a top drawer, and muffled rings would punctuate supervisions, always ignored. The telephone might ring on university business, but suggested also another, private life withheld from the social and the pedagogical setting. A more mysterious and deeper enclosure was the walk-in cupboard, of unknown depth, from which wine was produced, and into which an excitable Veronica Forrest-Thomson, the most poignant memoirist of "that room in Cambridge", was propelled by the exasperated occupant during a meeting of the Cambridge Poetry Festival committee ("you're going into the cupboard, Veronica!"). Largesse with secret enclosures described the occupant too, whose domestic life remained mysterious, and whose writing was at once evidently public in its address and ambitions, and at the same time hermetically reserved.

This evocation is written in the past tense, in part because it refers chiefly to undergraduate days, but because the room now is all but impenetrable, filled with the archive of its occupier's life-long correspondence and literary work. All records are enclosed in the pharaonic chamber but will be exposed. Hospitality and secrecy accommodate each other. Not completely though. There was another unknown enclosure under the eaves on the landing above, from which guests sometimes descended, so then presumably fitted out as a bedroom. Now this has become the occupied place where Jeremy Prynne works. I am grateful beyond words to have been taught and entertained on I Staircase, and to have been confirmed there in my own occupation.

Learning from Jeremy Prynne, 1963-1967
—An Autobiographicial Sketch—

JOHN HALL

I am seventy years old as I write this in honour of someone who will be eighty on the occasion for which it is written. Because of the task, because of the topic, I am also messily the age I was when I saw a good deal of Jeremy Prynne, from nineteen into my very early twenties. Within neither of these two ages can I write easily about him. There is a version of him in my head (why do I say 'head'?) that deserves something very particular, and I am not too sure what that could be or how—indeed, whether—to offer it. I still, all these years later, test such questions against the internalised, imaginary version of him that I carry around with me. Very few people have retained that kind of internal hold.

In those days he was my teacher, poet-mentor and guide to a world of writing in which poetry and knowledge were fully implicated in each other, necessary to each other. He must have been twenty-seven when I first met him and already seemed to have read more widely than I could ever imagine and, even more significantly, seemed to have all this reading and knowledge constellated on his own galactic intellectual map, always giving it meaning and purpose beyond the given instance. There was nothing, it seemed, that he just happened to know; all had its place. To be read by Jeremy, and therefore in relation to this map, and to have the reading responded to, was a rare privilege and sometimes an unnerving one. The reading would be precisely attuned to the text in hand and at the same time read off against the bodies of writing already in place, the forms of knowledge that different kinds of poems could shape. His own writing and his teaching offered insights into ways of knowing, of hearing, of seeing that felt necessary and very pleasurable. He seemed surrounded by legibility, and could speak it and yet never seemed to reduce that legibility to the pressures of a simplified prior logic. I know that I was far from being the only one who felt in his presence that I ought to learn to read and that this task would never to be over.

At the time his influence was already extending well beyond the university and he was becoming a very significant figure for a group of poets beginning to gather and meet in those parts of Cambridge that are neither university nor not-university, or temporary places of passage between, and was also in direct communication with poets the other side of the Atlantic, most notably perhaps Charles Olson and Edward Dorn.[1] He was anything but a loner as a poet, contributing then and later to the sense for many that writing and reading were part of an economy of exchange. Through his teaching this economy included the dead. Responding to the writing of others, whether alive or dead, is to contribute to the conditions in which writing can be made and constantly restored. At its worst this economy can be an unhelpfully restricted one, leading to imitation or a house style. Jeremy's attention was given to poets whose work was quite unlike his own, and I am glad to count myself among them.

§

the city

is the planned forest
of the dream, this morning.   green
hangs from all the branches & far blossom
thickens my breathing.   am I lost
in the enchanted wood
of my literal surrounds ?   do these sweet
sounds this morning seduce me
to my own wanderings, while, in the mantic eye, in
his sleep, shines
the wide sky, his serene year.

in the middle

of the green wood I look up & the blue
is white with an unserene brightness.   in his sleep, while
I tilt eagerly where my earth
points me, I hold my hopes in his dreams
that shine above these woods.

(Hall 1968, 40)[2]

§

Jeremy Prynne is one of the least autobiographical of poets and here I am needing the support of autobiography to say something about him that is specific to a time and a mode of connection, a time before the idea of a succession of 'Cambridge' poets, before a world sustaining poetry and a world designed for academic study could be uncomplicatedly thought to be the same thing.

§

I had applied to study English at Gonville and Caius College in the middle of an unplanned break in my education, caused in part by a mixture of indecision, failure to cope with entrance exams, exhaustion at the thought of continuing with school, and probably too by a very unrealistic set of expectations of what a university could be. I was working in a holiday hotel near my parents' home in Devon and, recovering from the excesses of looking after a bar whose closing time was whenever the last resident left for bed, I had been assigned the rehabilitation task of serving in the hotel's shop. The headmaster of a Plymouth independent school, never seen in the bar, was staying at the time. We fell into conversation over the shop counter, which ended up with advice that also sounded like an insider's tip. Try Gonville and Caius College, Cambridge, he said. I followed the tip for lack of any obvious alternative and was very pleased to learn that Donald Davie was looking after English in the college. I didn't know the other name, J.H. Prynne. I found *Force of Circumstance* (Prynne 1962) in a London bookshop and read it dutifully but it did not prepare me for what was to come.

I was called for yet another exam and an interview. The two of them were there in Davie's room. One of them must have started by asking me what I'd been up to since leaving school a year or so before and how did I feel that it—whatever it was—fitted in with studying literature. I'd had other interviews, unsuccessfully, and no one had asked me a question remotely like this. I told them that I had only been in England for about six years, mostly sequestered in a small boarding school and various rural homes. Conversations with the bar clientele had made me realise how little I knew about the country and that if I was going to go on living in it I'd better set about learning.[3] I can't remember details but I know that at that point it seemed to stop being an interview and to become a lively conversation, with the two of them getting up every now and again to pull a book out of one of the shelves, to bring another voice into the topic, and one from *literature*. I think Wordsworth came into it, perhaps the *Prelude*. Being asked if I'd read something felt like a genuine question rather than a test.[4]

This was my first encounter with Jeremy, a tall young man with a lisping voice, who seemed to belong in a room like this, a kind of book cave. I was excited. I'm not sure if I sensed any contradiction between the larger idea of lived context that we had been discussing and this richly shelved cave; if I did, I put it to one side, where it probably stayed for a few years. What mattered was that the interview had allowed for that contradiction, if that is what it was. It couldn't have differed more from the solemnity of the other interviews I had had. The assumption seemed to be that literature is something that *happens*, is part of lives and impacts on them; by implication, it must be sustained through further writing, not only studied, least of all as a fixed object. And it is a serious business.

§

By the time I started at Caius, Davie had gone as a pioneer to the new University of Essex and Jeremy was now Director of Studies for English. He was also a lecturer. At Cambridge University in those days, there was a programme of lectures that was university-wide and a set of supervisions organised at college level by a 'director of studies'. These—lectures and supervisions—all related to a syllabus whose main manifestation was a set of exam papers at the end of the year, most of them relating to literary periods, though one—am I remembering correctly here?—a practical criticism paper, in which the texts could be from any period. No one checked on lecture attendance but turning up for supervisions suitably prepared was expected. To use a term alien to this arrangement, supervisions were the main teaching method: teaching through a form of conversation that usually assumed prior reading and essay writing.

In the first year, Jeremy's supervisions were in practical criticism, and these were almost a sufficient education in themselves. First there was the choice of poems. In a drawer to the right of his desk was the reservoir. He would slide the drawer open on its runners and then crouch over it, peering in to select the poem (or prose text?) for the occasion. I never saw inside that drawer but the careful performance of abstracting from it suggested a spotless ordering, even that the set might constitute a condensed syllabus, following the hint perhaps of Pound's version of what Santayana is supposed to have said: 'It doesn't matter *what* so long as they all read the *same* things' (Pound 1950, 338).[5] I suspect that there are generations of Jeremy's undergraduate students who read, with the intensity of attention insisted on by his own reading, more or less the same poems. In this case, though, it did seem to matter what the poems were. I suspect too that over the years his own readings were incremental, drawing on everything that he had read and discussed since the previous encounter.

Here is Paul Ashton's recollection of some of the texts:

All I can remember of the poems in the Practical Criticism supervisions are: Campion's *When thou must home to shades of underground* and Yeats's *No Second Troy*; Auden's *The Capital*; Waller's *Go, lovely rose*; and Hopkins *(In the Valley of the Elwy, I think)*, Arthur Hugh Clough, and Hardy *(After a Journey)*.' (private email 27.08.2015)

Colin Still added: 'One practical criticism piece which Paul didn't mention—our second one, as I recall—was *On the Debt My Mother Owed to Sears Roebuck...*' This Dorn poem was first published in *The Nation* in September 1962, a little over two years before our session. Jeremy had also included it in the Spring 1964 issue of *Prospect*, which he edited (Dorn 1962: 944). The Campion (1966) was collected in the 1601 *Book of Ayres*, over three-and-a-half centuries earlier. The plan was obviously that the reading by the small group of the same poem should lead to discussion, with all of us contributing. There was too much awe in the air for that to be easy, though. Some of us might offer a few stilted remarks, knowing that sooner or later Jeremy would crack and would fill the silence with the most astonishing fluency and insight. I suspect that later he became more skilled at drawing the nervous in but I don't think any of us minded. We knew we were witnesses and beneficiaries of something very unusual and that we would best draw on it by listening as carefully as we could.[6] This inevitable inequality in the conversation may have anticipated what became so evident with the publication of the later 'field notes' and 'discursive commentaries', that a supposedly autonomous close reading was something of an illusion, that knowledge and prior reading were always also being brought to bear, and so this knowledge and prior reading might as well be apt to the specific demands of any one piece. There was and is a tension here: for the reading of poems *as poems,* a careful close reading is necessary but it is never sufficient. This insufficiency and the demands it implied were troublesome for some of us, especially those of us who later on were at some distance from well-resourced libraries and whose lives did not easily allow for the time required for painstaking philology, even if we had the competence.

§

Lectures in the Cambridge of that time (1964-67) were strange affairs. A.C. Spearing attracted enthusiastic audiences with what were mostly, as I recall, readings from Chaucer in an informed approximation of the poet's accent and intonation. Raymond Williams seemed bored with the business—perhaps, I realised later, uncomfortable with a mismatch between the material of his lectures and the still favoured young people in the audience. I can recall no conversation, no follow-up seminar at the end or after lectures. If the lecturers wanted to retain their audience they must have felt that they had to entertain or to offer something apparently indispensable for the syllabus, ideally both. Jeremy, who was still very new to all this, showed remarkable self-confidence. I can recall two or three different series: one on Victorian literature, though perhaps starting with Wordsworth, another unusual at the time in dealing with contemporary U.S. American writing—including, for example, Charles Olson. Jeremy didn't seem interested in either entertaining or proving indispensable to the passing of exams. Instead he appeared to count on the seriousness of what he was doing. The lectures were demanding in their range of reference, their conceptual precision and their expectation that the mostly young ears in the audience could be responsive to subtleties of poetic form; they were not aimed at simply filling out what might already be known or counting on angles of approach with which undergraduates would already be familiar. In each case audiences tailed off as the weeks went on. The handful of us who were still there towards the end would tell each other from time to time that these were the only lectures worth attending, with a troubling sense, so it seems to me now, of an elect or at least self-elect.[7]

§

Very early in my time as an undergraduate I came frustratingly up against my own no doubt naïve expectations of University study, feeling arrogantly that I already had a programme of what I thought I wanted to learn and that I was being foiled by the demands that I follow a syllabus and operate almost entirely through the limiting form of an academic short essay. It didn't occur to me that it was possible to treat these demands casually, with just enough attention to make an adequate if minimal response. I took the requirements seriously, which got in the way of what I thought I wanted to do, and led me to decide that I wanted to leave. If I had an alternative plan I can't think now what it was. I first of all had to go through a 'senior tutor', who must have sent me along to Jeremy. We talked and at some point he told me that, despite usual practice, the exam at the end of the first year wasn't obligatory, since it didn't contribute to final classification; why didn't I stay on until the end of the second year and see how things were looking?[8] He then said that I could see him once a week and he would give me things to read and we'd talk about them. I have taught in higher education for nearly forty years and I cannot begin to see how this could now happen. If I had nothing else to be grateful to him for, this would be enough. He rescued me from what might well have been a depressing set of consequences, and then offered me the most intellectually stimulating period of my early adulthood. Our weekly meetings became shaped around the reading I was doing, usually at his suggestion and often of copies of books from his own shelves. He leant me a number of still recent books which were not otherwise easily available, including his annotated copy of *Maximus Poems* and a large-format copy of Robert Duncan's *Letters*, John Lloyds Stephen's *Incidents of Travel in Yucatán*, Vols. 1 & 2 (1843)[9], and a typescript copy of Tony Ward's novel, *The River Lea*. Jeremy sent my comments on the last to the author and then delighted in showing me the irritated response.

Donald Davie had asked him to stock relevant sections of the new Essex library and seems to have given him a free hand. This was one explanation for what I was being lent. The Stephens, though, which may have been his own or from the Cambridge University Library, probably came out of his engagement with Olson's continuing Maximus project.

When I expressed some resistance to the *Maximus Poems*, Jeremy made no attempt to persuade me otherwise, as though a conversation about merit was beside the point. This had the effect of leaving me in the experience of resistance which soon switched all on its own into a perhaps excessive admiration. On one occasion, when I had been critical—judgmental—about some poem, he said that there was no such thing as a *bad* poem, just different poems. I have wondered since whether this was a pedagogic ploy but have myself remained ever since distrustful of the usefulness of negative judgments, of reading as a proxy for puritanical zeal, or as an exercise in taste or connoisseurship.

Apart from the weekly sessions there was pigeon-hole exchange, the antecedent of email. Notes on suggested reading and copies of poems would often be there.[10] Things didn't stop between supervisions. Most of what made Jeremy a remarkable teacher was beyond emulation, dependent as it was on his extraordinary gifts, and also, to an extent, on the context of Cambridge at the time. (I use the past tense since I can only speak of that time.) Those pigeon-hole notes, not what is in them but the fact of them, that indicate a reading—or a listening or a viewing—that is alert to quite specific other potential is something that can be emulated. I try to do it myself as both teacher and fellow-writer.

§

This was the period when Jeremy was writing the sequence of poems that became *Kitchen Poems* (Prynne 1968) and the earlier stretches of *The White Stones* (Prynne 1969). These—individual poems—too would arrive in my pigeon-hole, photocopies of immaculately handwritten texts, looking as though there was no other way for them to be. They stunned me. 'Moon Poem' especially.

And this was the time too of the first run of *The English Intelligencer*, edited by Andrew Crozier, but dependent in a number of ways on Jeremy, who got me on the circulation list. Those same poems that had been arriving in my pigeon-hole were included in a number of the issues. There was nothing else like them in the neighbouring mimeographed pages but nor yet were there any attempts at direct emulation. There was bafflement, of course, and irritation, even in response to poems that in the light of those written not many years later may seem to have a reassuring rhetorical coherence and surface lucidity, and there was admiration.[11] But the range of difference between the kinds of poems in the *Intelligencer* and the later poems of those involved was to prompt Andrew Crozier and Tim Longville to name their 1987 anthology *A Various Art*. No school, that was the hope. As I have suggested, Jeremy was always generous in his attention to poetry that was very different from his own.

§

Having decided to make an attempt at the second year exam (Part 1 of the 'Tripos') despite my only sporadic engagement with the syllabus, I saw out my allotted three years as an undergraduate. The company of poets who, with the exception of Jeremy, weren't part of the university, and many of whom didn't even live in Cambridge, was almost certainly more important to me, and the source of more learning too, than the formal university experience in that third year (ending in summer 1967). I had made no provision for my future and felt quite strongly that I should not try to find a way to stay in Cambridge (the place), despite the lure. I expected the friendships to last if in a very different form, but knew, I think, that a student–mentor relationship with Jeremy was over. He had future cohorts of students to respond to, in his remarkable conscientiousness as a teacher.

I don't suppose that I was the first to struggle after moving away from such strong support. I would go on to send Jeremy books as they came out—and to receive them from him—to look out for anything by him, whether poems or discursive prose, on more than one occasion to ask him for a reference, and to see him from time to time but I did not try to keep up a regular correspondence with him or even to try to see him when visiting Cambridge in recent decades. I may have felt my own work would not be of much interest to him, on the basis of my own sense of its marked difference from his own recent publications (this despite having received a very warm response to a 1999 collection of mine). I have not felt capable of turning my mixed compulsion towards and clumsiness with his more recent pamphlets into an adequate response: my readings, though compelled, are always incomplete, and by incomplete I don't meaning adequately provisional, good enough, where 'enough' might mean that even if only for the time being there is something to say. Both aspects of this polarity continue to prick at me. I read others on these poems and am sometimes dazzled by confident accounts of the poetics supposedly at work within and behind them—as though there is a clear programme for which the poems are instances—and also by sweepingly confident paraphrases (interpretations) of poems whose resistance to paraphrase seemed to me to be the point.

§

From a letter to Jeremy dated November 27th 1999:

> I have your *Poems* [Prynne 1999] and need much more than the 'quiet time' you needed for my book because I want to read the book through and it is a very very substantial body of work. The pamphlets as they have come—and for which very many thanks—have mostly unsettled me because of the need each time to re-recognise the form of ignorance that they occasion in me and that it is my intuition that you work with, now (that you have moved, I mean, in your poems, from an explicit epistemological cross-referencing to the linguistic *inside* of knowledge, where traces and anticipations are compacted into both lexis and syntax but where the knowledge can no longer know what it knows).
>
> I have been struggling recently with this word *ignorance*: a variable state of knowing/unknowing, in relation to a writing, quite specifically modulated to its means and going. So I haven't been trying to 'understand' your poems but equally I haven't been able to recognise and speak my ignorance, because that needed more time (yes) than I had.

§

Over fifteen years later:

6. emergency appeal

the little pamphlet by Jeremy Prynne
Al-Dente resting at a sliding angle
on a pile that includes the visible heading
Ebola Emergency Appeal and a letter from the
local MP inviting me and everyone else no doubt
in this corner of TQ11 to a meeting
that I can't get to it is
an autumn afternoon and my eyes
are heavy any effort
physical or mental is there
to be avoided I have read
the little book (Prynne) with
familiar puzzled pleasure
and even begun to trace patterns
in it that may well have been one
source of the pleasure the way they
can be with him but now looking at it with its
cover ajar through hooded eyes how
did I ever lift its
words to my ears and eyes and
how could I ever
do so again acuity
when it is in hiding is
difficult to recall or even suppose
its recovery to be
possible on another
table to my right is a *Collected Poems*
of Emily Dickinson these
can seem at first very
simple in comparison but even so
or especially this is not the moment
to get these poems singing
far from simply the way
they can to a clear-eared

reading but who knows
writing this has perhaps
a little unhooded my eyes [12]

§

So J.H. Prynne is eighty. In many ways that feels irrelevant for such a figure, just as autobiography has been an irrelevance for his practice. Those who have known him in all three capacities, as poet, as teacher, as commentator, have a triple cause to be grateful for his life so far. I have offered a sketch of what it meant to be one of those about fifty years ago, and of what has stayed with me from that time.

NOTES

[1] I first met Dorn when we were both waiting outside Jeremy's room while he overran an extended supervision, a familiar occurrence since for Jeremy things had to be brought to their own proper end, even if only for the time being.

[2] The second section of my 'Poem for Dreamers', from *Between the Cities,* a collection dedicated to Jeremy. The poem was also included in Hall 1999 (32).

[3] The 'country' was England. Despite strong family connections with Scotland I had been no closer to it than North Yorkshire where an uncle lived. I had travelled on a train through Wales on my way to the Fishguard ferry but no more than that.

[4] I asked Paul Ashton and Colin Still, two others in the same small Caius 1964 English group, to offer me any brief recollections of any or all of the initial interview, a practical criticism session (and what the texts were), a lecture by Jeremy. Paul gives an account of his selection interview in his autobiographical *A Puritan at Les Baux* (Ashton 2011: 145—146). Colin referred to his as 'intimidating'.

[5] 1950. *The letters of Ezra Pound, 1907-1941*. Ed. Paige, D. D. . New York: Harcourt, Brace & World, Inc.

[6] Here is Paul Ashton on these same practical criticism sessions: "In comparing the first two [Campion and Yeats, see above], which I think was our first ever assignment, I fell straight into the elephant trap and said the Campion was over-formal and lacking in feeling, while the Yeats was passionate and

deeply felt. Jeremy wrote at the end of my essay, 'Well, the issues are now squarely before us.' I was fascinated from the start by his exquisite handwriting (and copied it for years) and by his unchanging dress, with just the warm orange, or yellow, or red, of his tie against the white shirt and black jumper and jacket.

I remember my astonishment in supervisions that he could talk virtually uninterruptedly for an hour, and all one could do was go along with the ride, holding on for dear life. Nothing in my subsequent intellectual life has ever come near the impact of those sessions.' (private email, 27.08.2015)

Colin Still recalls: "[…] the supervisions in Caius Court in the book-lined room with the manifesto from BLAST on the wall outside, the reproduction of *Pallas & the Centaur*, the tapes of the Berkeley Conference (Dorn, Wieners, Creeley, Snyder, Olson) & the Tandberg tape recorder via which he introduced us to the 'plangent monodies' of Thomas Campion."
and adds:

"Later memories include his moving tribute at Roger Langley's memorial, at which he read *Tintern Abbey*, his reading of *Homage to Sextus Propertius* at Kettle's Yard, his lecture on Blunden & Poussin, the launch of the Chinese edition of his selected poems (which I filmed) &, that same week, walking with him through King's Backs & being presented (a reference, I think, to Xu Zhimo) with a sprig of willow leaves."

[7] Paul Ashton again, on Jeremy's lectures: "He seemed to hate lecturing, arriving ten minutes late, using up another ten minutes by writing the titles of relevant books and articles on the blackboard, and then ending ten minutes early. The lectures that influenced me most were on *The Prelude*, where his references to climate and geology made me realise what a vast knowledge of things outside literature he could bring to bear." (private email, 27.08.2015)

And Colin Still: "Also the handouts: 'Some Notes on the Scope & Scruple of the Post-Romantic Mind', for example, & the list of American publications (*Yugen* & so on) which he'd generously placed in the University Library."

[8] The first year examinations at Cambridge were known as *prelims*. According to the Wikipedia entry, 'While they do not count towards a student's final degree classification, a very poor performance in prelims can result in disciplinary measures and students may be required to repeat the exams until they receive a satisfactory grade.' (https://en.wikipedia.org/wiki/Prelims). This suggests that Jeremy had to exercise influence to ensure that if there was no performance at all, it couldn't be pronounced 'very poor'.

[9] It may have been *Incidents of Travel in Central America, Chiapas and Yucatán*, Vols. 1 & 2 (1841). I am working from memory and this was fifty years ago.

[10] Caius had installed a very large photocopier in a room of its own. Jeremy made good use of it.

[11] For an example of both irritation (Ian Vine's) and admiration (mine), see Pattison 2012: 12-15.

[12] From an as yet unpublished sequence tentatively called 'I'm on the train'.

REFERENCES

Ashton, Paul. 2001. *A Puritan at Les Baux* London: Bell Buoy, 2011

Campion, Thomas. 1966 (1909). ed. Percival Vivian. *The Works of Thomas Campion.* Oxford: The Clarendon Press

Crozier, Andrew and Longville, Tim (eds.). 1987. *A Various Art.* Manchester: Carcanet Press

Dorn, Edward. 2012. *Collected Poems.* ed. Jennifer Dunbar Dorn *et al.* Manchester: Carcanet Press

Hall, John. 1968. *Between the Cities* Lincoln: Grosseteste Press

Hall, John. 1999. *Else Here: Selected Poems.* Buckfastleigh: etruscan books

Pattison, Neil, Pattison, Reitha and Roberts, Luke (eds.). 2012. *Certain Prose of The English Intelligencer.* Cambridge: Mountain Press

Pound, Ezra. 1950. *The letters of Ezra Pound, 1907-1941.* ed. Paige, D. D. New York, NY: Harcourt, Brace & World

Prynne, J.H. 1962. *Force of Circumstance and Other Poems.* London: Routledge and Kegan Paul

Prynne, J.H. 1968. *Kitchen Poems.* London: Cape Goliard Press

Prynne, J.H. 1969. *The White Stones* Lincoln: Grosseteste Press

Prynne, J.H. 1999. *Poems.* Newcastle upon Tyne: Bloodaxe; South Fremantle, WA: Fremantle Arts Centre Press

If Flowers of Language Will (Have) Been a Language of Flowers: Trials of Florescence in the Poems of J. H. Prynne

Peter Larkin

And so I came to Fancies medow strow'd
With many a flower:
Fain would I here have made abode
But I was quicken'd by my houre.
George Herbert

J. H. Prynne's early mentor, Donald Davie, could make play with his own ignorance of botanical nomenclature ('That lime-tree—no, what is it? mulberry?'), names which for him were simply poetic appurtenances.[1] Prynne himself can write: 'The plants stare at my ankles in / stiffness, they carry names I cannot recognise'.[2] This needn't imply botanical indifference, so much as an irreducibility between what plant names might label and their blatant ankle-stare. A later, more sardonic Prynne will note that 'In the spray the choice herbs cluster, their / names a *de luxe* suppletion'(249). At the level of sheer imagery, this poet's references to flowers are intermittent. A greater commonality predominates with images of snow, stars, moon or even rain. As Nigel Wheale discerns, Prynne's language draws on 'a wide range of diction, specialisms and knowledge-bases, but there do not appear to be consistent image-clusters'.[3] I want to privilege what flower references there are, however, as underwriting the status of botany as itself a *technical* pastoral, richly symbolic yet accountable to exact description. Flowers are an inherent constituent of lyric language, and the status of specialist discourses in Prynne will simultaneously rebound on the status of poetic voice.[4] Prynne's flowery resources mesh within plant microbiology attracting their own coronas of complexity,[5] contributing to what David Caddy sees as a 'difficult poetry' now become a 'poetry of the desert'.[6] My essay considers what, if anything, can bloom in this desert as a distinct element never wholly purgatory. As such I write in homage to Prynne but seek to do the difficulty otherwise, keeping in mind how his work incorporates its 'matter and thinking with plant materiality', and the outcomes of that.[7]

Flowers once seeded in language rapidly spring up as 'flowers of language' (*flores rhetoricae*), innately metaphorical but figures of thought as well as of speech. Prynne's rhetoric is rebarbative and flowery, spiny but forms a rich syntactic composite. This will imply speech raised (or partially crazed) towards song, signalling the problem of lyric in Prynne from the outset. Robin Purves defines any lyrical re-approach to the notion of our world-as-home as strictly 'our current condition of bereavement, diminution' but at the same time affirms Prynne's own sense of the rightness of desiring as such, even if pastoral commits absolute mistakes over how its satisfaction can be mediated .[8]

Might not the flowery predilections of lyric also predict its resistance? In singing a home out, lyric renders home as beside itself, unfamiliar but a response to what is not yet fully given (including the contaminated nature of what is over-sold). The younger poet explicitly favoured Olsonian epic with its sense of a unique universal, to be distinguished from the metaphoric partiality of lyric.[9] Michael Stone-Richards doubts whether Prynne ever fully accepted Olson's projective prosody;[10] and Wheale notes the later Prynne's continuing (lyric) preference for collections of discrete poems gathered under one title. He also insists on the 'specific kind of music, of poetic beauty' in Prynne's work,[11] as well as seeing it as attempting 'a novel order of the beautiful'.[12] For Keston Sutherland, however, the 'semiotic concentration' of Prynne's later oeuvre is strictly 'unvoiceable' and Wheale will concede voice to be a 'text-voice' , *ie*, eking out a residue of vocality.[13] Sutherland is clear, though, that however much Prynne's lyricism is no 'petition', this doesn't amount to the 'refractories of a scientific realism rubbishing the lyricism on which they trespass'.[14] Though Prynne challenges lyric as unacceptable privilege of voice, he doesn't offer anything like a formal counter-lyric: his difficulty arises from his not doing so. We participate in the poet's trauma of having to refuse the urgent witness of what can only *be* lyrical.[15] John Wilkinson defiantly holds out for the truth of lyric in later Prynne, as a singing out of a 'reflex response to pain', even if this might be the final concession to a torturer.[16] He maintains the possibility that this singing out might also be a 'profound rejoinder to fear', however composed of the darkest, most compromised materials.

Even so, song turns towards a 'counterfactual universe' one that may 'flash with glimpses of other purposes'.[17]

My contention will be that Prynne's poetics don't evade the obstinacy of figuration as such, however much it might appear imagery has been taken hostage, but, nonetheless: 'we stay in the figure & can af / ford to count nothing else'(139) which affirms figuration even if simultaneously finance. Prynne's early predilection for the Olsonian universal as 'already the most complete prime particular thing' and therefore not open to substitution, for me begs the question of ontological gift, a particularity bringing with it a charged recognition placing the ordinary immediately alongside the extraordinary: what can only be the one can simultaneously only be the other, without being a work of substitution but enabling figures of relation.[18] Rod Mengham emphasises Prynne's early concern for an implicitly oppositional gift economy in which givers and receivers establish a more personal/universal bond than abstract exchange economies. Mengham also notes that as late as *Word Order* (1989) a whole series of language-constructs are being undone so as to follow 'the path of gift'.[19] Are we being nudged closer to some unconditional/vertical sense of gift at this point, despite Prynne's eventual substitution of Adorno for Heidegger: 'a rising vertical trust: enough to clear / line to line clasp essentials' (394)?[20]

Theresa M. Kelley affirms that botanical images can be conceptually informative and not merely decorative and Georges Bataille returned to a language of flowers as such. A rose can indicate love but a water lilly indifference, while the narcissus stands for egoism and the absinthe for bitterness.[21] For Hegel's *Geist* a flower religion with its egoless idea of the self necessarily gave way to the earnestness of a warring life and the guilt-conditions of animal religions. Above all, flowers can be gender-burdened, assimilated to a symbolism in which they scarcely participate to the extent they betoken beauty, innocence, virginity and passivity.[22] More distinctive for early Prynne is not petalic beauty, however, but curve as the circuit condition of space as a whole: 'That circular curve is an important condition of the lyric, because the cosmos...comprises the rearward time vector, back to the past, and all the space vectors extended until they go circular'.[23] One such circulation is how flowers of language are seeded by a language of flowers, not as a received symbolism but as part of a micro-biology that includes temporality. Sam Solnik identifies Prynne's interest in 'reverse transcription' as a biological and phonological process which re-runs identificatory and uni-directional flows of information. 'The *Plant Time Manifold* Transcripts' and *Bean News* first signalled this in terms of bi-directional sprouting patterns in which the 'roots and shoots open up the grammar of being and time'. A plant *is* its own past as a simultaneity-from below ground as much as it is a simultaneity-towards at above-ground stems. From this derives what Prynne was to call the 'will been' in the root systems and the 'is/has being' in the leaf and flower counterparts [24] This is plant-time moving both ways along the horizon of time's arrow, whereby plants have literal access to the past via a rooted 'positive mnemonic pressure'.[25] In this way, pastoral memory is radically implanted and actively transformative, not inertly nostalgic. Michael Stone-Richards comments how every living organism not only develops unique memory paths but may develop unforeseen possibilities from the feedback effects of its own autonomy.[26] What, then, is the ontological bearing of such an unforeseeable? Is this a genuine, tensional horizon of existence, or another tongue-in-cheek cult of diversionary energetics?

Can 'secondary noise' within a cognitive structure of itself respond to the formally useless gift of existence, so that no flower can be self-organising without also being self-offering? As such, this is not a one-way accumulation of future benefits: Prynne's 'will been' encapsulates a gesture of gift-making from a constant rebecoming of the 'is' out of what has been/will have been given. Earlier, Prynne had emphasised resistance as 'an inescapable sense of the *given*... hence the valid priority of substance'.[27] Prynne is reading the given as no neutral starting point but already implicated in a primary texture of aspiration and participation.[28] For John Milbank, 'codings in biology are never merely metaphoric, or metaphor operates only from within biological metamorphosis itself'.[29] Prynne himself writes:

> Do not take this as metaphor...
> look at the plants, the entire dark dream outside (166)

This is to glimpse flower as a novel ontology or sheer verticality of gift. Geoffrey Hartman speculates on the naming of flowers in the Linnaean system as itself aspiring to magic, a renaming of living things 'at once scientific and fantastic'. Even metalanguages, he claims, can feel the allure of pure signification, luring words and things into a single system so as to facilitate the exchange of feelings.[30] Claudette Sartiliot describes a 'botanical model of the flower' which proposes 'an extravagant reading which reveals… a waste, a squandering of seeds (and semes) out of which meaning is eventually gathered'.[31] Though Prynne once declared existence itself as 'thankfully beyond the condition of meaning'(where 'thankfully' implies a sense of gift) he has never valued textual autonomy as pure dissemination, cut off from its own philological history essentially one of partially submerged usages and relations.[32]

In looking in detail at how flowers feature in Prynne's poems, I cannot go much further than assembling an implicit cento of quotations from his work.[33] The macro-context is either omitted or unmastered, but the micro-contexts remain worth looking at in their own terms.[34] Prynne counts botanical terms among his many specialisms, so that 'stolons' (which can be thought of as coloured, above-ground rhizomes), 'stipules' and 'phloems' feature, as well as processes like 'nutation' (the bending of plant organs), 'intercostal' (anatomical, but equally the area between leaf-veins) and 'remontant' (a flower blooming more than once in a season). In the phrase 'invasive, ground cover / fire down below / vinca alkaloids' (376), the alkaloids so named are derived from the Periwinkle (often used for ground-cover) and are a chemo-therapy for cancers ('fire down below').

Some flower-allusions will perform to a post-pastoral sense of contamination and collusion and be succinctly ironised: 'Patience is / the sum of my inertia like the flower in / heaven'(69). This is a sublimated but wholly uprooted florescence, but (see below) also a possible reference to the orchid. There is a particular Prynnian reckoning underlying 'The muse / in reckless theophany gives a familiar yell: / juniper, moss agate' (155), the latter less a flowerless plant than a gemstone associated with healing. Theophany is risked in a radical participation in plant-life never entirely reckonable as history unmediated by ulterior cycles. If 'the idea of change is briskly seasonal'(112) and thus circuited rather than linear-historic, desire as such reaches only towards loss of focus: 'The wish is green in season, hazy like meadow-sweet' (172). What flowers here is already mediated by its ready absorption: florescence inflamed internally becomes icily fixating:

> a flowering spray in the glow of the mirror.
> The internal view burns at this frame,
> eyes frozen by calm' (332)

The distorting mirror doesn't just glow but over-colours what can never be a neutral love: 'In the margin tinted love breaks off / to spot bravura by scrub wintergreen' (326). Wintergreen is an aromatic plant but the addition of 'scrub' evokes a wasteland flower as well as cosmetic exfoliation. The poetry is more minatory than afflicted with pathos: 'Pity me! These petals, crimson and pink, / are cheque stubs, spilling chalk in a mist / of soft azure'(338). To 'plant orchid root' is to confront a 'Fixitive intrinsic. Resting allured'(541). We don't cease to register repose however allured, while having to continue attending: 'It must be the clasp of waiting hands / dipping to a flower print of the outcast' (350). At his most sardonic, Prynne can write: 'I saw the groves of acanthus rise up and bite / the lips of clear morning light' (506).[35] . The original Greek name signifies a prickly plant that might well bite at lips, though the Linnean *Acanthus mollis* is so called after its gentle leaves.

Are these 'flowers streams [as they] flow' little more than 'simple bright goods' which 'clutter the ravines' (26)? Early Prynne retains some lyric appetite ('I refer directly to my / own need, since to advance in the now fresh & / sprouting world must take in some musical / sense' (99)), and the later poet never quite abandons patience with florescence, even if depriving it of pathos and votive energy:

> take what you hear slowly
> as water makes the sun
> pale again, near the
> scabious pinned out for
> rescue. (163)

Scabious, however, is associated with mourning. A prolonged pastoral sensitivity can bear a mark of defiance, if not quite self-mutilation:

> A light wind crosses the fragrant waters;
> deaf to reason I cup my hands, to
> dew-drenched apricot flowers and their
> livid tranquillity (334)

Elegy itself seems timed out, nonetheless, for lines like 'sun gliding each / petal fringe just watch shrivel pit margins / pleat and plaint' are prefaced by an impotent marginalising: 'There's time but not much say // those whose time costs less' (560). If Prynne can note a proto- or counter-Romantic origin in 'Only plant systems remain functional on the pre-organic event horizon' (235) he is equally ready to echo a poetic write-off: 'Plant death is clearly a more complex event than in other life systems' (240), unless this reads as the 'pre-organic' side-stepping the unilateral finality of animal death. As an earlier phrase goes: 'biologic collapse is violence reversed' (21).

Allusions to the rose will emerge as over-determined. There can be apparent nostalgia: 'The white rose trembles by the step it is / uncalled for in the fading daylight' (119). The very image may be uncalled for in a poetry no longer teasing out twilight but emerging into 'daymare', given a white rose, itself by implication 'stunted by snow on a hip rose / and juice spurts' (304). At another moment:

> Over the rosy hedges the passions
> in their circuit feel for the safe
> edge of the hoop   (262)

Here, 'rosy' is set up as a rhyme-cue for 'cosy' but in the context of 'hedges' the image gets thornier: hedges with their dog-roses are a tangled edge never entirely safe to feel: 'as mother knows, there is no rose' (348) if it be exclusively a maternal symbol or one of forgotten passion. In 'Such shading / of the rose to its stock tips the bolt / from the sky' (190), the generic (commercialised) root of the rose ramifies into both rifle-imagery and divine retribution. The rose will attract its due of sardonic close-up:

> Hang down
> ye blood-red roses, hang down; there is no call
> for any other run on the town   (353)

Here 'blood-red' echoes Prynne's preoccupation with wound as both ethical protest and potential internal transformation.[36] The phrase 'Hang down / ye blood-red roses' evokes a world of oceans and whale-hunting, derived from the chanty or sea-shanty 'Go down, Ye blood-red roses' which featured in the 1956 film-version of *Moby Dick*. In that milieu a bunch of roses can also suggest a sweetheart or affection itself. That Prynne's roses 'Hang down' is more plant-specific, so that what droops is the deracinated outcome of love in the urban world, or: 'Injury too mounted in harm of sorts entrance docket' (545). Any rose as 'stock' in this latter line has mutated to an undrooping injury which is both deleterious choice of fate ('sorts') and a label of admittance draining (creating a run on) urban life itself.

Prynne can displace botanical names and their associations:

> the word is out
> at play in field dilemmas where they grow strong
> and split and multiply. Harrow at spiny rest (525)

The condition of the word at play is in negotiating a world-field where it risks being put out of play altogether. 'Harrow at spiny rest' performs something of this as the common name of *Ononis repens* is Restharrow, a once frequent cereal (and semi-parasitic) weed that lived up to its reputation for impeding farm machinery, though the pastoral 'rest' more acutely denotes 'arrest'. My interest in this theme was initially caught by the following passage from *For the Monogram* (1997):

> Afloat oblique and limping
> at this the monocline in agreement for interrupted
> wings, nodding thistle to melancholy orchid. (418)

I read this first as two thistle epithets (nodding and melancholy) coalescing and colluding in a partial displacement. Nodding thistle (*Carduus nutens*) is native to much of Europe and Western Asia but as an introduction is often regarded as a noxious weed with a similar obstructive profile to Restharrow. Its flower typically bends sideways or downward as if surveying the field horizontally. The Melancholy thistle (*Cirsium heterophyllum*) is unspiny but once sourced a potion thought helpful to depression. But the epithet is displaced to a plant (Melancholy Orchid) unknown to me botanically but which can be traced to a tune entitled 'Iou Lan' from the Tang period and rediscovered in 1885 in Japan. The melody for the chyn (ancient Chinese harp) was composed by Chiou Ming (493-590) and was intended to suggest the lofty character of a hermit retreating from court intrigue and corruption.[37] The flower itself is intended to evoke a pure and calm mind, however troubled in circumstance, while the corona symbolically floats in the heavens ('Afloat oblique and limping') detached from the rest of its plant body. More immediately, Prynne's erring botanical nomenclature defers to the predicament of a lyric tune while underwriting two thistle varieties which nod to each other across a Chinese elegy ('for interrupted / wings') swaying in the hinterland of chosen exile.

Flower allusions persist as ambivalences: 'pollen here is bright feeling, damp spores' (219) and can become as sardonically explicit as:

> He wanders in-
> ertly with a shrewd
> unattending absence,
> his being on a thin stalk
> ...   going black
> from the centre like
> a flower rotting (138)

In *Triodes* (1999), Irene, the figure of peace, is apostrophised as a 'plant group mother' but is equally one who 'infix[es] / shock limits' (481). Is her nurturing predefined by shock so that our hunger for tranquillity becomes fixated at that point or can the very community which a 'plant group' suggests modify the range of trauma itself? A similar undertone loosening irony from itself can be detected in *Red D Gypsum*: 'in parted stipules by allowance freshly done. Flow / flow my phloem dear ones' (443). The repetition of 'flow' is further transmitted into the sound of 'phloem'(the tissue which conveys plant sugars) amounting to a refrain for the pulse of the flow-er itself.

A familiar moment in 'On the Matter of Thermal Packing' runs:

> ah some modest & gentle
> competence a man could live
> with so little
>   more   (86)

The initial take offers 'a man could live / with so little' as an expression of beneficent frugality compromised by the lure of 'more', so that 'little' is never more than penultimate in terms of consumption. A further reading opens the perspective that what is offered is not a 'little more' but more of the little or a slightness of gift which pleads to be lived 'with' as its only addition. Commenting on a Hölderlin phrase crucial to Heidegger translatable as 'Full of merit, yet poetically man dwells', Stone-Richards detects an implication that the poetic hints at a diminution poised on the 'yet'. He links this to an immanence and transcendence not needing any ontological commitment.[38] Does this poverty of spirit include a radical sense of gift which exceeds the known except in so far as it is known as gift? And given the severe poetic/ ethical stalemate which Prynne's later work confronts us with, is there a way the lyrical can prevent this impasse from staling, so as to allow the 'little' to persist as desirable desire or a purification itself no purism? *Kazoo Dreamboats* insists on mediation whereby 'you do not see into the life of things, dimension- / less or not' (655), but here a language of gift might posit a not-seeing or one on behalf-of what has already been responded to, which is not a metaphoric mystique but a literal (though not exclusively lateral) participation.

Sutherland insists Prynne's project is governed by the possibility of recognising true contradiction which depends on 'getting the vectors of corruption right'. I read such vectors as over-determined, only to be resisted via a prophetic innocency of gift as ethical spring-board. Prynne doesn't ramp up lamentation, Sutherland declares, but evacuates it.[39] Fair enough, but sheer evacuation will leave debris marking a resistant path not identical to the original corrupt scouring, so that a lyric displacement hovers over the blocked imagery of a violated but unassimilated natural order. Where Prynne distrusts the interminable deferrals of paradisal attraction,[40] Milbank offers a more radical stance of redemption: the myth of a Fall itself denies we are still to a degree operating within the earthly paradise of unconditional gift and so has forfeited that perception. For Milbank there is the risk that unbridled horror in the face of extreme evil grants evil the ontological victory as sole unconditional presence.[41] Against this, Milbank reads Christianity as construing our universal tragic condition non-ontologically but as part of a contingent narrative upshot. Otherwise, whatever is abandoned or outside donation is only barely, giftlessly alive. Hence, he concludes, the 'private, supposed "free" gift of market society is identical, precisely *as* abandoned, with the commodity of the capitalist mode of exchange'.[42]

In this light, lyric is firstly offering rather than critique, on behalf of a radical equality of victimage, proclaiming how victims would cry out on our behalf if situations were reversed which they always might be. To refuse this in the name of derisive suspicion or as a soft option would exactly inhabit a negating ontology. The initial poverty of lyric averts traumatic self-maiming by affirming the co-insistence of joy alongside the very suffering that can no longer sing for itself. Prynne's work does do this but then defiantly damages this very acclamation in terms he might well acknowledge are strictly indefensible. A shared existential guilt (witnessed to in Paul Ricoeur's *The Symbolism of Evil*) is not reducible to sheer mechanistic complicity without a distinct cost that Prynne's work owns up to. It implies that no more than a brittle strategic advantage is gained.[43] Guilt and helplessness are common poverties but also the basis of a relation already partly reparative, a weaker part but more sustaining of relationality itself. Sutherland discerns that what he recognises as 'radical thinking' has at once 'a greater and a smaller object than religious thinking'. Thus, Prynne's later work offers less as well as more than normative communication.[44] For the younger Prynne, Sutherland explains, radical knowledge is an ontological augmentation, but what is more known is knowable of a world become lesser.[45] This may be because such knowledge lacks/ aborts any sense of unconditional gift, or knowledge of a world which invites an additionality neither wholly deterministic nor dogmatic but which needs to assert the difference of gift itself as its one condition of reception. Reception is then insistent enough to lyrically companion either encountered determinisms or the prophetic burden of belief.[46] A world become less offers to share more of itself, in the same way that Prynne's own poetic innovations demand to be received as less-than, as not without cost, one never fully recoverable by a reader.

> To be this with sweet
> song and dance in the exit dream, sweet joy befall thee is by
> rotation been and gone into some world of light exchange, toiling
> and spinning and probably grateful, in this song. (661)

These closing lines of *Kazoo Dreamboats*, with their (Biblical) echoes of Blake and Vaughan, ascribe to gratitude an uncertain object still probe-able by experience even though provable as gift. The exchange would be equally dubious if merely 'light' but owns a light lessened to exchange but assertively less than (*ie* distinct from) mere exchange. The features of flowers make a similar gesture, at once rare gestae or ironic jests only one of several nondescript registers in this poetry unless pollinated by a reader who can never wholly penetrate the work's corolla but does seek out its corollary designs:

face and flower shining each upon the other. (335)

NOTES

[1] See Andrew Crozier, *Thrills and Frills: Selected Prose*. Ed. Ian Brinton (Bristol: Shearsman Books, 2013), p.67.

[2] J. H. Prynne, *Poems* (Eastburn: Bloodaxe Books, 2015), p.123. All future page references to this edition are given in the text.

[3] Nigel Wheale, 'Crosswording: Paths through "Red D Gypsum"' in A *Manner of Utterance: the Poetry of J. H. Prynne*. Ed. Ian Brinton (Exeter: Shearsman Books, 2009), p.168.

[4] See Simon Perril, 'Hanging on Your Every Word: J.H.Prynne's "Bands Around the Throat" and a Dialectic of Planned Impurity' in A *Manner of Utterance: the Poetry of J. H. Prynne*. Ed. Ian Brinton (Exeter: Shearsman Books, 2009), p.93.

[5] Nigel Wheale commenting on the 'Crown' (116-7) writes that 'human sovereignty is the gathered body of what is commonplace as well as the composite flower of what might be: "corona" could mean "a collection of men"'. *Groseteste Review*, 12 (1979),p.115.

[6] David Caddy, 'Notes towards a Preliminary Reading of J.H.Prynne's "Poems"' in A *Manner of Utterance: the Poetry of J. H. Prynne*. Ed. Ian Brinton (Exeter: Shearsman Books, 2009), p.24.

[7] See Theresa M. Kelley, 'Botanical Figura', *Studies in Romanticism*, 53 (Fall 2014), 343-368 (365).

[8] Robin Purves, 'A Commentary on J.H.Prynne's "Thoughts on the Esterhazy Court Uniform"' in *On the Poems of J.H.Prynne*, ed. Ryan Dobran (Brooklyn, NY: Glossator, 2010), p.84.

[9] J.H.Prynne, 'Jeremy Prynne Lectures on "Maximus IV, V, VI"', Simon Fraser University July 27 1971 http://charlesolson.org/Files/Prynnelecture1.htm (accessed June 22, 2015).

[10] Michael Stone-Richards, 'The Time of the Subject in the Neurological Field (I): a Commentary on J.H.Prynne's "Again in the Black Cloud"' in *On the Poems of J.H.Prynne*, ed. Ryan Dobran (Brooklyn, NY: Glossator, 2010), p.190.

[11] Wheale (2009), p.166,169.

[12] Nigel Wheale, 'Expense: J.H.Prynne's "The White Stones"', *Grosseteste Review*, 12 (1979), 103.

[13] Keston Sutherland, 'XL Prynne' in A *Manner of Utterance: the Poetry of J. H. Prynne*. Ed. Ian Brinton (Exeter: Shearsman Books, 2009), p.118; Wheale (2009), p.168. Simon Perril reads the poetry of the 1980's as wrestling with issues of voice and address as necessary impurities. See Perril, p.83.

[14] Sutherland (2009), p.108.

[15] Prynne's 'perjoracratic' stance seems an ironic mode resigning itself to didactic brittleness but in fact takes an intensively sonic path through its own paratactic meta-paralysis. Prynne conjures us to acknowledge poetry is the field in which to do this, and this must always be part of his meaning.

[16] John Wilkinson, 'Heigh Ho: a Partial Gloss of "Word Order"' in *On the Poems of J.H.Prynne*, ed. Ryan Dobran (Brooklyn, NY: Glossator, 2010), p.299.

[17] Wilkinson, p.300.

[18] Prynne, 'Maximus'.

[19] Rod Mengham, '"A Free Hand to Refuse Everything": Politics and Intricacy in the Work of J.H.Prynne' in A *Manner of Utterance: the Poetry of J. H. Prynne*. Ed. Ian Brinton (Exeter: Shearsman Books, 2009), p. 75-6. Mengham adds, that for Marcel Mauss, gifts once in circulation set up 'a pattern of spiritual bonds, a perpetual transfer of "spiritual matter"'.

[20] Sam Solnick questions the degree of Adorno's influence on Prynne. See 'Poetry in the Anthropocene: Ecology, Biology and Technology in the Work of Ted Hughes, J.H.Prynne and Derek Mahon', unpublished thesis, University of London, 2013, p.132. For me, Adorno's sense of the damaged life itself expresses a loss of participatory donation and not just frustration with impotent political agency. Only such a vertical gift, one could say, glimpses the range of what might be a meaningful (*ie* non-autonomous) historical response.

[21] Kelley, p.343; quoted in Claudette Sartiliot, 'Herbarium Verbarium: the Discourse of Flowers', *Diacritics*, 18, 4 (1988), p.68.

[22] Sartiliot, p.68

[23] Prynne, 'Maximus'.

[24] Solnick, p.114. Solnick sees this as a materiality of language 'running inwards to its roots and outwards to its surface' so as to establish a distinct ontogenesis exceeding textual instrumental transfer (p 148).

[25] See Justin Katko, 'Relativistic Phytosophy: Towards a Commentary on "The Plant Time Manifold Transcripts"' in *On the Poems of J.H.Prynne*, ed. Ryan Dobran (Brooklyn, NY: Glossator, 2010), p. 268.

[26] Stone-Richards, p. 164.

[27] Quoted in Solnick, p. 171.

[28] The 'given' here is not understood as a bare Cartesian naturalism but as an active perception of and participation in the life-world of objects, which also includes the sedimented cultural tradition in which/out of which they appear amid the experiences of fault, hope and history.

[29] John Milbank, *Being Reconciled: Ontology and Pardon* (Abingdon: Routledge, 2003), p.188.

[30] Geoffrey Hartman, *A Critic's Journey: Literary Reflections, 1958-1998* (New Haven: Yale UP, 1999), pp. 228, 236.

[31] Sartiliot, p.72.

[32] Prynne, 'Maximus'. Stone-Richards insists Prynne is not a nominalist despite the power his poetics accord to language, a power that also accepts the existence of an independent world. Stone-Richards, p. 187.

[33] Ryan Dobran writes: 'the fulfilment… of quotations… by commentary only deepens the sense of their embeddedness: once extracted and commented upon, they do not fit back into their original places'. *On the Poems of J.H. Prynne*, ed. Ryan Dobran (Brooklyn, NY: Glossator, 2010), p.9.

[34] Robin Purves points to the dangers of 'citation' or 'fanciful improvisation' which lack context but also shows how any reading of Prynne will fail to pay dividends and argues a general apprehension of difficulty as such is not automatically retrievable as critical insight. See his 'Apprehension: or, J.H.Prynne, his Critics, and the Rhetoric of Art', *The Gig*, 2 (1999), pp.45-60.

[35] Why 'groves' for a non-woody plant (though Strabo mentions a sacred grove of 'gum-producing Acanthus' and there was a city of that name)? Otherwise, the association of acanthus leaves with Corinthian capitols might be in play here.

[36] See Stone-Richards, pp.149-244.

[37] I am very grateful to Dr Fay Yao for this information.

[38] Stone-Richards, pp.206-7, 233.

[39] Keston Sutherland, in *On the Poems of J.H.Prynne*, ed. Ryan Dobran (Brooklyn, NY: Glossator, 2010), p. 131.

[40] In a letter to Drew Milne, Prynne insists any definition of paradise always implies indefinite postponement. Quoted in Perril, p. 92.

[41] Milbank, pp. 154-55.

[42] Milbank, p. 152.

[43] Prynne's poetry senses as a matter of rhetorical texture that rigidly suspicious arguments develop their own preciosity of revelation, one always counter-prophetic.

[44] Similarly, Katko describes Prynne's plant-time axis as representing less than what is being proposed but making possible an otherwise impossible higher analysis. Katko, p. 264.

[45] Sutherland (2009), pp. 105, 113.

[46] For Katko, Prynne's quasi-parodic plant-time speculations do not offer extrapolated figuration reducible to nineteenth-century naturalism, but punctuate latent cracks which allow for the vertical flight or slip. Katko, pp. 284-6. This could coincide with flower imagery as no fixed hierarchy but still an ontological opportunity offering relation to a divinity both more and less than any whole.

madrigalian / brightness
Renaissance Prynne

NIGEL WHEALE

A lot depended on which texts you were given for 'practical criticism'. Some poems, which you might spend days and nights thinking about, would stay with you for the rest of your days, many of the nights. Reading Shelley's 'Mont Blanc' to the point of snow-blindness, that particular shelleyan sublime, forever beyond reach: which was the point, the agonised tutorial concluded.

> The everlasting universe of things
> Flows through the mind, and rolls its rapid waves,
> Now dark—now glittering—

Some academic careers began thanks to the author offered for analysis, other kinds of career were inspired in different ways: Simon Russell Beale describes the practical-critical tutorials as 'an incredible privilege' that informed his own work—'Acting is three-dimensional lit. crit.'.[1] Sometimes a tutorial would be on an individual basis, time seemed to expand, way beyond any notional fifty minutes. The session on Shake-speare's Sonnet 94, 'They that haue power to hurt, and will doe none', was one of these, the linguistic and moral finesse of that sonnet summoned huge issues, so much was at stake—ethical and expressive questions of the subtlest, most urgent kind. Get this right, everything will follow: inspirational teaching, in so many ways. Not least, that poetry could be supremely important, as an achievement, a practice.

The *Specimen of a Commentary on 'Shake-speares Sonnets', 94* (Cambridge 2001), first of three essays of sustained analysis, eighty-seven pages, was so compelling, engaged in ever more detailed textual and contextual nuance, rigorous scholia word by word, way beyond what the tutorials could deploy. A bravura reading, followed by *Field Notes: 'The Solitary Reaper' and Others* (2007, 134 pp.), and *George Herbert, 'Love [IIII]': A Discursive Commentary* (2011, 92 pp.), repeated scannings of those poems, to teach dozens of practical-critical tutorials, lectures and seminar-based discussions, across decades.

I went 'up' across for interview at Gonville & Caius in October 1968, on the way reading Kenneth Allott's *Penguin Book of Contemporary Verse 1918–60* (1950; 1962 selection). I gazed from train windows at a strange new landscape, horizontal black fen, compelling austere, after red, gently modulated midlands. Allott's survey was exactly the right collection, gathering all of the poetry that was left behind, at speed: Wain, Gunn, Thwaite, Hill, Hughes... Plath. One of them would return, at high speed, from an unanticipated angle. Roger Langley, my sixth-form and Cambridge scholarship teacher, had talked a good deal about 'Prynne', seemed to take a lot of intellectual bearings from him, some in frank reaction, I arrived with a lot of presumptions. The first collection I bought was *Kitchen Poems* (1968), I'd already seen some of the texts in copies of *The English Intelligencer* that Rog had shown me; I had a few gratis numbers, having tried to join that tightly corresponding, mimeographed circle, but been declined membership— just a callow sixth-former, after all.[2] *Kitchen Poems* was way over the fen horizon, as far as Allott's Penguin *Contemporary Verse* was concerned, a distance that became the next acceleration. Prynne's collections that appeared during this undergraduate time, after *Kitchen Poems*, were *Aristeas* (1968), *Day Light Songs* (1968), *The White Stones* (1969), *Fire Lizard* (1970), *Brass* (1971), *Into the Day* (1972), and just afterwards, *A Night Square* (1973).

To read through this work now, at another distance, less bound in—I can't say free of—the immediate urgencies of what kinds of poem these might be, how might they relate to the current sense of poetry that they were so obviously refuting, their implications for the practice of writing—What comes across so vividly is the range of concerns vigorously worked through, worked over, in these books, an intellectual project uniquely ambitious. Who else was trying to think on this scale, in poetry? It has never halted: China. Read the collections, bracketing them as a variant on poetic convention, approach them as a thought-agenda that depends on a particular kind of writing. Even if you are unable to follow a consecutive argument, line to line, sometimes from word to word, within a phoneme, the sense of intellectual challenge is heady enough. *Kitchen Poems* may be the ostensive book of this project. Exasperated, impatient, baffled, by tracts of the writing, Prynne's notion was a comprehensive way of being interested in the world, and in poetry—all of it. The everlasting universe of things, flowing through the mind.

The four apparently separate texts, *day light songs*, *Fire Lizard*, *A Night Square* and *Into the Day* intrigued, maybe because they looked 'easier' to read and hold in attention, though still dispersing, evading every attempt to cohesion. The first efforts to write about Prynne's work were around, passionately debated; *The White Stones* seemed readable within some contexts, but then there was *Brass*, an outrageous 'going-beyond' the cohering voices of *Kitchen Poems* and *The White Stones*.[3] Rog was excited and appalled simultaneously: '"Love holds me to the mallet path"—Terrific! But what's a "mallet path"?!'.[4] Between these three, absolutely distinctive collections, the four pamphlets could get overlooked. I happened to be there and then, so I read them in the original formats, often beautiful as book-objects, where the meaning of the text has come to be instinct within their forms. Reading the collections as reproduced in the monumentally reprising editions of *Poems* (1982, 1999, 2005, 2015), I miss their supra-textual tones and glosses.

day light songs and *Fire Lizard* are as simply—cheaply—made as possible, the least sophisticated sort of self-publication that the hosts of aspiring 1960s poets would crank out: typed and mimeographed (stencil duplicated) with stapled card covers, a trimmed octavo in 'landscape' aspect, wider than high. There is information in the colophon matter of these serial poems not given in the collected editions. *day light songs* was 'written on 15th june 1968. / this is a first edition of 250 copies / produced by R. now at beech lane…'. These are poems of a day, specifically, occasional to that moment. It is the day before Bloomsday, the diurnal instant for *Ulysses*; in 1215, same day, King John ratified Magna Carta, and in 1968, one year after 'the Summer of Love', 'Jumpin' Jack Flash' was at no. 2. The date doesn't seem to be referencing these kinds of temporal resonance, unless it's proud to just sneak in front of *Ulysses*. Any local, personal or historical significance is occulted. Here is the walking persona of *The White Stones*, divagating, continuous, though textually complicated by elisions and non-sequiturs. A text voice penetrated by the world's (mostly natural) details, there is rapturous address:

> the mountain
>> respires, is equal to
>>> the whole   *(Poems* 2005: 26)

Line breaks point or ambiguate sense, 'we walk slowly if it / hurts we rant it / is not less than true oh / love I tell you so' (29). There is a climax, emphatic in some way, and ecstatic, you might say: 'The whole cloud is bright / & assembled now'—I see the billowing cumulus of Samuel Palmer's ink drawing for 'The Bright Cloud', its shepherd and shepherdess, intimate foreground. I hear an 'assembled crowd' to which we are drawn 'by simple plea', but these may just be my own occulted meanings; the poem ends so openly, (we) 'touch the / air streaming away' (31). Do 'we' stream, or does the air? The lovely (Rog word), open lightness of this sequence, through which so many connotations flow, was and is compelling, at the time, there was nothing to compare with it.[5]

> …the
>> twigs are inside
>> us, we the
> branches beyond which
>> by which through which
>>> ever the
>>> entire brightness ex,
>>> tends   *(Poems* 2005: 28)

Did *day light songs* inspire Edward Dorn's *Songs, Set Two—A Short Count,* 'This volume is to honor the Scald'? Dorn's first Set was *Twenty-four Love Songs* (1969), passionately addressed *'for* JD'—Jennifer Dunbar. Dorn's second sequence is still flagrantly erotic, but from a pulled-back perspective, outraged at US grosser political formations, attentive to the resourcefulness of migrant lives, across the Mex/Tex Border. Both Dorn's print-objects were beautifully designed by Graham Mackintosh's San Francisco-based Frontier Press (1970), in poignant contrast to the Cambridge UK formats. Dorn's lyric is sure, swift, dropping big ideas from ancient lexes:

I
The resin of the Pine
white cast in amber
planted and watered
in the river of the blood
across the bench
of the mountain
in the full mirage of the world
grove where the gnosis
lets go into hold of creation

14
...Our World
is the news of Strife's wandering[6]

Peter Riley's *Strange Family. 12 Songs*, also acknowledges *day light songs*. Beautifully designed and printed by Rosmarie Waldrop, for Rosmarie and Keith Waldrop's heroic Burning Deck press, then in Providence RI (1973), the colophon states, 'the present work is an imitation or parody in terms mainly of sonic and lexical structures'; '*These poems were written on 17ʰ September 1968*':

intending to fall
into the brightness
bending to touch the leaf
on the ground   the drop
of moisture on the bank
tending to force
brightness into the soil
touch of a finger   (vi)

Roger Langley's 'Matthew Glover', his first, declared poem, was also written around this time. Rog passionately lectured on Olson's 'The Kingfishers', citing *Mayan Letters*, to we captive, avid sixth-formers during Wednesday afternoon 'general studies' sessions. He gave me a copy of 'Matthew Glover', full of demur, disclaiming, said it was a poem inspired by all this 'Terrific'—Rog acclamation—writing going on:

a fine, detailed bush, dead,
a wicker cage now

here three or more warblers
hawk at the flies.

and, as the light changes, they are soft
brown or soft yellow with such restraint

that their flanks
shew like ice

as they shift
the small fizz

of their flight
breaks into

your thoughts... [7]

Fire Lizard has a similar format to *day light songs*, but already slightly sophisticating, an ochre, printed card cover, another precise date: 'Written in Cambridge, New Year's Day 1970'. These discrete sequences are 'diurnal', written down within a single day..., a sustained, through-composed meditation: a diurnal is the record of daily experience, can be a book of and for devotional exercise; diurnal is daily and commonplace, but embraces the movement of planets and stars (*OED*). All of Prynne's texts have been unrevisable, his copy is never blotted, their final enscripting to page is definitive to that moment, day or night. *Fire Lizard*, salamandrine, is written in short, sharp sentences, compacting humane issues, fragmenting glances to the whole deal:

The broken dangerous cup
is not mended.
The point of the sky has
all that in sight but
optics apart. Parsecs
fiddle the onion,
don't you know?   (*Poems*: 145)

Parsecs, light-over-distance speeds, deflect down through the layerings of the worlds, the cosmos, glancing off, giving sheen to the skins, the spheres, as they burn down—making that largest music, don't you know? (I'm writing this to Tallis, perfect backing-track to this thought. Stephen Hawking needs to know.)[8]

A Night Square in format puns on the title, seven and one quarter inches square, and a square line-block around the title-page text, 'A NIGHT SQUARE / CANDLEMAS 1971 / by J. H. Prynne'. Candlemas, 2 February, the winter midpoint between shortest day and spring equinox, an ancient festival of lights, the presentation of Jesus in the Temple and the ritual purification of Mary, forty days after giving birth. Also Groundhog Day. Eleven poems each of eleven lines, printed blue, lower case except for the initial, mid-page, recto only, scattering, irregularly spaced lines within the tight format. Written fourteen months after *Fire Lizard*, *A Night Square* was published a year after *Into the Day*, colophon: 'A NIGHT SQUARE takes its place / in a diurnal sequence / which already comprises: / DAY LIGHT SONGS (R Books, 1968) / FIRE LIZARD (The Blacksuede Boot Press, 1970) / INTO THE DAY (J. H. Prynne 1973).' The first collected *Poems* (1982) adds another, unpublished sequence, *Voll Verdienst*, between *day light songs* and *The White Stones*.

Into the Day (1972) is a beautiful trimmed octavo, dark cerulean blue, textured card with a flagrant black circle impressed front and back cover, also title and final page, which informs, *Achevé d'imprimer en juillet 1972; édition de 500 exemplaires. Printed by the Saffron Press, Saffron Walden.* What does this add to the spin of the work? Cambridge didn't alas have a Graham Mackintosh and his Frontier Press, but the Saffron Press took great pains with several of the self-published chapbooks. *Into the Day* isn't just a scaling up of format, the poem operates in the registers of *Brass*, by strategies, reference, ambition, the longest, most complex of the poems to that date. The variety of 'verse forms', disposition of text, is beautiful, matched to sense you sense; there are twenty-four strophes, divided twelve and twelve at mid-point of the booklet. In dialogue with Dorn—'his hope / strikes zero and is caught, as / by the shade, so slowly / from out of that bright hall he came.' (213), off, 'Oh my darling kid my darling thing / My darling twin

/ And your offspring / From out of the dark hall we came' (*Songs Set Two*: 3: *Collected Poems*: 251). It provoked: John James, *Striking the Pavilion of Zero* (1975), Andrew Crozier, *High Zero* (1978). At mid-point, between 'No resented banter takes' and 'See that you see', where in the collected editions there is a blank, unnumbered page (*Poems* 2005: [208]), the chapbook has a blank leaf, then a leaf with a luminous chrome yellow circle, recto and verso, impressed upon cream laid paper, a blazing interlocutor to the black circles that open and close the sequence, then another blank leaf. The circumference of these shapes is not perfect, but irregular, somehow artisanal, hand-cut. They summon Kazimir Malevich's supreme formalist works, 'Black Circle', 'Black Square', 'Black Cross' (c. 1913), radical aesthetic statement, the new ultra-art of Suprematism:

> In naming some of these paintings, I do not wish to point out what form to seek in them, but I wish to indicate that real forms were approached in many cases as the ground for formless painterly masses from which a painterly picture was created, quite unrelated to nature.[9]

Enter and leave *Into the Day* by way of these burning dark, burning chrome sunbursts, koranic verse markers, 'Occulted by the great disk :' (212). The play of the lines throughout is tinted by these superbly blank emblems. The black and the chrome radiances may denote entire ranges of cultural reference, frankly cosmic resonances. So, before the 'rising' of the chrome sun, 'fixed in- / justice gives the orange its / juice' [Tesco seriatim], mid-sequence,

>   ... the sky
> in chance halo, cadentia
> sydera caelo. Close by
> the pit the punter stands,...   (*Poems*, 207)

I read through here, from a glance at Vergil's [old-style spell, like 'shew', '&'] paean to oncoming night, *Aeneid* IV.81, then to Dante's *Inferno*, the 'punter' being led by Vergil himself to the edge of that infernal pit, all those last-century body holes, at furthest extreme from his mentor's

121

beautiful, pagan sky dome. Or is that, just a punter, on the Cam? 'Trailing / in the water, his hand / in the field of seed.' (206). Like you do. Vergil's lovely sky was then shining above Dido, agonised in her love for Aeneas, he determined to leave Libyan Carthage to achieve his founding mission in Italica. At the end of Book IV, dying from her self-inflicted wounds, Dido seeks release, desperately looking to the same sky, 'oculisque errantibus alto / quaesivit caelo lucem' (691–2). Simultaneously in reading time, the black and the chrome yellow circles are just that, mute non-denotational signs, demanding the play of inferences, necessity to read the world, inescapable, in question from moment to moment.

As you waited outside the double doors, some kind of intellectual compression/decompression device, there were two images framed on the wall, may still be, to contemplate. Satan, very much a falling angel, treads the fiery waves in Hell, first plate to Milton's *Paradise Lost* from one of the late seventeenth-century folio editions 'with sculptures'. The plate is unsigned, perhaps because it might have attracted censorship and punishment: in the dark background lurk a king and queen enthroned, condemned to the lowest depth of Inferno. And a much smaller reproduction. Piero del Pollaiuolo's 'Apollo and Daphne' (1470/80), National Gallery. Daphne flowers, wing-like, fretted dark green laurel branches, uplifting from her shoulders, she seems ok with this, she avoids Apollo's imploring gaze offered in right profile. The god, *per me concordant carmina nervis* (518), by whom, through whom, the sinews of song accord, is losing his beloved, or the one he needs, at least, as she ascends. 'And the bark grew and grew.'[10] Transitioning to and fro between RFL and JHP, I went after Strange Gods for light relief: European cinema; pursuit of (actually-existing) Socialist Realism, via Raymond Williams (didn't, haven't found it); the latest word from Paris, Roland Barthes and *Tel Quel*, thanks to Stephen Heath's vespertine seminars on Proust–Semiotics–Deconstruction; the Reverend Kenelm Foster leading us through Dante's *Inferno* in his cigarette-singed (we took them for infernal fires survived) donkey jacket; Helena Mennie Shire's all singing, dancing and poetry party in the Court of Scotland under James VI[11]; Peter Dronke's lectures and seminars on medieval latin lyric, Notker (Balbulus) of St Gall's *Liber Hymnorum* (881/87), and its *sequentiae*.[12] Patrick White (a JHP enthusiasm, then), Solzhenitsyn (not), Cervantes (ah, La Mancha, al-Andaluz) and…. This was not a modularised degree course, understand.

Mr Prynne's poetry fascinated and exasperated me, it was beautiful and occulted, by turns. One of his practical-critical sessions that set me on track was to read George Chapman's *Ouids Banquet of Sence. A Coronet for his Miftreffe Philofophie, and his amorous Zodiacke* (1595). The forcible 'energia' of this poem became a way to approach the overdetermined text of *Brass*, and the four *sequentiae*. The *Banquet of Sence* compelled me to Shakespeare, *Venus and Adonis*, then its compulsive dark pendent, *The Rape of Lucrece*. In a visionary night, I took to my heart, Renaissance, Shakespeare, Freud, European *rinascità*, and poetry, all of it. I have hoped to pass on all of this, ever since. *Futurum inuifibile.*

NOTES

This essay is declared Heidegger-free.

madrigalian / brightness: *Into the Day* (1972): [24]; *Poems* (2015): 210.

[1] Mick Le Moignan (2004), 'Generations in Harmony', *Once a Caian…* vol. 15 (Michaelmas 2015): 13.

[2] 'CAMBRIDGE INTELLIGENCER. Some time since we received a Letter signed Y. Z.—the writer of which recommended to our notice and reprobation, the *Cambridge Intelligencer*, as a Paper which, from its "rancour and scurrility, might do much mischief among the Yeomanry and Peasantry of the Northern Counties, if not properly checked and exposed."'

'We were not inattentive to our Correspondent; we immediately purchased the *Cambridge Intelligencer*, and found it infinitely more vile and detestable than we had been led to surmise. It contained a mass of loathsome ingredients, a sort of "hell-broth," made up of the worst parts of the worst public Papers that ever disgraced the Metropolis of any Country, with added filth and venom of its own … a Print so decidedly hostile to the Religious and Political Establishments of this Country, so rancorous and malignant in its language, and so diabolical in its principle, must either be confined to a few Readers, as mad and wicked as its Conductors; or must be soon suppressed by those Laws which its purpose was to revile … We know from certain information, that the *Cambridge Intelligencer* is *dispersed gratuitously* in the most unfrequented parts of the Country. We see that it has somehow or other the means of supporting itself without the aid of Advertisements. Our Readers must be left to guess at the source of these supplies.' *The Anti-Jacobin, or Weekly Examiner. In Two Volumes. 'Sparsoque Recolligit Ignes'* [Lucan, *Pharsalia*, I 155: 'and scatters the gathered fires']. Fourth Edition, Revised and Corrected. London: Printed for J. Wright, Piccadilly. 1799. Notice for 7 May 1798, vol. 2: 263–5.

The Anti-Jacobin was founded by George Canning, Under-Secretary of State for Foreign Affairs, and edited by the 'cold and saturnine' satirist, William Gifford; Pitt the Younger wrote for *The Anti-Jacobin*, James Gillray contributed cartoons; it ran from 1797 to 1798. Gifford was wrongly thought to have written the 'Cockney poetry' notice attacking Keats' *Endymion*, which, in the view of Shelley and Byron, destroyed the poet. The notice was written by 'the talking potato', John Wilson Crocker, denounced by William Hazlitt: Walter Jackson Bate, *John Keats* (Chatto & Windus, 1979): 369. See also, Emily Lorraine de Montluzin, *The Anti-Jacobins, 1798–1800. The Early Contributors to the Anti-Jacobin Review* (1988).

[3] Veronica Forrest-Thomson, *Poetic Artifice. A Theory of Twentieth-century Poetry*, (Manchester University Press, 1978): 'Sonnet 94 and what it has taught us': 'It has shown that neither the thematic, nor the formal/conventional, nor the semantic level working on its own is sufficient to embody the range of ideas and of reactions to ideas that most competent poems and any great poem would require language to embody.' (15–6) … 'Neither the psychopathological and political emphases of French literary theory associated with the journal *Tel Quel* nor our native breed of rank theoretical ignorance will explain why the idea that poetry gives us special contact with external reality has been so popular in the past.' (135). The 'tendentious obscurity' of Prynne's 'Of Sanguine Fire' discussed 142–6. David Trotter, 'A Reading of Prynne's *BRASS*', *PN Review* 5.2 (6) (1978): 49–53, and *The Making of the Modern Reader: Language and Subjectivity in Modern American, English and Irish Poetry*, 'Language, Discourse, Society' Series, (Palgrave Macmillan, 1983). Nigel Wheale, 'Expense: J.H. Prynne's *The White Stones*', *Grosseteste Review* 12 (1979): 103–18. Around this time, Richard Read came across: 'Of course, it is not that formal values are imperceptible in Giorgione's art…. The miracle is of bonds as naturally borne as the one of the air we all must breathe, of the freedom in subject-matter under the poetic aegis of affinities and reciprocal relations; of the just and sanguine fire in an unaccustomed mood.' Adrian Stokes, *Art and Science. A Study of Alberti, Piero della Francesca and Giorgione* (Faber and Faber, 1949): '[37]'.

[4] 'Royal Fern', line 8, in *Brass* (1971): '[20]'; *Poems*: 159. Discussed in N. H. Reeve and Richard Kerridge, *'Nearly Too Much'. The Poetry of J. H. Prynne*, Liverpool English Texts and Studies, 26 (Liverpool University Press, 1995): 77–102. A sceptical review of this—the first book-length study of the poetry?—by Tim Love, is at *litrefsreviews.blogspot.co.uk* (12 January 2009), sceptical of the

poetics *passim*. I always associated 'mallet path' with those uncomfortable flint-cobbled pavements of college courtyards; Google offers the pioneering expedition of Pierre and Paul Mallet, from the Missouri River to Santa Fe, 1739, guided along existing Indian trails by 'first Americans'.

[5] See now, John Wilkinson, 'Heigh Ho: A Partial Gloss of *Word Order*', Ryan Dobran (ed.), *Glossator 2: Practice and Theory of the Commentary: On the Poems of J. H. Prynne*, (2010): 295ff., for sources in Wordsworth, Hölderlin's 'rhapsodic prose fragment' 'In Lieblicher Blaue', Heidegger, and other texts. PDF at the Glossator site, solutioperfecta.files.wordpress.com.

[6] Edward Dorn, *The Collected Poems 1956–1974* (Four Seasons Foundation, Bolinas CA, 1975): 250, 256.

[7] R.F. Langley, *Complete Poems*, Jeremy Noel-Tod (ed.), (Carcanet, 2015): 26.

[8] Reeve and Kerridge: 'These poem-sequences express what the speaker of *Fire Lizard* calls 'my love of the corners'—a phrase in which subject and object positions flicker to and fro in a protracted perceptual labyrinth.' (50).

[9] Camilla Gray, *The Russian Experiment in Art 1863–1922*, revised and enlarged edition by Marian Burleigh-Motley, (Thames & Hudson, 1986, first edn 1962): 161.

[10] Ovid, *Metamorphoses* I 449–569. 'And the bark...', *Into the Day*: [5], *Poems*: 206.

[11] Helena taught from home, summer terms, to the sound of F. R. Leavis mowing his lawn (rigorously, shirt open, no tie) beyond the beech hedge. She was wonderful, though declined to teach *Piers Plowman*. She had taught Thom Gunn a few years before, sprang an obscure mediaeval lyric on you, demanding—'Solve it, Tom did!' She edited *The Wrong Music. The Poems of Olive Fraser, 1909–1977* (Canongate, 1989), beautifully celebrated by Ali Smith, *Shire*, (Full Circle Editions, 2013).

[12] Peter Dronke, *Medieval Latin and the Rise of the European Love-Lyric*, (Clarendon, two vols, 1968; second edn, one vol., 1999). Read this.

J.H. Prynne and Grid

Masahiko Abe

The first impression matters in poetry. When you pick up a collection of poems written by someone not familiar to you, the voice you hear at the moment of encounter flicks on a switch. It helps you adopt a new mode and transform yourself into a receptive organ specially arranged for that new poet. You discover your new self then.

Indeed, this was how I came across Jeremy Prynne's work. His name had been unknown to me until I applied for a place in the graduate school of Cambridge University. In application I did not specify the name of the supervisor I wanted to work with, mainly because I was yet to decide what subject to focus on in the doctoral course after having studied T.S. Eliot in the M.A. course at Tokyo University. Apparently, however, the office of the English faculty of Cambridge University filled in the blank space for me. A few months later, a letter of acceptance arrived with the name of the supervisor: J.H. Prynne. This was the first time I ever saw the name. *They* decided for me whom I should work with, and now I know how luck favoured me.

Immediately after receiving the letter, I tried to find out who this person was. A swift answer came from an Englishman teaching in our department. He had a Ph.D from Cambridge and knew who the person in question was. 'You are lucky. Jeremy Prynne is legendary as supervisor; also, he is very well known as an experimental poet.' Since our library in Tokyo University did not hold any copy of his work, I had to wait till I arrived in England.

When I picked up *Word Order* at Heffer's on Trinity Street in Cambridge, the following passage, taken from the first page of the collection, worked in double ways.

> As you knew why
> you took me for
> just as well you knew
>
> you I took, as you
> could hardly, with
> me if you offer

126

Firstly, I felt that this was exactly the kind of poem I wanted to study. The sharp edge of the words, the radical challenge to syntax, and the grip you feel despite the disjointed, fragmentary appearance—all this seemed miraculous to me. Naturally, if you are faced with a miracle, you want to enjoy it more. My way of enjoyment almost always involves thinking. Prynne's poems loomed in front of me as a question to be answered. But you cannot carry out research *on* the poet while you are working *with* him. So eventually I decided to write on another miraculous poet, Wallace Stevens, in my doctoral thesis. I thought I could wait till I finish this project.

The passage from *Word Order*, however, had another different kind of impact on me. The lines were part of a poem, but it also signalled a human existence behind it. Of course, the author is dead, as Roland Barthes famously declared. We can forget about the author's intention in reading the text. But still I could not completely ignore the authorial existence especially when he is sitting just in front of me. I had numberless conversations with Jeremy Prynne, mainly in the academic, but also in more relaxed and casual, contexts; the poet Prynne seemed to be more visibly there, I felt, when we were not discussing my drafts on Wallace Stevens. It became increasingly difficult for me to dissociate one from the other, that is, the poet from the person. When I talked to Jeremy, I thought of the poet who wrote *Word Order*, and when I read his poems, not surprisingly, I thought of Jeremy. The lines from *Word Order* seemed to echo in some obscure way what Prynne, the person, embodied.

As I went through his works, my interest grew. I frequented the West Room of University Library, where you can consult books, magazines and pamphlets not easily available at ordinary bookshops and libraries. I was struck by the way Prynne's style changed. His early days were represented by *Force of Circumstance and Other Poems* (1962), where his cautious balancing act was almost indistinguishable from those of his immediate conservative precursors, while more radical experiments were carried out in *Day Light Songs* (1968), *The White Stones* (1969), *Fire Lizard* (1970) and *Brass* (1971). But my favourite books remained to be *The Oval Window* (1983) and *Word Order* (1989), collections marked by frugality and rigour.

At that time I was reading through materials that focus on the painterly imagination of poets in the modernist period. I thought that

Innovative styles in painting, particularly cubism and abstraction, were likely to give us hints for understanding the syntactical experiments carried out by poets such as Ezra Pound, T.S. Eliot, Wallace Stevens, William Carlos Williams and Gertrude Stein. I came to be attracted by the concept of grid in this context. Rosalind Krauss's fascinating works on grid led me to see the continual crossing of vertical and horizontal lines on the canvas as an ultimate reductive gesture, which help us transcend everyday orders including syntactical constructions. Prynne's poetic achievements, too—particularly those in *Word Order*—could be explained if we set painterly grid side by side with poetic one.

Well, more than twenty years have passed since I decided the idea of grid can serve as a good introduction to the difficult poems of J.H. Prynne. I have not finished my project yet. I did publish an essay on the issue, but I do not think just highlighting the reductive aspect of grid is good enough. For Prynne's works do not end up as a mere demolition of English syntax. They go beyond that. It is likely to take some more time for me to make a convincing argument on this issue.

So, did I manage to forget about Prynne the person when I was engaged with the idea of grid? Perhaps not. But, when I was sitting in front of the poet, I rarely managed to talk about his poems. One of the few questions I asked was: do you give readings of poems? I still remember his answer: there are poems which are meant to be read aloud in public; but there are also those which are supposed to be perused silently. The implication, I thought, was that his poems belonged to the latter group. Interestingly, however, he hastened to add, 'I don't mind reading in front of foreign audience.'

I had to wait for more than twenty years before the opportunity came. In the spring of 2013 Jeremy Prynne visited Japan for the first time and made a tour round Kyushyu Island. The event was sponsored by a private university in Japan and for some reason poetry reading was not part of the programmes. I was not that disappointed, though. I flew over to Kyushyu and attended one of his lectures on Wordsworth. He said he would rather remain standing than sit down during the talk. It was at this instant that a problem arose. Prynne, when he stood, was too far away from the table where his paper lay. Now you can look at the photo printed below and see how he solved the problem by putting a chair on top of the desk. It was a beautifully illustrative scene of grid: a compensation, perhaps, for what we could not really experience in the form of poetry reading.

'Assuming banishment for lost time back across nullity'[1]: on opening *Acrylic Tips*

Matthew Hall

In 2002 Barque Press published Prynne's *Acrylic Tips*, a slender edition with an earthen-red cover. Inside the small book, on the unpaginated third page, there is the dedication, "For: S.K.", and on the fifth page there is an unattributed epigraph, "The murderous head made from a motor car number-plate."[2] Running from the seventh to the sixteenth page, inclusively, are ten pages of six stanzas each, the stanzas composed of quatrains with regular and patterned bilinear indentation.

Prynne's poetic works released throughout the 1990s and the early twenty-first century exhibit a marked obduracy which operates through the systematic incorporation of disparate discourses. The excess of signification stems from an excess of lexical and discursive elements imbuing the poems with a sense of language existing under pressure. *Acrylic Tips* elides the enclosed semantic and semiotic space of *Triodes* (1999) and draws the reader back to Prynne's work in *Her Weasels Wild Returning* (1994). As Rod Mengham writes on *Her Weasels Wild Returning* in his essay 'After Avant-gardism',

> With the exception of one or two fragments, it is composed in a language which resolutely and systematically excludes any phrasing that retains the balances and tensions we would normally be able to detect in the manner of a speaking voice. What we get instead is not a discursive free-for-all filling the vacuum—not an intensifying of fracture and dispersal—but, off-puttingly, a weird concerted texture, that works hard to make the separate parts of the whole comply with one another. The language is more bizarre than ever, but it is also more heavily synthesised, more systematically correlated, simply more commensurable.[3]

In *Acrylic Tips* poetic language exists under pressure, as the concretion of discourses is lineated across the transmigratory space of the poem. Both

Acrylic Tips and *Her Weasels Wild Returning* contain thematic threads that unify social ritual with song; in *Acrylic Tips* this song extends to Indigenous Australian ritual and song lines as mythic narratives of creation patterned on the landscape. From *Her Weasels Wild Returning* concepts of nomadicism and exile carry through to *Acrylic Tips*, where they are read through the traditional Indigenous and colonial milieus of Australian history. Another element that has carried through from *Her Weasels Wild Returning* is the attention given to the politics and lexical complexity of the female pronoun.

Andrea Brady's brief essay 'No Turning Back: *Acrylic Tips*' examines the forced transmogrifications of the feminine and the natural as inherently paralleling territorial and geographic division. Brady writes that the feminine is "associated with the lineated and amputated body, the bound and divided land, is lyric".[4] I will propose an alternative reading suggestive of the ongoing ramifications of colonisation and the increasing technological means of dominance both in social structures and cultural formations. This analysis is structured on concepts of social and technological advancement, and is incorporative of pathological models of harm and genetic engineering contrasted with notions of an Indigenous experience of the natural. Brady's assertion that "the bound and divided land, is lyric", must be balanced against the 40,000 plus years in which Indigenous Australians have used song as a cultural and spiritual practice establishing a relationship with and building knowledge of the land. For Indigenous Australians, knowledge of land and its traversal is a pathway to spiritual embodiment and replenishment. At issue are postcolonial concepts of territorialisation and contemporary land usage, but also poetic language history as it corresponds to Prynne's definition of poetic thought, "as brought into being by recognition and contest with the whole cultural system of a language".[5] The poetic language used in the poem embeds and articulates patterns of colonial and argotic usage, demonstrative of its etymological antecedents as well as its potential to evolve and adapt to new models of meaning, as constituted by a localised, Australian English.

In his reading of *Her Weasels Wild Returning* Mengham discusses the poem's gendered language and its representation in landforms:

So what I am suggesting is that the peculiarly powerful abstractness of the language in *Weasels* represents an attempt to deterritorialize both masculine and feminine, not by neutralising their differences, but by at least proposing to equalize them; by demonstrating how the only viable *terra nullius*, previously unoccupied, unsettled, unowned, is one that can be projected in a synoptic language that shows remarkably little interest in either *écriture feminine* or the masculine tradition.[6]

Acrylic Tips presupposes a nature, not explicitly Edenic, but which speaks to the origins of knowledge possessed by traditional owners of the land. This connection is made explicit in *Acrylic Tips* by contrasting a Western and culturally imperialistic position inherent in an account of colonisation with an Australian Aboriginal understanding of land use and ritual in the mythopoetic space of the poem. The exploitation of the earth endemic to patriarchal societies is contrasted with the Australian Indigenous perspective which traditionally understands the land as a living, identificatory embodiment of the people.[7] The forced adaptations to a technologised pastoral represent a discontinuity from an ecological-based reading and the exposition of nature as feminine. The text expresses a legacy of imperial dominance as it is represented against the Australian landscape and Indigenous culture, a power dynamic that has its nascent structure in an anthropocentric colonialism which entails dominance over, exploitation of and barbarity towards nature.

Though Mengham talks about *Her Weasels Wild Returning* as introducing a "synoptic language" that may be the only exemplary form of a "*terra nullius*, previously unoccupied, unsettled, unowned" land, it is only in *Acrylic Tips* that this position is tested against the application of *terra nullius* in the establishment of Australia on sovereign, Indigenous land. In *Acrylic Tips* the contestation of the land and its 40,000 year history of use and ritual is contrasted with the theoretical space of which Mengham writes. This comes to fruition in *Acrylic Tips* through representations of Australia, where Prynne and Mengham both spent time in 2002.

John Kinsella's 'Oxidia: Go', which was published in *Quid 17*, provides details about Prynne and Kinsella's trip to Country Peak and Yenyenning, prior to Kinsella's still more detailed account of Prynne's visit to Australia in *Fast, Loose Beginnings*.[8] Aside from 'Oxidia: Go', other works of Kinsella's through which parallels can be drawn stem from *The Hierarchy of Sheep*. The poem from which the book's title stems, 'The Hierarchy of Sheep—a report from my brother', details in four parts the treatment of rams, ewes, wethers and lambs in the processes of mulesing, shearing and slaughter. The parallels between the situation described in Kinsella's 'The Hierarchy of Sheep' and *Acrylic Tips* make it likely that this was a report retold to Prynne, during his time in Australia. To provide a preliminary view of these parallels as they relate to pastoral violence, it will serve to contrast Kinsella's wordings with Prynne's in their respective poems.

John Kinsella's 'Ewes' begins,

All cut by a shearer at one time or another-
sewn together with dental floss or wearing their scars
gracefully [...]

Later in the poem, Kinsella writes that "older ewes", "all of them full with young, milk veins / up and pumping hard to udders— / somewhere a nick with a blade has a vein / knotted off with needle and thread, / the myth declaring another will take its place".[9] These lines are tied into what Prynne relates of an infant that thirsts for an "abrogated breast", the expectant wait for "milk / at a lip trickle", with "needlepoint decision", "engorgement", "grapple juices" and a mythic teat regrown in a "post-hormone limb crisis."[10] Immediately apparent in the description of the animals is the problematisation of the feminine as bound and divided, and of the female body as the site of harm. It should be noted that very similar cross-readings can be made with John Kinsella's seven-part poem 'The Epistemology of Sheep'. Approaching *Acrylic Tips*'s opening line with this in mind, the reader may begin to acknowledge and understand a number of the informational axes and discourses upon which the poem communicates.

While there remains little critical attention paid to the poem *Acrylic Tips*, there is an essay by Andrea Brady and an examination of the poem by Jon Clay, in his *Sensation, Contemporary Poetry and Deleuze*. Aside from Brady's reference to Woomera asylum seekers, no mention of Australia is given in any of the critical literature on the poem to date. I would argue that the structural patterns of landscapes, argot, botanical studies and Indigenous knowledge presented are uniquely tied to the Australian continent and Prynne's experiences there. Established in this manner, issues of systemic (colonial and techno-capital) violence will be implicitly detailed against Australian colonial and Indigenous history, tracing the foundations of dominance and violence as a socio-historical construct. The "synoptic language"[11] of the poem will be weighed against the history of Australia, starting with the land's designation as *terra nullius* by the British to give themselves grounds for colonial settlement of the continent.

Acrylic Tips represents and utilises an Australian English loaded with the complexities and connotations of colonisation. It functions, as Prynne argues, through "the pragmatic history of [...] the social and generically coded uses of a specific language".[12] The observational thread that continues throughout the poem reflects Prynne's position as an outsider, but the colloquialisms, argot and socio-historical operations of language in *Acrylic Tips* position its poetic language as co-existing with Australian history. It is in this manner that the trans-historical aspects of the poem show that "poetic thought is brought into being by recognition and contest with the whole cultural system of a language".[13] The epigraph of *Acrylic Tips*, from Donald Stuart's *Yandy*, allows the reader to glimpse the transformation of the ritual hunt through a suturing of the material and cultural advancements prescribed by the dominant Western force, as the quote contrasts forms, registers and government control of transport and food procurement between cultural epochs. "The murderous head made from a motor car number-plate"[14] applies not only an ameliorative positioning of cultures, but also suggests a culture of adaptation and survival, positioned at the margins of society. The vectors of speed demonstrated in the epigraph entail a destabilisation of cultural norms, rituals and cultural identity. Post-contact Aboriginal culture has undergone change; subjective identity, physical and social environments continue to adapt, and traditions alter based on dynamic and responsive social formations.[15]

Reading the first line of *Acrylic Tips*, "Assuming banishment for lost time back across nullity" (537), through an informational matrix rooted in Australian history allows the reader to immediately unpack certain thematic threads of the poem. "Assuming banishment" contains obvious referential allusions to being banished from the Garden of Eden and to life after the fall. It also implies an ethnographic position of observation and categorisation, a condemnatory set of relations through which Prynne signifies the irony of assumed cultural hierarchies. That the loss of the Edenic is signalled from the outset adds weight to the line "his right arm / tied to creation" (540), which implies humankind's involvement in manifesting their way of life. This line may also be indicative of artificial insemination, linking man directly to the genetic manipulation present in the creation of sheep with culturally desirable characteristics, which the poem goes on to explore. The "[r]ibs of possession" (537) connote an implicit need for control and show an *a priori* link between the technological and the feminine pronoun through the transformation it undergoes in the course of the poem. The emphasis on "his right arm" as "tied to creation" details a masculine register of possession which affects our understanding of control, dominance and the division of land within the poem. In such lines, the gendering of the natural within the poem juxtaposes culturally divergent knowledge of the land and its embodiments.

One could also establish a linkage between the registers of control over movement established in the epigraph, through the car's registration plates, and the car scenes in the poem. The practice of registering one's possession may also relate to early maps where land is not "named" but numbered or referred to only by coordinates, where Indigenous place names and traditions were erased and reinstated in familiar, colonial contexts. In this case the "banishment" from the poem's opening line may speak to the marginalisation of Indigenous culture within Australian society.

If the reader allows the word "nullity" from the poem's opening line its full weight it provides not only a colonial depiction of the Australian landscape but also, from a Western perspective, one of legal and foundational origins. To provide some insight into the sovereign authority of command in the decree of *terra nullius* over Australia, it will serve to examine this notion and its use in colonisation. In 1770 Captain James Cook anchored outside what is presently called Botany Bay, then sailed north, around the Cape York Peninsula, and proclaimed the land he sighted as belonging to the expansive British Empire.[16] The legal rationale upon which the convention of colony acquisition was founded was one in which claims of ownership could be based on discovery and effective possession.[17] As Attwood contends,

Aboriginal hunter-gatherers were adjudged to have no property rights because of the way in which their place in time was constructed by major seventeenth- and eighteenth-century philosophical and legal authorities which, in turn, drew upon historical theories regarding human society. In the opinion of Grotius, Pufendorf, Locke and others, hunter-gatherers (or "savages" in their terms) had no concept of property because they were in the original state of nature. This assessment was founded upon one or more 'historical' sources: the representations of antiquity found in classical history and the representation of the Americas as "the beginning [of] all the World".[18]

These laws demarcated the stages through which a society should pass, each stage being characterised by particular concepts and institutions regarding law, property, government and commerce. At the lowest stage, that of the hunter-gatherer—in which the occupants of a land lived as part of nature—it was determined that there existed no concept of property, and therefore the lands of the Australian Aborigines were declared by British colonialists as "waste" or "desert".[19] The decree of *terra nullius* over the already occupied land of Australia, whose Indigenous people Cook encountered, was upheld until the Mabo-Wik Judgement of 1992, with the recognition of land rights and the recognition of generational ownership.[20] Thus New Holland was declared, subsuming the subjective status of the Indigenous population to the category of the continent's flora and fauna. It was to remain this way until 1949, when the rights of full citizenship were granted to Australian Indigenous people. Equal voting rights for Indigenous Australians was only finally given in the 1967 Referendum.

The first line of *Acrylic Tips* and the connotations of "lost time" evoke the racist notion of "lost time" and the supposed "primitivisms" observed by the first colonial fleet.[21] Reading Mengham's proposition about *terra nullius* in *Her Weasels Wild Returning* through the transhistorical structure of Australian Indigenous and colonial history allows the reader to arrive at the conceptualisation of poetic language as determined co-extensively with national history. Mengham writes that

> [t]he peculiarly powerful abstractness of the language [...]
> represents an attempt to deterritorialize both masculine and
> feminine, not by neutralising their differences, but by at
> least proposing to equalize them; by demonstrating how the
> only viable *terra nullius*, previously unoccupied, unsettled,
> unowned, is one that can be projected in a synoptic language.[22]

As Prynne claims in 'Mental Ears and Poetic Work', "I want to present
experimentally a scheme for the description and analysis of poetic
language mounted in the domain of poetic discourse. The specific
domain is that of English poetry and the English language considered
as a system and as a history."[23] The poetic language of *Acrylic Tips* exists
as co-extensive with and determined by the physical landscapes and
colonial history of the Australian continent. This is a language that has
developed under the pressures of colonisation, to become a "synoptic
language". The poem focuses upon the adherence of a language
"which [is] cross-wired into the cultural history of a ramified national
identity".[24] Prynne's interest is in the depiction of language existing
under pressure and through the rubric of a language history, sutured
to national history. The compression of discourses into an incalculably
integrated register shows the implications of "[h]uman language [as]
the tribal continuity of expressive human behaviour".[25] For Prynne,
imperialist control entails within it the mindset established during
Australia's colonisation upon a campaign of dominance and sustained
systemic violence, and it has been integrated into power relations which
exist in cultural relations, religious fervour, the pastoral industry and
language itself. *Acrylic Tips* operates between and across disciplines and
discourses, demonstrative of a linguistic system that creates its own
operative language and spatial relations.

Poetic language in *Acrylic Tips* functions as a system under
pressure, a pressure which it partly self-creates, forcing the linguistic
pattern away from the constructs of customary discourse towards an
"inclusive conjunctive synthesis",[26] or what Mengham identifies as
"synoptic language". Linguistic integration in *Acrylic Tips* gives rise
to and strengthens Prynne's descriptions of the forced adaptations of
the natural through the rubric of the technological. As Prynne writes
in the essay 'Poetic Thought', "Poetic thought is empowered within
and through energies of language under pressure", and as it informs

or commands the linguistic form and structure of the text, "the language of poetry is its modality and material base, but whatever its relation with common human speech, the word-arguments in use are characteristically disputed territory, where prosody and verse-form press against unresolved structure and repeatedly transgress expectations".[27] Thus the language of *Acrylic Tips* enacts in its linguistic deployment an actuated sense of the forced adaptations of the poem's thematic threads.

Notes

[1] J.H. Prynne, *Poems* (Hexham, Northumberland: Bloodaxe Books, 2015): 535-546, 537. All references to Prynne's *Acrylic Tips* will cite page number in parenthesis from the 2015 edition unless otherwise noted. Note that the poem as collated in *Poems* does not include the dedication as per the Barque Press edition.

[2] *Acrylic Tips*'s epigraph, from Donald Stuart's *Yandy*, is also indicative of the construction of the transhistorical space of the poem.

[3] Rod Mengham, 'After Avant-gardism: *Her Weasels Wild Returning*', *Assembling Alternatives; Reading Postmodern Poetries Transnationally*, ed. Romana Huk (Middletown, CT: Wesleyan University Press, 2003) 384-88, 384-5.

[4] Andrea Brady, 'No Turning Back: *Acrylic Tips*', *Quid*, 17 (2006) 82.

[5] J.H. Prynne, 'Poetic Thought', *Textual Practice*, Vol. 24 No. 4 (August 2010) 595-606, 598.

[6] Mengham, 'After Avant-gardism: *Her Weasels Wild Returning*', 387.

[7] A.P. Elkin, *The Australian Aborigines* (Sydney: Angus and Robertson, 1976) 186. See also, Deborah Bird Rose, *Nourishing Terrains* (Canberra: Australian Heritage Commission, 1996) 39. In the subchapter titled 'Centres of Life', Rose writes, "Daly Pulkara told me that his people are 'born for country'. In many parts of Australia Aboriginal people believe that the spirit (or one spirit) that animates a foetal human is a spirit from the land: an ancestral Dreaming spirit, or a human spirit (baby spirit) resident in a particular locale. [...] That is, country gives forth life, and included in that life are the people of the country." (39)

[8] John Kinsella, *Fast, Loose Beginnings: A memoir of intoxications* (Carlton, Vic.: Melbourne University Press, 2006) 120-138.

[9] John Kinsella and Coral Hull, 'The Hierarchy of Sheep—a report from my brother,' *Zoo* (Sydney: Paperbark Press, 2000) 125-127, 126.

[10] These references stem from pages 544, 538, 540, 539, 543 and 545, respectively.

[11] Mengham, 'After Avant-gardism: *Her Weasels Wild Returning*', 387.

[12] J.H. Prynne, *Stars, Tigers and the Shape of Words; The William Matthews Lectures, 1992* (London: Birkbeck College, 1993) 32.

[13] Prynne, "Poetic Thought," 598.

[14] Donald Stuart, *Yandy* (Adelaide: Rigby, 1978) 89. [originally published in 1959]

[15] Ernest Hunter, *Aboriginal Health and History: Power and Prejudice in Remote Australia* (Cambridge: Cambridge University Press, 1993) 203. Hunter argues that the most telling adaptation necessary to Aboriginal culture was the understanding of historical time, as opposed to the subjective link to the mythic past, which was materialised through land and family moieties. Hunter writes, "The upheavals accompanying European colonisation transformed their physical and interpersonal environments, demanding a new level of adaptation. What was introduced was time—historical time. An examination of emerging constructions of self, of personal and group identity, necessarily requires both longitudinal and horizontal perspectives: 'the development of society is both synchronic and diachronic [...] We have to think of societies in terms of both a set of simultaneous institutions (synchronism) and a process of historical transformation (diachronism)' (Paul Ricoeur, *Time and Narrative*, 3 vols. Trans. Kathleen McLaughlin and David Pellauer (Chicago: University of Chicago Press, 1984) 38) 203. The notion of historic time is also discussed in Bain Attwood, *In The Age of Mabo: History, Aborigines and Australia* (St. Leonards, NSW: Allen and Unwin, 1996) 42-46.

[16] Peter Russel, *Recognising Aboriginal Title* (Toronto: University of Toronto Press, 2005) 39.

[17] Attwood, *In the Age of Mabo*, ix.

[18] Attwood, *In the Age of Mabo*, ix.

[19] Attwood, *In the Age of Mabo*, ix.

[20] Attwood, *In the Age of Mabo*, xvi.

[21] Remarking upon acts of "primitivism" and accounts of encounters with Indigenous Australians can be found in *The Journals of Captain James Cook on his Voyages of Discovery*, Vol. 1, *The Voyage of the Endeavor* 1768-1771, ed.

J.C. Beaglehole (Cambridge: Cambridge University Press, 1968): 305-306; *The Endeavor Journal of Joseph Banks: Vol. 2*, ed. J.C. Beaglehole (Sydney, NSW: Angus and Robertson, 1962): 111-12, 123-30.

[22] Mengham, 'After Avant-gardism: *Her Weasels Wild Returning*', 387.

[23] J.H. Prynne, 'Mental Ears and Poetic Work', *Chicago Review*, 55.1 (2010) 126-57, 126.

[24] Prynne, 'Mental Ears and Poetic Work', 127.

[25] J.H. Prynne, 'A Quick Riposte to Handke's Dictum about War and Language', *Quid*, 6 (2000) 23-26, 24.

[26] Jon Clay, *Sensation, Contemporary Poetry and Deleuze: Transformative Intensities* (London: Continuum, 2010) 40.

[27] Prynne, 'Poetic Thought', 598.

wynsum wong: J.H.Prynne
Inside and Outside *The English Intelligencer*

Anthony Mellors

A shared belief in the free circulation of literature and ideas based on the pastoral anti-commercialism that was a motivating force behind little magazines and presses in the 1960s meant that the *Intelligencer* was regarded by its editors as 'produced' information rather than 'published' material. Andrew Crozier says that 'I've never regarded what was circulated in [*TEI*] as *published*', and Peter Riley claims that 'Last month's sheets of *TEI* should be almost as dead as yesterday's papers... *TEI* is a move toward a print-free method of distributing information'.[1] Mr. Prynne expresses this in his acerbic manner when he remarks in a 1968 letter that 'the syllables of a child's world are more than the adverts for Summer County would have us believe.'[2] Indeed, indeed. The alternative, ideal economy guiding these remarks are made explicit in a letter by John Hall, responding to Ian Vine's claim that Prynne's 'Moon Poem' is 'pretentious nonsense', an 'incredible creation which takes over fifty lines to say round about nothing as far as I can see.'[3] Hall argues that the 'global' movement of Prynne's work

> gives him the authority to the <u>word</u>, what has to be <u>earned</u>... by the achievement of just such an honour; and <u>honour</u> is just such a word, as <u>hope</u> and <u>love</u> are—to get the constant breathing of such is song—and out of context, outside of that movement these words ought not really to be mentioned. For they become something quite different. And that's just what I've done here, and what many of us are doing with our poems, getting in without the earning power, other people's hard-earned cash.—I've abandoned that sentence as I hope you will have done.[4]

Abandoned or disavowed, perhaps, because the argument veers from the transcendental to carping about the kind of earning poetry ought to avoid. The discourse here seems to me typically Olsonian in its appositional constructions, which urge abstractions into the concrete, and its heavy, repeated stress on key terms. And Olson's rhetorical tics are the currency which drives critical exchange throughout the *Intelligencer*. Since the journal is dedicated to an Olsonian project of reverting continental drift, this is hardly surprising; re-forming the U.K. and the U.S.A. as part of an unbroken landmass would be one way of getting rid of the Brit parochialism the contributors are at pains to overcome. Hall wants to drop the Eng from England in the hope that we can begin to contemplate Land as an inclusive spiritual entity, for '[w]hat we are after is something much more proper, to us, our own, purity: the nomadic purity of "who we are", all flags left outside.'[5] Yet later, in a letter to Crozier, he is troubled by the generality, 'since the politics of that drift are very recent in one sense and so possibly the political name there shd stay.'[6] Less equivocal in this respect is Ralph Maud's letter on Peter Riley's archaeological 'Working Notes' , where Riley's description of flint-mining is seen as

> ...literally sexual. It took Olson to give me that insight: metaphor as decoration & not what we want in poetry any more, since it tends to keep us at too safe a distance from the truth—the passionate & physiological truth—of such things as mining or horse-riding, say.'[7]

The rejection of metaphor as decoration is clear enough as an essential component of Anglo-American late modernism. As in Olson's writings on poetics, however, the substitution of literal references as facts, truths, energies, purities, becomes incoherent because it cannot prevent the transfer of these 'facts' into abstractions. Other than in anything but the most prurient terms, what does it mean to say that flint-mining is *literally* sexual? The desire to return to an international or cosmic sense of purity, property, and community, which Prynne evokes in his philological excursus 'A Pedantic Note', with its emphasis on 'proper names' modulating into 'the sounds of our proper selves', is underwritten by this organic metaphorization of the literal.[8] Riley, confronted with Jim Philip's eulogizing of Lévi-Strauss's *The Savage Mind* as a programme 'to breed out of the interactive past and present a new common humanity that could be the basis of communicative and peaceful operations over a huge field' is 'convinced that the whole ethos is the <u>complete</u> antithesis to <u>everything</u> I have gained from the work of such men as Olson' because 'it puts the shape/plot/structure/form <u>before</u> the living content…'[9] Since for Olson, following Creeley, 'FORM IS NEVER MORE THAN AN EXTENSION OF CONTENT', Riley is right to be suspicious of a structural anthropology that rejects the organicist theories of language on which this credo is based.[10]

While constantly taking issue with what he regards as the sentimental and nostalgic tendencies of other contributors to the *Intelligencer*, Prynne is far from being immune to the traits he deplores. As early as the journal's first run he berates Crozier, whose Elizabethan delicacies have too much of the glister of the falsely 'authentic' , and soon the entire journal is taken to task:

> I am frankly bored to death by the total contrast between the discrete sequence of good and interesting things—separate, house-proud, often so local as to be without any force as risk—and on the (t)other side an almost complete lack of momentum, of culmination or exchange…the 'Intelligencer' has come up into a thick cloud of inconstancy; where, wryly, we 'prefer' to live. What does such a thing mean? Nothing, I suppose, and one would be foolish to admit the poignancy of alternatives…[11]

'[W]ithout any force as risk' is revealing in its implication that the Olsonian 'local' has been reduced by British poets to provincialism, short-circuiting the enterprise from the start. The targets here are Riley and Crozier, but probably Gael Turnbull too, whose demand for clarity of private expression is far removed from Prynne's notion of poetry as being the point of concentration for a 'shared' yet necessarily dense and non-expressive language. A 1968 letter on poems by Ray Crump takes up this issue:

> Rhyme is the public truth of language, sound paced out in the shared places, the echoes are no one's private property

143

or achievement; thus any grace (truly achieved) of sound
<u>is</u> political, part of the world of motion and place in which
language is like the weather, the air we breathe.[12]

The holistic sentiment is checked at various points in poems that will
appear in *Kitchen Poems* and *The White Stones*; 'Numbers in Time of
Trouble', for example, suggests that we 'move / right out of range of those
sickening and / greasy sureties—like "back to our proper / homes"...'
At times, however, it is reaffirmed in the numerous invocations of 'love',
such as

> It *may* all flow again if we suppress the
> breaks, as I long to do,
> at the far end of that distance
> and tidings of the land...
>
> ...that we be
> born at last into the image   of love[13]

This poem, 'The Wound, Day and Night', is glossed in 'A Communication' as a

> consequence in some sense at least of the Royal Society
> Symposium on <u>Continental Drift</u> (London 1965). And more
> especially, Miller's paper on geochronology. I say this mainly
> as propaganda, since the political & personal relevance of this
> volume has to be seen to be believed. As with the migration
> of peoples, the earth too has her movements. Not that we
> easily know this: 'According to Tomaschek's measurements in
> Marbury, <u>M</u>2 land tide has an amplitude of .5m, i.e., the earth's
> surface rises and falls twice daily by .5m (20 inches). Naturally,
> this rise is imperceptible, as there is no fixed point from which
> to measure the fluctuations, since the observer standing on the
> earth undergoes the same motion' (Defant, <u>Ebb and Flow</u>, p.
> 114). Yet the priorities of such knowledge are clear...[14]

A Latin passage from the *Astronomicon* of Manilius follows, translated
as

> And since it is from high heaven that poetry descends and fate's established order comes to earth, the very pattern of nature must be my verse's first theme and I must set out the whole universe in its proper guise.

Here we are in classic Olson/Prynne territory: the leap from empirical to mystical revelation presented as a conjunction clear as day. I take it that Prynne means in the most basic sense that since the earth's motion is not experienced as such by a subject, poetic enquiry must go beyond subjective experience; therefore the objective conditions of nature become the starting-point from which any recursive meditation on experience takes place. As Michael Stone-Richards says in a recent essay, 'always at issue are questions of newness and subjection the basis of which are states of embodiment marked by dispossession which serve to problematize the subjective appropriation of experience', and 'the language of objectification is indeed explored in Prynne's oeuvre for the question of what such a discourse might be like if regulated however tenuously by the idea of a non-intentional universe which finds its models not merely in scientific discourse, but closest to discourse of the body.'[15] But does it follow that setting out the universe in its 'proper guise' is predicated by poetry descending from heaven and the established order of fate? Reading Prynne always involves these difficult negotiations, and the unspecified content of 'political and personal relevance' seems as evasive as it is thetic. In the context of the *Intelligencer* debates, the political remains an unfocused something on the horizon, no doubt because the question throughout is *how* the political takes place in poetry rather than *what* it is (though let's not forget the Editorial Note of March 5th, 1968: 'We shall be attending the Anti-Vietnam War demonstration in London on Sunday, 17th March.') The rejection of decoration is crucial. Riley's 'Communication' railing against A Level stock responses wants 'poems which cannot be broken down into their component parts any more than a piece of wood can, with a saw; therefore organic in some sense other than haphazard'; therefore political views in the poems should be directly stated rather than something projected or dramatised.[16] Similarly, Prynne states that if 'a set of language is to need and deserve confidence it must keep its own kind of fidelity: it must be true to its purpose.'[17] Yet the call for fidelity and purpose is itself conceptually vague, anything but the direct statement Riley demands. 'Need and deserve confidence' in what or for whom? Isn't 'confidence' a notoriously slippery term politically; and can language have its own fidelity? Fidelity to what?

It's only later in Prynne's writings that we can begin to give definition to these moral abstractions. The recent lecture 'Mental Ears and Poetic Work', for example, picks up on almost all the topoi mentioned in the *Intelligencer*, broadening them into an historical and politicized poetics, and shows that Prynne has never stopped thinking through the journal's exchanges. The following remark restates the 1966 letter I have just quoted:

> [t]he active poetic text is… characteristically in dispute with its own ways and means, contrary implication running inwards to its roots and outwards to its surface proliferations: not as acrobatic display but as working the work that, when fit for purpose, poetry needs to do.[18]

Fit for purpose means neither decorative expression nor the simplicity of direct, supposedly literal, statement, but the textual effects of passionate engagement with the sonorities and sedimented sense-patterns of language as historical record. The point is not merely to affirm and extend existing poetic tradition but to intervene creatively within it, exploiting the fault-lines which inevitably separate intentional structures from the complex reality outside them. Poetry therefore

> comprises at its most fully extended an envelope which finds and sets the textual contours in writing of how things are; while also activating a system of discontinuities and breaks which interrupt and contest the intrinsic cohesion and boundary profiles of its domain, so that there is constant leakage inwards and outwards across the connection with the larger world order.[19]

Reality, politically and ethically, is messy, and the poet's job is not to suture it with an overlay of committed effusion but to expose its wounds and leaks.

Now, I would say that this is a fundamentally ethical rather than political position, and one that is problematic in terms of its own claim to value. As Prynne argues in his detailed discussion of the philological connection between Wordsworthian 'blessing' and blood-sacrifice, we need to understand the consequences of deeply-embedded ritual institutions, which persist even in *The Prelude*'s joyful invocations, for 'the condoned spillage of innocent blood is everywhere around us, now, and the artificers of consolatory blessing who are the leaders of organized religion are up to their dainty necks in this blood.'[20] A note cites Chomsky on the British involvement in Iraq. Clearly, then, Prynne does not condone the spillage of innocent blood; yet his evolutionary and archetypal discourse, supported here by Walter Burkert's sociobiological account of ritual, gestures toward an underlying structural reality, more Hobbes than Marx, which cannot say why these acts of human cruelty should be seen as wrong. In other words, from what source does the commitment to political 'fidelity' derive? Moreover, Prynne's dialectical position works as a form of *ascesis* which always checks its own motives: the commitment is to recursive complexity rather than to political *praxis*.

This is why the experience of reading Prynne's poetry, always from the outside, as it were, if one is to remain true to its disclosure of a non-intentional, non-identical universe, involves constant double-take. And Prynne's critical work sometimes performs that double-take for us. Re-reading 'The Wound, Day and Night' after 'Mental Ears' suggests that the 'I' who longs to suppress the breaks is ironic, because making it all flow again is not poetically fit for purpose. What, then, of being born into the image of love? Love here, as elsewhere in *The White Stones*, is presumably that spiritual mantra of the '60s rather than desire or narrowly envisioned romance. 'A Pedantic Note' had spliced Olson's concept of field poetics with the *wynsum wong* or 'blissful field' of the OE Cyenwulfian poem *The Phoenix*, implying that 'the field is more extended than the garden, since it <u>includes</u> the whole range of love, desire, the pursuit of happiness; it is the nomadic or excursive condition of <u>longing</u> fulfilled and completed.' The faked pastures of Summer County margarine yield to a 'spatial & historic metaphor, in "desire" separated by exile from "fulfilment", as a <u>literal</u> component of the land...'[21] 'Mental Ears' continues the meditation on longing and loving, but now longing is a finite span linked with memory and love via 'mind' (OE *myne*), less concerned with desire than with affection. 'For Wordsworth... little nameless acts of kindness and love were "unremembered", not held in finite recollection, so that their influence can still flow onwards when the specific occasions have been lost to mind and memory; they form the tacit habitual prosody of a man's ethical character.'[22] But later, when a note on Freud and Jonathan Lear's *Love and its Place in Nature* seems about to conclude that '[l]ove is... a self-concept, endued with a function similar to Coleridge's imagination, to promote a noble resolving unity, "a certain harmony in the soul" ', Prynne rounds on his/Lear's surmise by remarking that 'validation of autonomy by these procedures can in last resort only be circular and self-fulfilling, because the baseline order of material reality has been pre-emptively subsumed into the drama of uplifted human purpose.'[23] The literal, the real, and purpose itself is now suspect, being too involved in the rationalizing-phantasizing process of human motives to be able to analyse the 'real' nature of love as self-transcendence. The suspended ('love in the air') signifieds displayed across the poetic field represent the possibility of this kind of dialectical reading, and readers must intervene in the text just as the poet intervenes in the historical record. As Allen Fisher suggests in *Necessary Business*, 't]he realizations can only be with the participating reader who interferes and brings noise: brings a dictionary, or a biography of Wyndham Lewis, or notes on crystallography.'[24] Except that this intervening—as disruption and interference, to change the course of events but also to protect one's own interests—might itself pre-empt the baseline order of material reality. Reading is a necessary disruption of poetry, but one which inevitably rationalizes or humanizes the material field of the poem. 'The discourses of modernism in Western poetics', Prynne declares,

> make steeper descents into sub-intelligibility; and in my own case I am rather frequently accused of having more or less altogether taken leave of discernible sense. In fact I believe this accusation to be more or less true, and not to me alarmingly so, because what for so long has seemed the arduous royal road into the domain of poetry ('what does it mean?') seems less and less an unavoidably necessary precondition for successful reading.[25]

In an essay on the *Intelligencer*, Alex Latter argues that Prynne's poetry of the late 1960s can be usefully anchored in the context of the journal's debates, and that readings of complex works such as 'Aristeas' have failed to take account of Prynne's position with regard to the journal's community. By ignoring the original appearance of 'Aristeas' in Series 2, without its scholarly notes, he argues, Simon Jarvis overestimates the poem's heuristic aims, when much information is contained within Prynne's response to Riley's 'Working Notes' on prehistory, while Anthony Mellors wrongly treats the poem's historical mediation of shamanism as romantic self-identification: '[r]ather than blindly trusting the figure of the shaman to offer some kind of redemption', Latter argues, deferring to Jarvis's materialist reading, the passage on bone 'explicitly counts "the cost of such trust by recounting the material needs and desires which such motifs support and depend upon."'[26] Well, I'm inclined to agree with this, partly because in *Late Modernist Poetics* I too hastily reduced the poem to Eliotic 'mythic method', and partly because of what I've just said about the problem of intervention. Yet look at the key passage Latter quotes from Prynne's disillusioned letter to Crozier of 1966:

> I had thought that perhaps something might <u>move</u>, if there were perhaps some initial measure of trust, so that the community of risk could hold up the idea of the possible world; we could approximately and in some sense or other mostly be <u>in</u> it, or moving in part across the same face, giving out something and who am I to care how it might be done? Get back the knowledge, the purities, the lightness of language, whatever it is.

Getting back the knowledge and purities—the hectoring Olsonian imperative again—is little more than modernist nostalgia and hardly supports claims for Prynne as a rigorous materialist. Two months later, though, Prynne is insisting that he doesn't want back the culture that existed prior to exchange economies, 'nor any version of cultural nostalgia.' (quoted in Latter) If 'Aristeas', then, 'counts the cost' of trust rather than what Latter calls 'blindly trusting' in a redemptive figure, it shows that Prynne's demand to 'take knowledge back to the springs' has undergone revision. Presuming, of course, that Prynne's call to get back the knowledge and purities is more than a snipe, which, the more I look at it the more it seems to be, and what Prynne later calls his 'pyrrhonic tirade' attests to the disappointment with what he perceives as the *Intelligencer's* 'thick cloud of inconstancy; where, wryly, we "prefer" to live.'[27] Simon Jarvis is right, I think, to say that 'a recursive pattern is set up whereby the poem extends trust to apparently fictional and archaic religious motifs' but then subjects that trust to historical and economic scrutiny. It still seems to me that Jarvis achieves his beautifully coherent reading by way of a dialectical method that will always sublate extreme parataxis and multiple referents to a desired end, though the strength of his commentary is its ability to factor-in crucial objections, e.g., '[d]o not the italicisations, '*life* and not value', 'Royalty as *plural*', seem to urge us towards the recidivism into the direct exercise of power which Adorno warns is the price of a glorification of the irreducibly qualitative?'[28] What the *Intelligencer's* exchanges tell us is that Prynne's poetry of this period, like his letters, might not be entirely the product of a coherent poetics but the record of a gradual movement from a residual modernist mythos to a conception of spirit as bone, 'the truth that subjective spirituality is a temporalised moral finitude alienating itself within a series of reified figures.'[29] Or, in Prynne's words, '[w]here-as for any reader thereafter, the way into poems is by retrospect and from the finished outside, through the shell of the boundary layer.'[30]

Notes

[1] Andrew Crozier, letter to Peter Riley, *TEI*, Series 1, 24.1.67; Peter Riley, letter to Andrew Crozier, Series 1, 29.1.67.

[2] J. H. Prynne, letter in *The English Intelligencer*, Series 3, unnumbered pages, 14.3.68. Summer County margarine, which is still available today from wholesale suppliers, was one of the first products to take advantage of television advertising in the mid-fifties. Prynne might be referring to a particular advert, which I've not been able to trace, but I suggest what he's attacking here is the 'jingle', which sets the pattern of patronising patter TV advertising continues to use today by aping nursery rhymes and simple songs designed for infant minds. See Prynne, *Stars, Tigers and the Shape of Words*: 'The vast scale and remoteness of phenomena are potentially frightening, as also the imminent loneliness at bed-time;

but each word reduces this scale to the friendly and protective charm of little things.' (10). As margarine, Summer County itself is a typical embodiment of advertising's desire to represent culture as nature, which then has to be re-packaged as culture in order to avoid the negative implications of the rude and perishable: 'it's foil-wrapped to keep it country-fresh'.

[3] Ian Vine, letter, *TEI*, Series 1, 1966, p. 84. 'Either my critical intelligence is going to pot, or it's pretentious nonsense.'

[4] John Hall, reply to Ian Vine, *TEI*, Series 1, 1966, p. 86.

[5] John Hall, 'Some Notes to the Biographies of Poems Written and Unwritten', *TEI*, Series 1, 1966, pp. 105-7.

[6] Hall, letter to Crozier, *TEI*, Series 1, 18.ii.67, pp. 225-6.

[7] Ralph Maud, *TEI*, Series 2, 29.iii.67, p. 286.

[8] Prynne, 'A Pedantic Note in Two Parts', *TEI*, Series 2, 1967, pp. 346-51; p. 348.

[9] Jim Philip, *TEI*, Series 2, pp. 520-1; pp. 521-3.

[10] Charles Olson, 'Projective Verse', in *Collected Prose*, 240.

[11] Prynne, letter to Crozier, *TEI*, Series 1, 13.ix.66; letter to Crozier, Series 1, 27.xii.66. Is Prynne making 'wryly' a homophone for 'Riley', I wonder?

[12] Prynne, letter, *TEI*, Series 3, 5.iii.68.

[13] Prynne, 'The Wound, Day and Night', *TEI*, Series 1, 1966, pp.74-6; 17. An insert in the trial proof of *Brass* (1971) in the UCLA archive includes a poem by Nick Totton, 'The Overcoat of Mr. Prynne': 'We apply whatever adjective in the air'.

[14] Prynne, 'A Communication', *TEI*, Series 1, 1966, p. 27.

[15] Michael Stone-Richards, 'The Time of the Subject in the Neurological Field (I): A Commentary on J.H. Prynne's "Again in the Black Cloud"', *Glossator*, 2 (Spring 2010), p. 233.

[16] Peter Riley, 'Communication', *TEI*, Series 1, 1.2.67, p. 184. The piece of wood analogy is to some extent another ventriloquism of the Olson of 'Projective Verse': '...a word to be taken to stand for the kind of relation of man to experience which a poet might state as the necessity of a line or a work to be as wood is, to be as clean as wood is as it issues from the hand of nature, to be as shaped as wood can be when a man has had his hand to it.' (Olson, *Collected Prose*, 247.)

[17] Prynne, letter to Crozier, *TEI*, Series 1, 13.ix.66.

[18] Prynne, 'Mental Ears and Poetic Work', *Chicago Review*, 55: 1 (2010), p. 141.

[19] Prynne, 'Mental Ears', p. 126.

[20] Prynne, 'Mental Ears', p. 141.

[21] Prynne, 'A Pedantic Note', p. 350. 'From the moment he ventures into FIELD COMPOSITION—puts himself in the open—he can go by no track other the the one the poem under hand declares, for itself'; '...we now enter... the large area of the whole poem, into the FIELD, if you like, where all the syllables and all the lines must be managed in their relations to each other.' (Olson, *Collected Prose*, 240; 243.)

[22] Prynne, 'Mental Ears', p. 139.

[23] Prynne, 'Mental Ears', p. 153.

[24] Allen Fisher, *Necessary Business* (London: Spanner, 1985), 33. (My offprint of this long essay, which has been 'amended' over the years, may not be reliable as to page numbers. It is already a revised 1990 text from the author, and I have consulted also a new chapter version, *Necessary Business: aesthetics and patterns of connectedness: reading works by cris cheek, Eric Mottram, and J. H. Prynne*, which is part of a forthcoming book from University of Alabama Press (the quotation is at p. 129).

[25] Prynne, 'Mental Ears', p. 132.

[26] Alex Latter, 'Scheming for the Possible World: J. H. Prynne's *The White Stones* and *The English Intelligencer*', *Intercapillary Space*, 2010, unnumbered pages.

[27] Prynne, letter to Drew Milne, 21.03.1993, 'J.H. Prynne/Drew Milne: some letters', *Parataxis*, 5 (1993–1994), p. 58; letter to Andrew Crozier, *TEI*, Series 1, 27.xii.66.

[28] Simon Jarvis, 'Quality and the Non-identical in J.H.Prynne's "Aristeas, in Seven Years"', *Jacket*, 20 (December 2002), unnumbered pages.

[29] Adrian Johnstone, *Zizek's Ontology: A Transcendental Materialist Theory of Subjectivity* (Evanston: Northwestern University, 2008), 236.

[30] Prynne, 'Mental Ears', p. 127.

BIBLIOGRAPHY

The text of *The English Intelligencer* I have used throughout is the one held in the Bodleian Library, Oxford. Its editors and dates are as follows:

Series 1, ed. Andrew Crozier, March 1966–February 1967.

Series 2, ed. Peter Riley, March 1967–December 1967.

Series 3, ed. Andrew Crozier, December 1967–April 1968.

Fisher, Allen, *Necessary Business: A text regarding the poetry of new pertinence produced from the works of cris cheek, Eric Mottram & J. H. Prynne.* London: Spanner, 1985.

Jarvis, Simon, 'Quality and the Non-identical in J.H.Prynne's "Aristeas, in Seven Years"', *Jacket*, 20 (December 2002). (http://jacketmagazine. com/20/pt-jarvis.html) Originally in *Parataxis: Modernism and Modern Writing*, 1 (Spring 1991), pp. 69-86.

Johnstone, Adrian, *Žižek's Ontology: A Transcendental Materialist Theory of Subjectivity.* Evanston, IL: Northwestern University, 2008.

Latter, Alex, 'Scheming for the Possible World: J. H. Prynne's *The White Stones* and *The English Intelligencer.*' (http://intercapillaryspace.blogspot. co.uk/2010/04/scheming-for-possible-world-j.html)

Olson, Charles, *Collected Prose*, ed. Donald Allen and Benjamin Friedlander. Berkeley, CA: University of California Press, 1997.

Prynne, J. H., 'J.H. Prynne/ Drew Milne: Some Letters', *Parataxis*, 5 (1993–1994), pp. 56–62.

'Mental Ears and Poetic Work', *Chicago Review*, 55: 1 (2010), pp. 126-157. (https://english.duke.edu/uploads/assets/Mental%20Ears%20Prynne. pdf)

Stars, Tigers and the Shape of Words. The William Matthews Lectures. Birkbeck College, London, 1992.

Stone-Richards, Michael, 'The Time of the Subject in the Neurological Field (I): A Commentary on J.H. Prynne's "Again in the Black Cloud"', *Glossator*, 2 (Spring 2010), pp. 149-244. (http://michaelstonerichards. com/downloads/PrynneGLOSSATOR.pdf)

Notes on 'Es Lebe der König'

MICHAEL TENCER

'Es Lebe der König' was written, according to J.H. Prynne's remarks at a poetry reading in 1971, 'immediately after hearing of the death of the Romanian-German poet Paul Celan, who, as the French language so discreetly puts it, "gave himself to the River Seine" last year. Everyone knew he would sooner or later, but it was somehow shocking when finally a man who had survived the concentration camps as a Romanian Jew, and exiled himself to Paris, and lived in a condition of such attenuated and rarified misery that anything so carelessly physical as death would seem a kind of almost humorous afterthought... But he did anyway.'[1] Celan likely drowned during the night of 20 April 1970, though several weeks passed before his remains were identified and his death confirmed. Celan's obituary was printed in *The Times* on 23 May 1970, and the clipping was included in a letter from Prynne to the American poet Edward Dorn.[2] Prynne's poem was published several months later, in *Collection*, 7 (Autumn 1970).[3]

The implication that the poem was composed quickly seems plausible alongside some of Prynne's other occasional public descriptions of his compositional practices, from the period of *Force of Circumstance and Other Poems* ('I don't revise very much, because a poem that needs extensive revision, on the whole, I try not to allow to get written at all.'[4]) to at least *Bands Around the Throat* (published 'about 24 hours before Margaret Thatcher won her extended term as the prime minister of the United Kingdom. I knew it was going to happen, obviously it inevitably was going to happen. So I wrote these poems in a hurry, just before the results could be declared, and published them in a little pamphlet from a Xerox machine in order to get them out before she got in.'[5]).

A further plausible implication of the immediacy of 'Es Lebe der König's composition would be that reference materials were unlikely to have been consulted during the writing process. This practice would again be consistent with Prynne's occasional public statements on poetic composition, from his earliest (only after 'the poem is written', undergoes 'a certain amount of small adjustment', and is put 'into some form of print', is the poem then reread 'to see which words are really carrying the nodal weight': 'My most valuable aids are the etymological dictionaries, and this is perhaps a kind of minor vice. Once a poem gets written and I have located a word which this poem has given to me, I've won out of the English language another word for my small vocabulary of words that really mean and matter to me. [Then I go] back to the etymological dictionary [...]'6) to some of his most recent ('I composed [*Kazoo Dreamboats; or, On What There Is*] in a condition of complete isolation, totally and deliberately separated. I had one book only with me when I wrote this. So the material that is in the reference section is a kind of memory bank—which I had to verify some of by prowling around the internet—but basically it's remembered bits and pieces.'7).

Regardless of whether or not we assume these implications of speed and relative independence from source materials during the poem's composition—partly contingent, I suppose, on whether we could imagine such characteristics as applying consistently to more than half a century's highly variegated shifts and developments—certainly no lack of premeditation could be inferred, particularly in regard to the poem's vocabulary.

The vocabulary of the poem appears to be partly composed of embedded references or part-translations from numerous sources, including Celan, Georg Büchner, Martin Heidegger, the Old and New Testaments, and Tacitus; though beyond direct reference, the vocabulary bears indelible traces of its previous historical and literary usages. It would be absurd to attempt to decipher or explain away the poem as though it were merely a collection of weighted words, but not to take account of at least some of the vocabulary's previous resonances would be to neglect a set of its inherent significations. To a poet who does not 'believe in the unconscious'8, the '[f]acts dredged up from the world and facts also dredged up from language, the great body of language, reaching back, down into the past'9 count for a lot—but only insofar as they serve as a nourishing source of active intellection; poetic thought requires more than simply the faithful reproduction of where language has already been. Prynne articulated this creative dynamic in a recent discussion in the People's Republic of China:

The story is sometimes said about [the] great [Chinese] poet Du Fu that when he was sitting in front of his writing desk composing a poem, and he came to a point where he had to choose the next character for the line that he was composing, that he would run in his mind through the alternative characters that might occupy the position in that line at that point; and he would survey in his mind the entire literary and social history of each of the alternative characters—that is to say, he knew the corpus of traditional Chinese poetic composition so well that he could look at each possible character and say 'Oh yes, oh yes, oh yes,' and follow its history right through the canon of Chinese poetic writing up to his time. I have something of that feeling myself—that is to say, when I use a word I'm very conscious of where it's been and what it's done, how much dirt it has on its shoes, how much stardust it has on its upper crust, because that's part of the way in which one makes a decision about one's vocabulary. But one has to be conscious of the fact that if one becomes too aware of the history of words then that becomes a kind of mannerism—you may have to force it or shake it off, or abandon it, in order to keep the language somehow alive.[10]

The following materials, then, should not be regarded as annotations, 'decrypting' the poem via meticulous and reductive literalism. They consist, instead, of a small portion of the historical, etymological and literary context relating to the poem's vocabulary. These are also considered alongside apposite suggestions or speculations made by the poet, his critics, and critics of Celan; and occasional impossible correspondences, in which images and terms travel the wrong way through time to influence events before them. In the spirit of Prynne's caveat to one of his own recent poetic seminars, I would stress that this approach 'is not designed to harass you into a particular channel of consideration, but rather to open perspectives that each of you may treat differently, as part of your own discoveries.'[11]

A Note on the Text, Dedication and Title

The text of 'Es Lebe der König' has remained almost entirely stable since its first publication in 1970. There are only two minor variants from the version printed in *Brass* to the most recent [2015] edition of *Poems*: the poem's first appearance, on p. 22 of *Collection, 7*, included one word not featured in subsequent printings (the first line of the third stanza read 'we hear of your' rather than 'we hear your'); and the 1999 edition of *Poems* erroneously changed the comma at the end of the second stanza to a full stop.[12] Given that the version in *Poems* in 1982, 2005 and 2015 is identical to the version printed in *Brass*, we can safely regard that version as the poem's definitive form.

'Es Lebe der König' is Prynne's only poem prior to 2014 to feature a specific dedication. (The final poem of *Al-Dente*, 'For Tom', was evidently dedicated to fellow poet and friend Tom Raworth, who at the time of the book's publication was undergoing a series of life-threatening surgeries). Individual books by Prynne have also featured dedications,[13] but the dedications of individual poems have otherwise only been implicit.

The title 'Es Lebe der König', as Prynne noted in the aforementioned 1971 Vancouver reading and as many others have noted since, is a line from Georg Büchner's play *Dantons Tod*, and the line was discussed by Celan in his acceptance speech for the 1960 Georg Büchner Prize, 'Der Meridian'.[14] As Geoffrey Ward succinctly summarised it, 'At the end of the play Lucile is left alone, her lover Camille and his friends having gone to the guillotine. A citizens' patrol passes, and in response to their automatic "Who goes there?", she answers, deliberately, "Long Live the King!", signing her own death-warrant. Celan argues that this utterance, an apparent statement of fealty to the *ancien régime*, is in reality "an act of freedom ... a step ... It is homage to the majesty of the absurd which bespeaks the presence of human beings." It is "poetry", he goes on: yet in the same address poetry is termed "an externalization of nothing but mortality, and in vain".'[15] Andrew Ross, in an utterly contradictory reading, viewed Lucile's closing line as an 'involuntary gesture [considered by Celan] an act of pure dissent because its political agnosticism terrorizes the public with nonmeaning'; and Ross likens this gesture to Celan's own poetry as a 'long guerilla war against the

German language [that] rests upon his own Nazified experience of a privatized terror which language seeks to generate all on its own. The increasingly hermetic cult of idiosyncrasy which marks his dealings with language may itself be an act of dissent, but there is no doubt about where it leads us—beyond the social altogether, toward a state, we could say, of extreme privation. [...] For all its politically charged power it does not, however, offer a discourse *of* or *about* individualism which we are going to be able to find socially useful.'[16]

While there are certainly a wide range of interpretations possible, Ward's reading of Lucile's final line and of Celan's use of it in theorising his poetics seems more relevant to Prynne's poem, not only because Ross's reading disregards Celan's own vehement refusal of his characterisation as a 'hermetic poet',[17] but because Ross seems to neglect any possibility, such as that discussed by Prynne in his review of Jean Bollack's *Poésie Contre Poésie; Celan et la Littérature*, that Celan's ostensibly private poetry of 'what are most often taken as his prevailing signs: darkness, negation, silence'[18] could simultaneously be rife with the results of philological research, acute sensitivity to social utterance, and embedded ironies, including that bitterest irony of Celan's choice to write poems exclusively in the language of his oppressors. Such layers of meaning, shaped by a paradoxical combination of interiorised discourse, formal experimentation and philological history in a variety of languages and fields of study, would indicate significantly more in Celan's work than what Ross views as 'only *one*, highly idiosyncratic [...] *individual discourse*'.[19] Prynne's later public discussions of Celan confirm his view of Celan's work as complex and dynamic, embracing contradiction in an ambiguity 'fraught with enigma and equivocation but also direct to its task of questionings',[20] and Prynne's use of Lucile's exclamation as the title of a poem dedicated to Celan likewise appears to function dialectically, in the sense that Prynne would later describe as 'the working encounter with contradiction in the very substance of object-reality and the obduracy of thought; irony not as an optional tone of voice but as a marker for intrinsic anomaly.'[21]

1. Fire and honey oozes from cracks in the earth; / the cloud eases up the Richter scale. Sky divides [...] Give back the / fringe to the sky now hot with its glare, turning / russet and madder, going over and over

> And hee opened the bottomelesse pit, and there arose a smoke out of the pit, as the smoke of a great fornace, and the sunne and the ayre were darkened, by reason of the smoke of the pit.

The Holy Bible, King James Version [1611]: *Reuelation*, Chapter IX, verse 2. The imagery recalls also *Genesis*, Chapter XIX, verse 28 ('and loe, the smoke of the countrey went vp as the smoke of a furnace') and *Exodus*, Chapter XIX, verse 18 ('And mount Sinai was altogether on a smoke, because the LORD descended vpon it in fire: and the smoke thereof ascended as the smoke of a furnace, and the whole mount quaked greatly'). The character Woyzeck, in Georg Büchner's unfinished eponymous play, quotes this in confused hysteria in Scene Three:

> Woyzeck: 'Isn't it written: "And there arose a smoke out of the pit, as the smoke of a great furnace"?'
> Marie: 'Oh, Franz!'
> Woyzeck: 'Shh! Quiet! I've got it! The Freemasons! There was a terrible noise in the sky and everything was on fire! I'm on the trail of something, something big. It followed me all the way to the town. Something that I can't put my hands on, or understand. Something that drives us mad. What'll come of it all?'

Georg Büchner, *Woyzeck* [*Complete Plays and Prose*, tr. Carl Richard Mueller (New York: Hill and Wang, Inc, 1963): 113 [German orig. *c.* 1837]].

Celan's experiences during the Holocaust, witnessing the cremation of fellow prisoners, are clearly of direct relevance as well, considering the recurrence of the imagery of burning bodies, ash and smoke throughout his work (most famously in 'Todesfuge' [from *Mohn und Gedächtnis* (Stuttgart: Deutsche Verlags-Anstalt, 1952): 37-39 [though the poem was likely written *c.* 1945]], and in the poem which is frequently regarded as a revisitation of or response to 'Todesfuge', 'Engführung' [from *Sprachgitter* (Frankfurt am Main: S. Fischer Verlag, 1959): 55-64 [the poem was written in 1958]].

2. technical

> In 'The Question Concerning Technology', Heidegger explores the way in which *techne* has lost its primary sense of revealing, being "at home in something", which links it to *poiesis*. In modernity, appearance submits to a technology which "pursues and entraps nature as a calculable coherence of forces."

Matt ffytche, 'Es Lebe der König (for Paul Celan, 1920-1970)', in *For J.H. Prynne: In Celebration, 24th June 2006*, [ed. Keston Sutherland] (*Quid*, 17; Falmer, Brighton, 2006): 19-23 [24], quoting Martin Heidegger, *The Question Concerning Technology and Other Essays*, tr. William Lovitt (New York/London: Garland Publishing, Inc., 1977): 3-35 [13, 21], German orig. published as *Vorträge und Aufsätze* (Pfullingen: Verlag Günther Neske, 1954): 9-40. See also Birgitta Johansson, *The Engineering of Being: An Ontological Approach to J.H. Prynne* (Umeå: Umeå University; *Acta Universitatis Umensis*, *Umeå Studies in the Humanities*, 135, 1997): 134-46 [135]; Matthew Hall, *On Violence in the Work of J.H. Prynne*, op. cit.: 33; and D.S. Marriott, 'The Rites of Difficulty', in *fragmente*, 7 (1997): 118-37 [128], where Marriott posits that 'the knowing exactitude of the poem in its references to sky, earth, technical, flags, wire, animals, suggest that the poem is also in dialogue with [Celan's 'Meridian'] speech's own engagement with the ontological poetics of the German philosopher, Martin Heidegger…'—though note that of this list of terms, only 'sky' appears in the 'Meridian' speech, in relation to Büchner's *Lenz* ('a man who walks on his head sees the sky below, as an abyss.' [*Collected Prose*, tr. Rosmarie Waldrop, op. cit.: 46, and referred back to on 52]).

3. starlight becomes negative

> Starlight becomes negative because light from stars no longer exists at its source […] But starlight becomes negative in a second way. All stars become signs, all prints are divisive. Star of general, of jew.'

Matt ffytche, 'Es Lebe der König (for Paul Celan,1920-1970)', op. cit.: 25.

4. you [...] we

The dedication raises the first enigmatic question of many produced by the poem: to what extent is this poem an encounter with an other, a 'you'? and is the referent of that other, that 'you', Celan himself or some other unspecified addressee?

D.S. Marriott, 'The Rites of Difficulty', op. cit.: 128. Many critics of 'Es Lebe der König' have noted resemblances between the poetics of estrangement and unrepresentability in Prynne and Celan, and have speculated that Prynne's poem enacts the type of encounter with otherness discussed by Celan in the latter half of 'Der Meridian'.[22] While such an encounter with otherness could be read as literal, reading the 'you' of the poem as Celan and 'we' as his readers, the use of deictic ambiguity combined with an often elusive but persistent sense of import in recurring common nouns (*e.g.* 'snow', 'window', 'water', 'star') may seem too deliberate and consistent an effect to warrant a simple narrative explanation.

5. If you / are born to peaks in the wire

Denk dir:
der Moorsoldat von Massada
bringt sich Heimat bei, aufs
unauslöschlichste,
wider
allen Dorn im Draht.

Paul Celan, 'Denk dir', in *Fadensonnen* (Frankfurt am Main: Suhrkamp Verlag, 1968): 121. In Susan H. Gillespie's English translation: 'JUST THINK: / The *Moorsoldat* of Masada / acquires a homeland, most / unquenchably / against / each barb in the wire.' [in Celan's letter to Ilana Shmueli, 27 June 1967, in *The Correspondence of Paul Celan & Ilana Shmueli* (Riverdale-on-Hudson, New York: The Sheep Meadow Press, 2010): 3-4 [3]; German orig. published in *Paul Celan/Ilana Shmueli:*

Briefwechsel (Frankfurt am Main: Suhrkamp Verlag, 2004):7]. Gillespie adds a note on her translation: '*Moorsoldat*: a "peat-bog soldier," from a song composed by prisoners in a German concentration camp and later revised by Hanns Eisler and recorded by Paul Robeson.'

6. we too are numbered

He telleth the number of the stars: he calleth them all by *their* names.

Psalmes, CXLVII, verse 5; recalling *Genesis*, Chapter XV, verse 5: 'And he brought him forth abroad, and said, Looke now towards heauen, and tell the starres, if thou be able to number them. And hee said vnto him, So shall thy seed be.'

Matthew Hall gives a literal reading of 'we too are numbered' as alluding to 'the physical branding and systematised deaths [of] the interned prisoners' in concentration camps [*On Violence in the Work of J.H. Prynne*, op. cit.: 25-29 [26]].

7. the / fish dying in great flashes

Thus saith the LORD, In this thou shalt know that I am the LORD: behold, I will smite with the rod that is in my hand, vpon the waters which are in the riuer, and they shalbe turned to blood.
And the fish that is in the riuer shall die, and the riuer shall stinke, and the Egyptians shall loathe to drinke of the water of the riuer.
[…]
And Moses and Aaron did so, as the LORD commanded: and he lift vp the rod and smote the waters that were in the riuer, in the sight of Pharaoh, and in the sight of his seruants: and all the waters that were in the riuer, were turned to blood.
And the fish that *was* in the riuer died: and the riuer stunke, and the Egyptians could not drinke of the water of the riuer: and there was blood throughout all the land of Egypt.

The Holy Bible, King James Version [1611]: *Exodus*, Chapter VII, verses 17-18, 20-21. Consider also the lines of the character Camille just prior to being led to the guillotine, in Büchner's play *Dantons Tod*:

> Is the ether with its golden eyes nothing but a bowl of golden carp, set on the table of the blessèd gods, so that the blessèd gods can laugh eternally, and the fish die eternally, and the gods amuse themselves eternally with the play of colors of the death agony?

Act IV, Scene Five, [*Complete Plays and Prose*, op. cit.: 67].

'flashes' could also indicate the use of explosives, as in blast fishing, an illegal, environmentally destructive, but quite common form of fishing in impoverished communities throughout the world, most notably featured in the 1957 Italian film *La grande strada azzurra* [= *The Wide Blue Road*], based on screenwriter Franco Solinas's only novel, *Squarciò* (Milano: Feltrinelli Editore, 1956). Alongside this maritime reference, note also, in the poem's previous stanza, the 'landing-stage': 'a flat structure, often wooden and floating, that acts as a bridge with the land when taking goods on or off boats or ships' [*Cambridge Advanced Learner's Dictionary*, 4th ed. (Cambridge: Cambridge University Press, 2013): *s.v.*].

Also, though Prynne could not have had access to this text at the time of the composition of 'Es Lebe der König', see Ingeborg Bachmann's letter to Celan of 24 June 1949, written nearly 21 years before Celan would drown himself in the Seine and 24 years before Bachmann died, possibly by her own hand, as well: 'Take me to the Seine, let us gaze into it until we become little fishes and recognize each other again.' [Ingeborg Bachmann and Paul Celan, *Correspondence*, tr. Wieland Hoban (London/New York/Calcutta: Seagull Books, 2010): 11-12 [12]; German orig. published as *Laß uns die Worte finden. Ingeborg Bachmann—Paul Celan. Briefwechsel* (Frankfurt am Main: Suhrkamp Verlag, 2008)].

8. the plum exudes its / fanatic resin [...] the plum is a nick of pain

ein
Fruchtblatt, augengroß, tief
geritzt; es
harzt, will nicht
vernarben.

Paul Celan, 'Stimmen', in *Sprachgitter*, op. cit.: 7-9 [9]. In John Fel-stiner's English translation: 'a / carpel, eyesize, deeply / nicked; it / resins, will not / scar over.' [*Selected Poems and Prose of Paul Celan*, tr. John Felstiner (New York/London: W.W. Norton & Company, Inc., 2000/2001): 90-93 [93]]. Each fruit of the plum tree develops from a single carpel, the female reproductive organ of the flowering plant. Of possible relevance in relating these lines to the opening of 'Es Lebe der König' ('Fire and honey oozes from cracks in the earth'), Felstiner's biography of Celan, *Paul Celan: Poet, Survivor, Jew* (New Haven, Connecticut/London: Yale University Press, 1995/2001): 100, adds a note on Celan's poem: 'This fruit-leaf, like the nettle path and gallows tree, bears a wound but still lives: it oozes resin and "won't / scar over," will not forget.'

9. the plum exudes its / fanatic resin and is at once forced in, pressed / down [...] the alder'

Du Tausendgüldenkraut-Sternchen,
du Erle, du Buche, du Farn:
mit euch Nahen geh ich ins Ferne, –
Wir gehen dir, Heimat, ins Garn.

Schwarz hängt die Kirschlorbeertraube
beim bärtigen Palmenschaft.
Ich liebe, ich hoffe, ich glaube, –
die kleine Steindattel klafft.

Paul Celan, 'Kermorvan', in *Die Niemandsrose* (Frankfurt am Main: S. Fischer Verlag, 1963): 61. These two stanzas in Michael Hamburger's English translation:

You tiny centaury star,
you alder, beech and fern:
with you near ones I make for afar, –
to our homeland, snared, we return.

By the bearded palm tree's trunk
black hangs the laurel-seed grape.
I love, I hope, I have faith,—
the little date shell's agape.

Poems of Paul Celan, 4th ed., op. cit.: 181. Compare with the first two stanzas of Geoffrey Hill's poem 'Two Chorale-Preludes on Melodies by Paul Celan', 2. 'Te Lucis Ante Terminum', subtitled 'Wir gehen dir, Heimat, ins Garn…':

Centaury with your staunch bloom
you there alder beech you fern,
midsummer closeness my far home,
fresh traces of lost origin.

Silvery the black cherries hang,
the plum-tree oozes through each cleft
and horse-flies syphon the green dung,
glued to the sweetness of their graft:

Tenebrae (London: Andre Deutsch Limited, 1978): 35-36 [36]. Hill's poem, it is clear, is partly a translation of Celan's, with a few intriguing exceptions: Celan's 'beim bärtigen Palmenschaft', translated 'black hangs the laurel-seed grape' by Hamburger, becomes 'the plum-tree oozes through each cleft' in Hill—peculiarly close to Prynne's construction 'oozes from cracks in the earth', though Prynne was unlikely to have been a direct influence on Hill [at least judging by Hill's recent dismissive comments on Prynne, in Dominic Hand and Sofía Crespi de Valldaura's '"If I write about destruction it's because I'm terrified of it": An Interview with Geoffrey Hill'. *The ISIS*, (27 April 2015), online at http://isismagazine.org.uk]. Possibly drawing inspiration from the image of the nicked carpel in Celan's 'Stimmen' (cited in Note 8, above), Hill seems to envision a cherry tree grafted onto and growing out of a plum tree, with the resin oozing from the cut in the rootstock (the 'cleft'). This image of grafting certainly applies also to Prynne's 'the plum exudes its / fanatic resin and is at once forced in, pressed / down', albeit envisioning the plum as the scion (upper portion) rather than the rootstock (lower portion) of the graft; still, the reason for Prynne's and Hill's grafted 'plum' trees to both be independently derived from Celan's quite different 'Kirschlorbeertraube', cherry laurel, remains intriguingly unclear. [The comparison between Prynne's and Hill's poems was pointed out by John Armstrong, 'Paul Celan and Breathturn (Atemwende)'. *Bebrowed's Blog*, (6 October 2011): online at https://bebrowed.wordpress.com/2011/10/06/paul-celan-and-breathturn-atemwende/].

10. The long-tailed bird / is total awareness, a forced lust, it is that / absolutely

> When the most High diuided to the nations their inheritance, when he separated the sonnes of Adam, hee set the bounds of the people according to the number of the children of Israel.
> For the LORDS portion *is* his people: Iacob *is* the lot of his inheritance.
> He found him in a desert land, and in the waste howling wildernesse: Hee ledde him about, he instructed him, hee kept him as the apple of his eye.
> As an Eagle stirreth vp her nest, fluttereth ouer her yong, spreadeth abroad her wings, taketh them, beareth them on her wings:
> *So* the LORD alone did leade him, and there was no strange God with him.

The Holy Bible, King James Version [1611]: *Deuteronomie*, Chapter XXXII, verses 8-12. As a possible reference connecting 'The long-tailed bird' with the poem's opening line ('Fire and honey oozes from cracks in the earth'), note also the subsequent verse of *Deuteronomie*: 'He made him ride on the high places of the earth, that he might eate the increase of the fields, and he made him to sucke hony out of the rocke, and oyle out of the flintie rocke [...]', particularly in relation to the description of the Lord at the beginning of Moses's song (Chapter XXII, verse 4):

'*He is* the rocke'.

Matthew Hall, *On Violence in the Work of J.H. Prynne*, op. cit.: 42, reads 'the long-tailed bird' as 'a reference to the German coat of arms', the *Parteiadler* of the Nazi Party which featured an eagle with its long wings spread above a wreath encircling a swastika. If Prynne's poetic image is in reference to this emblem, it is possible that it is the swastika alluded to as the bird's 'long tail'. For tangential evidence of this reading, note also the alternative definition of 'flag' as 'The quill-feathers of a bird's wing' [*Oxford English Dictionary,* 2nd ed., 'flag' *sb.*[3] def. 1].

Both allusions, to the Lord of the children of Israel and to the Nazi *Parteiadler*, may be intentional, as the Nazi's grab at the 'total awareness' of absolute power travesties the image of the Lord as the Eagle protecting, taking and bearing up her young.

11. Give us this love of murder and / sacred boredom

Giue vs this day our daily bread.

The Holy Bible, King James Version [1611]: *Matthew*, Chapter VI, verse 11, as part of the Lord's Prayer [verses 9-13]; included also in a variant of the Lord's Prayer in *Luke*, Chapter XI, verses 2-4 [2]: 'Giue vs day by day our dayly bread.'

12. boredom

Oberlin told him to turn to God; this made Lenz laugh and say:
How I wish I were as fortunate as you to have so comfortable a pastime. One could very easily spend his time that way. Everything for idleness' sake. After all, most people pray out of boredom, others fall in love out of boredom, some are virtuous, some vicious, and I am nothing, absolutely nothing! I don't even want to take my own life: it would be too boring!

Georg Büchner, *Lenz* [*Complete Plays and Prose*, op. cit.: 160 [German orig. published 1835]]. 'boredom' here translates the German term 'Langeweile', also sometimes translated as 'ennui'; this 'curious spiritual indolence' [Prynne, 'Reading in Vancouver, 1 August 1971, part 2', op. cit.: [18.15-18.20]] appears in every one of Georg Büchner's works, and often as something of a root principle of human life.

Celan, in 'Der Meridian', refers to a specific instance in Büchner's play *Dantons Tod* just prior to the execution of Danton and his fellow prisoners:

> Lacroix [to the PEOPLE]: 'You killed *us* on the day when you lost your Reason; you will kill *them* on the day when you regain it.'
> Some Voices: 'Ha! We've heard that one before; try again! How boring!'

Büchner, *Complete Plays and Prose*, op. cit.: 69 (Act IV, Scene Seven, at the Place de la Révolution) [German orig. published 1835; Celan's reference to these lines is in *Collected Prose*, op. cit.: 39].

On specifically 'sacred boredom': 'The earth and water down below are like a table on which wine has been spilled, and we lie upon it like playing cards which God and the devil play with out of boredom [...]' [Büchner, *Leonce und Lena*, from *Complete Plays and Prose*, op. cit.: 93 (spoken by 'Valerio' in Act II, Scene Two) [German orig. written 1836, first published in abridged form 1838]]; and, later in the same play: '... in the beginning before the world was... [...] ... the Lord God found that He was bored ...' [op. cit.: 103 ('Valerio' in Act III, Scene Three)].

13. the / white cloth spread openly for the most worthless / accident. The whiteness is a patchwork of / revenge too, open the window and white fleecy / clouds sail over the azure; // it is true. Over and / over it is so

> Tacitus gives a careful description of <u>casting the runes</u> or <u>spelling</u>, from which it can be seen that the "white cloth" is the circle, which is the sky (the heavens), which is <u>the total presence of fortune</u>:
> 'For auspices and the casting of lots they have the highest possible regard. Their procedure in casting lots is uniform. They break off a branch of a fruit-tree and slice it into strips; they distinguish these by certain Runes and throw them, as

random chance will have it, on to a white cloth. Then the Priest of the State if the consultation is a public one, the father of the family if it is private, after a prayer to the gods and an intent gaze heavenward, picks up three, one at a time, and reads their meaning from the runes scored on them. If the lots forbid an enterprise, there can be no further consultation that day; if they allow it, further confirmation by auspices is required.' —Tacitus, _Germania_, X, trans. H. Mattingley [*sic*] (Harmondsworth, 1948)

J.H. Prynne, 'A Pedantic Note in Two Parts'. _The English Intelligencer_, 2nd ser., 4 (*c.* June 1967): 346-51 [346]. [part one [pp. 346-48] is dated 7th June 1966, part two [pp. 349-51] 6 June 1967]. Tacitus's Latin original was written 98 CE; Prynne's citation was from H. Mattingly's translation of _Germania_, printed alongside his translation of _Agricola_, in _Tacitus on Britain and Germany_ (Harmondsworth: Penguin Books, 1948): 109.

Tangentially, for a further instance of Prynne's poetry expanding upon a specialised use of vocabulary introduced in his earlier work, consider his recent poem 'Alveolar Shunts' (in _Poems_ [2015]: 636) alongside the poem from which it seems to derive much of its vocabulary, the sixth page of poetry in _Pearls That Were_ following the epigraph (*i.e.*, _Poems_ [2015]: 460). As with 'Es Lebe der König', it seems possible at times that translation from an unnamed source could also be the origin of some of the poems' vocabulary.

14. accident:

J'apporte en effet des nouvelles. Les plus surprenantes.
Même cas ne se vit encore. Ils ont touché au vers.
[...]
Il convient d'en parler déjà, ainsi qu'un invité voyageur tout de suite se décharge par traits haletants du témoignage d'un accident su et le poursuivant.

Stéphane Mallarmé, 'La Musique et les lettres', in his _Oeuvres complètes_ (Paris: Gallimard (Bibliothèque de la Pléiade), 1945): 643-44 [Mallarmé's original lecture, delivered at Cambridge University and

Oxford University, published in 1895]. In Shoshana Felman and Dori Laub's English translation: 'In effect I am bringing news, and the most surprising. Such a case has never been seen. They have done violence to verse […] It is appropriate to relieve myself of that news right away—to talk about it now already—much like an invited traveler who, without delay, in breathless gasps, discharges himself of the testimony of an accident known, and pursuing him.' [Felman and Laub, *Testimony: Crises of Witnessing in Literature, Psychoanalysis, and History* (New York/Milton Park, Abingdon: Routledge, 1992): 18; 'They' refers to Mallarmé's fellow late-19th-century French poets whose free verse innovations he discusses with his English audiences]. Felman and Laub go to great speculative lengths to argue, throughout Chapter V (Poetry and Testimony: Stéphane Mallarmé, or An Accident of Verse) [pp. 18-24], that Mallarmé's poetics, and indeed politics, are founded upon just such a 'testimony of an accident'; and then continue to extend this argument through the following chapter (Poetry and Testimony: Paul Celan, or The Accidenting of Aesthetics) [pp. 25-40] to encapsulate the oeuvre of Paul Celan as well, particularly in relation to his experience of World War II and the Holocaust: 'In exploding, once again—in the footsteps of the lesson taught by Mallarmé—its own poetic medium, in dislocating its own language and in breaking its own verse, the poetry of Paul Celan gives testimony, in effect, no longer simply to what Mallarmé refers to as an undefined, generic "accident," but to a more specific, more particularly crushing and more recent, cultural and historical breakdown, to the individual and the communal, massive trauma of a catastrophic loss and a disastrous fate in which nothing any more can be construed as *accident* except, perhaps, for *the poet's own survival.*' [p. 25; italics in the original].

15. The whiteness is a patchwork of / revenge too

> der ungeküßte
> Stein einer Klage
> rauscht auf,
> vor Erfüllung,
>
> er befühlt unsre Münder,
> er wechselt
> über zu uns,

eingetan ist uns
sein Weiß,
wir geben uns weiter:

Paul Celan, 'Wir, die wie der Strandhafer Wahren', in *Zeitgehöft* (Frankfurt am Main: Suhrkamp Verlag, 1976): 36. In Susan H. Gillespie's English translation: 'the unkissed / stone of a lament / rushes up / with fulfilment, / it feels our mouths, / it changes / over to us, / into us / its whiteness enters, // we pass ourselves on:'. [in Celan's letter to Ilana Shmueli, 3 November 1969, in *The Correspondence of Paul Celan & Ilana Shmueli*, op. cit.: 17-18; German orig. published in *Paul Celan/ Ilana Shmueli: Briefwechsel*, op. cit.23-24 [23]] Pierre Joris, in notes on his translation of the same poem, [in Paul Celan, *Breathturn into Timestead: The Collected Later Poetry* (New York: Farrar, Straus and Giroux, 2014): 619] explains that 'On October 9, 1969, Celan had very briefly visited the Wailing Wall, which pious Jews traditionally kiss. Shmueli remembers him saying "no excavations, please."' [quoting, in Joris's own English translation, Shmueli's *Sag, daß Jerusalem ist: Über Paul Celan, Oktober 1969–April 1970* (Aachen: Rimbaud Verlag, 2010): 25]. Note that the poems included in Celan's posthumous *Zeitgehöft*, Celan's letters with Shmueli, and Shmueli's personal reminiscences of Celan, would all have been unavailable to Prynne at the time of writing 'Es Lebe der König'.

16. revenge

Like the pelican he nurses his own wounds with gruesome constancy, because he must. Even to imagine otherwise in his case would be to falsify his destiny. But poets who carry any kind of destiny around their necks must labour under a heavy burden. Somewhere in between the exacting sparsity of lexical reduction and the unsayable enormity of vast crimes lies the everyday political world, of what it is possible to do: the crimes to be found here are no less fearful and oppressive for being idiomatic to the day-to-day. Who can doubt that the prisoner of Ramallah is locked into heroic ignominy by a pursuit of vengeance, one itself avenged by daily self-sacrifice, one killing after another; and that the unsolved hatred and misery of camps and settlements comprise the long but evident shadow of what for Celan was the memorial project of his writing life and scriptive drowning departure?

J.H. Prynne, 'Es Stand Auch Geschrieben: Jean Bollack and Paul Celan', op. cit.: 105. Note also, from Moses's song in *Deuteronomie*, Chapter XXXII, alluded to in Note 10 above in relation to 'The long-tailed bird': 'Reioyce, O ye nations *with* his people, for he will auenge the blood of his seruants, and will render vengeance to his aduersaries, and wil be mercifull vnto his land, *and* to his people' [verse 43]: hence, vengeance also functions as a component of the Lord's covenant to the children of Israel.

17. clouds sail over the azure

> rollt Azur
> über dich hin

Paul Celan, 'Ein Stern', in *Zeitgehöft*, op. cit.: 29. In Michael Hamburger's English translation: 'azure rolls / along over you' [*Poems of Paul Celan*, 4th ed., op. cit.: 329]. Though note that the poems in *Zeitgehöft*, the final posthumous collection of Celan's late work, could not have been available to Prynne at the time of writing 'Es Lebe der König'.

18. and the water is not quiet

> The 'water' into which Celan threw himself is 'not quiet' [...]

Geoffrey Ward, 'Nothing but Mortality: Prynne and Celan', op. cit.: 150. A literal reading of Celan's 'Der Meridian', with Celan as the figure of otherness which the poem encounters and returns from anew: 'The poem intends another, needs this other, needs an opposite. It goes toward it, bespeaks it. For the poem, everything and everybody is a figure of this other toward which it is heading.' And later, towards the end of the same speech:

> I had ... encountered myself.

Is it on such paths that poems take us when we think of them? And are these paths only detours, detours from you to you? But they are, among how many others, the paths on which language becomes voice. They are encounters, paths from a voice to a listening You, natural paths, outlines for existence perhaps, for projecting ourselves into the search for ourselves … A kind of homecoming.

Collected Prose, tr. Rosmarie Waldrop, op. cit.: 49, 53. Reading Celan himself into the end of the poem might be overly literal, but perhaps in this case it is appropriate to bespeak this one voice, and meaning, among many others.

Notes

[1] 'Reading in Vancouver, 1 August 1971, part 2' [at York Street Commune], online at http://www.archiveofthenow.org/authors/?i=77 [17.05-18.05]. In the following essay, transcriptions of recordings are my own; and, unless they are in square brackets, the ellipses indicate pauses in the original rather than editorial omissions. Quotations have been provided in their original language whenever such sources have been available to me.

[2] Keston Sutherland, 'Hilarious absolute daybreak', *Glossator: Practice and Theory of the Commentary*, 2 (2010: On the Poems of J.H. Prynne, ed. Ryan Dobran): 115-47 [125]. Online at https://solutioperfecta.files.wordpress. com/2011/10/g2-sutherland.pdf . The letter is presumably one of the hundreds between Prynne and Dorn collected in the Edward Dorn Papers, Archives & Special Collections at the Thomas J. Dodd Research Center, University of Connecticut Libraries, though the letter's location and postmarked date are not cited in Sutherland's essay.

[3] The journal, edited by Peter Riley, was co-edited with John James for this seventh and final issue.

[4] Prynne interviewed by Peter Orr, *The Poet Speaks* [Programme 39], recorded 6 January 1964 as part of the British Council's *The Poet Speaks* series [11.35-11.45].

[5] Unauthorised video of a poetry reading by Prynne and Sutherland at the University of Chicago on 16 April 2009, online at http://www.youtube.com/watch?v=Q1PRMeeFpwA, and also at http://news.uchicago.edu/multimedia/poetry-reading-jh-prynne-and-keston-sutherland [54.25-54.50].

[6] Prynne interviewed by Peter Orr, *The Poet Speaks*, op. cit. [11.05-13.00].

[7] 'from "Kazoo Dreamboats; or, On What There Is"' [a reading at the student-occupied Lady Mitchell Hall, University of Cambridge, 27 November 2011], online at http://www.archiveofthenow.org/authors/?i=77. [7.10-7.40].

[8] Private discussion in a Brighton pub, 12 February 2013, with Prynne, Keston Sutherland and several other British poets the night before the symposium on the recent poetry of J.H. Prynne held at the University of Sussex.

[9] Prynne interviewed by Peter Orr, *The Poet Speaks*, op. cit. [12.30-12.40].

[10] Prynne's response to an audience member's question during the discussion period following Prynne's talk in Guangzhou, 20 December 2012 [from an unpublished audio recording by Justin Katko] [13.40-15.05].

[11] 'A Tailpiece to "Listening to All"' [photocopied handouts prepared January 2014 for a discussion at the University of Sussex in March 2014] (distributed through Barque Press (London) as a special issue of the journal *Quid* as of July 2014): [fascicle '0' [the first page]].

[12] a feature read as significant by Matthew Hall in *On Violence in the Work of J.H. Prynne* (Newcastle upon Tyne: Cambridge Scholars Publishing, 2015): 17 and 30.

[13] Specifically, *Force of Circumstance and Other Poems* was dedicated to 'B.W.F.H.'—that is, Basil Harvey, the English teacher at St. Dunstan's College whom Prynne credits with first inspiring in him a love of poetry; *The White Stones*, 'for Sue', Prynne's wife; *Word Order*, 'for J.P.'—so far unknown, though perhaps a daughter or other relative…; *Not-You*, 'For Che Qian-zi and Zhou Ya-Ping and for the ORIGINALS', Chinese poets featured in *Original: Chinese Language-Poetry Group*, (Brighton: Parataxis Editions, 1994; as *Parataxis*, 7 (Spring 1995)), translated by Jeff Twitchell-Waas and (nominally) edited by Prynne; *Poems* (1999), 'A la mèmoire de Bernard Dubourg', French poet and translator of Prynne and others; *Acrylic Tips*, 'For S.K.', convincingly posited by Matthew Hall in *On Violence in the Work of J.H. Prynne*, op. cit.: 131-32, to be Stephen Kinsella, didgeridoo player, sheep-shearer and brother of Australian poet John Kinsella; *Furtherance*, 'For Marjorie Welish', American poet; *Poems* (2005), 'For Edward Dorn his brilliant luminous shade', American poet; *Kazoo Dreamboats; or, On What There Is*, 'For the Jinling Patriots'—uncertain, but likely Chinese scholars who had studied abroad in America and England prior to the founding of the People's Republic of China, who then returned to China to teach with creative methods neither specifically Western or Eastern but influenced by both. This group of individuals is partly documented in Stacey Bieler's book *"Patriots" or "Traitors"?: A History of American-Educated Chinese Students* (London and New York: Routledge, 2004/2015). Tao Xingzhi, one such educator,

founded the Xiaozhuang Normal College, a teacher's college that encouraged the 'little teacher model' in which pupils taught their families what they had just learned, and the 'each one teach one' technique of organised teaching networks. 'Jinling' is one of a number of ancient names by which the city of Nanjing has been known; and *Poems* (2015), 'For the Future'—and you know what that is.

[14] First published as *Der Meridian. Rede anlässlich der Verleihung des Georg-Büchner-Preises, Darmstadt, am 22. Oktober 1960* (Frankfurt am Main: S. Fischer Verlag, 1961), and cited throughout this essay in its English translation by Rosmarie Waldrop, 'The Meridian', in Celan's *Collected Prose* (Manchester: Carcanet Press Limited, 1986/2003): 37-55.

[15] Geoffrey Ward, 'Nothing but Mortality: Prynne and Celan', in *Contemporary Poetry Meets Modern Theory*, eds. Antony Easthope and John O. Thompson (Hemel Hempstead, Hertfordshire: Harvester Wheatsheaf, 1991): 139-52 [150], quoting from Celan, *Collected Prose*, op. cit.: 40, 52.

[16] Andrew Ross, 'The Oxygen of Publicity'. *Poetics Journal*, 6 (1986): 62-71 [64-65].

[17] Note particularly Michael Hamburger's 'On Translating Celan', part of the postscript to his translations of *Poems of Paul Celan*, 4th ed. (New York: Persea Books, 1972/1980/1988/2002): 346-62 [351-54], which recounts how Celan forbade Hamburger to translate Celan's poems in the last years of his life purely due to the mistaken belief that Hamburger wrote an anonymous review in the *TLS* [*Times Literary Supplement*] which had described Celan as a 'hermetic poet'.

[18] 'Es Stand Auch Geschrieben: Jean Bollack and Paul Celan'. *CCCP*, 12 (2002): 104-06 [105].

[19] Andrew Ross, op. cit.: 64.

[20] 'Huts'. *Textual Practice*, Vol. 22 No. 4 (December 2008): 613-33 [624], in reference to Celan's poem 'Todtnauberg' [first published in the posthumous volume *Lichtzwang* (Frankfurt am Main: Suhrkamp Verlag, [July] 1970): 29-30]. In addition to the statements quoted in this essay, Prynne's later discussions of Celan also include 'A Letter about Paul Celan' [letter to Anthony Barnett, 28th March 1983]. *Snow, lit rev*, 1 (Spring 2013; eds. Anthony Barnett and Ian Brinton): 73-77; and an unpublished talk in Guangzhou, P.R. China, from The Third National Conference on English Poetry Studies, 20 December 2012, recorded by Justin Katko [19.35-20.25].

[21] 'Poetic Thought'. *Textual Practice*, Vol. 24 No. 4 (August 2010): 595-606 [597].

22 cf. particularly David Trotter, *The Making of the Reader; Language and Subjectivity in Modern American, English and Irish Poetry* (London: Macmillan Press, 1984): 218-20; D.S. Marriott, 'The Rites of Difficulty', op. cit.: 118-37 [esp. 127-33]; Anthony Mellors, *Late Modernist Poetics: from Pound to Prynne* (Manchester: Manchester University Press, 2005): 186-99; Matthew Hall's *On Violence in the Work of J.H. Prynne*, op. cit.: 19ff.; and, focusing on Prynne's 'From End to End' rather than 'Es Lebe der König', but still directly relevant in its philosophical argument, Nicola Thomas's 'Meridians: the poem as a place of encounter in Paul Celan and J.H. Prynne'. *Tropos*, Vol. 2 No. 1 (2014): 68-79. Online at http://discovery.ucl.ac.uk/1469479/1/Tropos-Thomas.pdf.

It was also…

PETER RILEY

It was also the coast of East Anglia, worn down to the sea, sliding and crumbling, in poor visibility and cold. The sparseness. A bare and isolated chapel called, I think, St Peter's, at the back of the fields, on a cliff edge. But it was also the stonework of eastern England, at Lincoln a figurative plenitude, human figures worked into strata, all bending to the same tasks; Kings College Chapel, floral geometry bursting out of vertical stone. Places where this edge-line escaped from the insular circuit.

I arrived in 1959 with one poem in my sack, curricula aside. It was called *In Romney Marsh* and was by John Davidson and began "As I went down to Dymchurch Wall…" Coming down from the west side of north this sweep of land which I'd never seen was spread out like pastry, like pie crust. And when it said "I heard the South sing o'er the land", it was the *wire* singing, ringing out, *Within the wind* in the form of *a core of sound*. This just needed a guide or bus conductor, who shortly turned up, to lead it into the work of poetry. And when it said "knolls where Norman churches stand" there was a temporary lodging. In the cadence of folksong (As I went out) unrecognised at that time, the venture had realised a kind of inn, or a cabaret, on the way to somewhere. The question was whether it was open. When Jeremy arrived three years later (he had been in U.S.A.) all this began to align to some purpose. The wire was ringing with messages, sometimes more and wider messages than a wire could be expected to cope with.

The teaching method, as I remember, consisted usually of persuading you into a channel the borders of which had immense entailments, but then at some point deflecting you out of that into an open question which remained objectively sited. Must have been the very opposite of Olson's follow-my-leader or zeppelin airlift to everywhere at once by being-me.

More important were the sparse sounds of that Chinese zither, and what sprang out of that sparseness, what chaconnes, what tarantellas, what football chants! all balanced on a slight twist and slip of the finger, carefully foreseen. Cruelly foreseen… Verse was beginning to cut.

Which was its way of homing. "oh love be so blind to send to not roam alien in cornfields, again."

'Possente spirto' —On First Reading Prynne

Peter Hughes

I suppose you could have diagrams of words with text boxes all around notating their valencies and baggage, their histories and associations. To interweave and plait all these bristling connotations, as Prynne so often does, is pretty amazing and gives the lines their peculiar mass. It means you hardly ever get a line freeing itself and taking off in lyric light-headedness, or plodding along with stolid narrative purpose. Instead the language is rooted in specific and sometimes incommensurable contexts which preclude neutrality or closure, and sustain tension. This can create an almost polyphonic effect, easier to achieve in music than in a poem. Different instruments doing different things is obviously one of the joys of music (though fans of Bach's solo partitas, or Evan Parker, for example, will know that an entire three-ring circus can be proceeding full-pelt in the hands of just one player). I think of a choir on board a deep-sea survey vessel improvising upon language itself, and its location.

As I was preparing to move to Italy in 1983 Nigel Wheale generously gave me his *TLS* review copy of Prynne's *Poems*. Nigel already had one of his own. My case already bulged with the *Shorter Oxford English Dictionary*, Dante and a pre-hated copy of *Teach Yourself Italian*. In the startling clarity of autumn in L'Aquila I was therefore ready to explore unfamiliar worlds and learn two new languages. Guides to new languages tend to start with the self. You learn to say who you are, where you come from and what you do. You learn to ask others for the same information. You learn how to find the nearest station, bank and chemist. By the time you finish volume one you may be able to express the notion of the past and future, some opinions and preferences, and be able to describe in basic terms some of the things and people around you. It is worrying to think that at this stage you are already equipped to write many of the more successful poems currently doing the rounds.

But when you land up in another country or a Prynne text, everything is already going on all at once and you haven't done that bit yet, or this vocabulary, or this other form of the verb, or the specialised usages associated with specific trades, sciences, philosophies or other forms of enquiry. Everything is going on around you and you do your best to go with the flow and pick up what you can. There will be failures and frustrations but the process is exhilarating, revitalising and real. You will never really feel at home because you and the world are constantly changing and this cannot be captured intellectually or otherwise. Ejected from old habits, you see the world anew. You hold one thread and it's connected to everything else.

> You see
> as in late spring, shrouded in mist,
> the bright smooth water. The price
> is right, *eau minérale naturelle*
> from the hypermarket and thousands
>
> Of feet of glacial sand. Ten thousand
> families in the mountains, starved
> on mountain grass: and made me eat
> both gravel, dirt and mud, and last
> of all, to gnaw my flesh and blood.

This short passage from 'Marzipan' (*Bands Around the Throat*, 1987) begins with an apparently lovely landscape image which could come from any old poem. The reader may cock an eyebrow at 'The price is right'. Isn't that a rubbish game show on TV? The natural mineral water sounds reassuring and even more sophisticated, being in French. Hypermarket? OK—it must be bought somewhere. Then all that sand. Does the water filter up through great stretches of strata and sediment? Or is it, as Simon Perril suggested, the sand dumped on the Chernobyl reactor following the accident? Suddenly families are starving, as if in the Irish famine, reduced to eating grass. And why does it end up with me eating my own body? If we read it again, the words 'shrouded' and 'smooth' have become sinister. We are aware of a complex and damaging relationship between environment, local inhabitants and consumerism. It includes us. The poem is nearly thirty years old but more relevant than ever. You will recall that the chairman of Nestlé, which pays about $500 to extract over 25,000,000 gallons of water from drought-stricken

California to bottle and sell on at a staggering profit, has said "Human beings don't have a right to water". The system destroys the earth: we consume our world and selves.

The breadth of Prynne's web of reference is helpfully suggested at the end of his 2011 *Kazoo Dreamboats* (Critical Documents, Cambridge). After Prynne's text there is a page of 'Reference Cues'. Here, on a list which includes Leucippus, Parmenides, Aristotle, Boethius, Shakespeare, Wordsworth, Shelley and Alban Berg, we find contemporary scientific books on Van der Waals Forces, Condensed Matter Field Theory and Pore Geometry. The truth is constantly unfolding and the poet wants to check the latest sources. Reality evolves.

The information and being of these poems is to unweave the spells of corporate advertising and political disingenuousness. In *Wound Response* (1974) there is a poem called 'Cool as a Mountain Stream'. The words come from an advertising slogan for a particularly unpleasant brand of menthol cigarette called Consulate. The posters used to show happy, sexy young couples in idyllic surroundings in order to encourage addiction to burning, toxic substances.

This seriousness in Prynne's work suffuses a verbal texture and rhythmic drive which constitute a compelling music. But the pleasurable music has a message which keeps reminding you to pay attention. Watch what's going on. Keep listening carefully. Don't be distracted by sales talk. It could cost us everything. Focus (to quote the subtitle of *Kazoo Dreamboats*) *On What There Is*.

'*Brass* Nearly Off'

Ian Brinton

Andrew Crozier's Ferry Press championed the new world of British poetry towards the end of the sixties producing John James's *Mmm... Ah Yes* in 1967 and both John Temple's *Rothschild's Lapwing* and Chris Torrance's *Green Orange Purple Red* in the following year. 1968 also saw the Ferry Press publication of Prynne's *Aristeas*, which had originally appeared in *The English Intelligencer*, and then *Brass* in 1971. The stormy story behind the appearance of this second Ferry Press volume highlights the careful manner in which Crozier and Prynne, two dedicated and highly professional workers in the fields of poetry and its publication, worked together.

At the end of 1970 after it had been agreed that Ferry Press would publish the sequence of poems to be titled *Brass*, Prynne wrote to Crozier to ask for a further poem to be included:

> Meanwhile I'm afraid I've now written another piece which clearly belongs in this book & not in the next. If it is at all humanly possible to do so I should like it to be fitted in somewhere. Ideally I'd prefer it to come just before (or, just after) L'EXTASE DE M. POHER; but I don't want to be choosy at this late stage. I'm enclosing two copies in case the trick can be done.

This was in fact the second occasion that a late inclusion of a poem had been asked for prior to publication since Prynne had requested room for an extra poem to be included in Crozier's first issue of the magazine *Wivenhoe Park Review* which was to appear in January 1966. This first issue, jointly edited by Andrew Crozier and Tom Clark from the Department of Literature in the University of Essex, was, in Crozier's words, 'a disaster, inadequately perfect bound because the cover didn't include a spine and copies quickly disintegrated'. However, it contained an astonishing collection of work by both American and British poets ranging from Olson and Dorn, Spicer and Wieners, Eigner and Blaser to Tom Raworth and Jeremy Prynne. Perhaps most interestingly the Prynne poems which appeared there in that 1966 magazine were all to re-appear in *The White Stones*: 'Airport Poem: Ethics of Survival', 'A Figure of Mercy, of Speech', 'The Stranger, Instantly', 'Living in History', 'On the Anvil', 'The Holy City', 'How It's Done', 'If There is a Stationmaster at Stamford S.D. Hardly So', 'Song in Sight of the World'. In a letter to Crozier from November 1965 Prynne had sent 'another poem, which if you've room I would like to see in front of the others, i.e., the first in the group' and the urgent importance of this request was highlighted in a further letter from December in which he emphasized 'I do very much want 'Lashed to the Mast' in with those other things, preferably to stand first in the order of them'. The importance of this Odyssean figure who is enabled to hear what others can not is reflected in the fact that he pasted a vase painting of the scene on the inner cover of his own copy of Pound's *Cantos*.

When a similar request was put forward for an extra poem to be given room in *Brass* Crozier's instant response was to tell Prynne that 'The Five Hindrances' would indeed be fitted in although this might lead to a minor delay in making up the page proofs. However, there were to be more than minor delays in the production of this, the most ambitious and handsome of the Ferry Press publications to date. In a waspish note to the Director of Compton Press of Salisbury who was responsible for the printing of this unusually formatted volume, Crozier wrote 'about the standard of type-setting evinced by the proofs we have seen so far'. Compton Press had been chosen by Crozier on the understanding that the Press 'maintained a particular concern for high quality letterpress book production'. He was therefore dismayed to discover that, 'rather than setting the text yourselves, you were employing a commercial firm of typesetters'. The two sets of proofs which had so far been seen had fallen short of expectations since mistakes had occurred in between the first and second proof stages:

> 'Corrections to the first set of galleys have been ignored, and in general there has been demonstrated none of that sensitivity to the typographical demands of exceptional texts which I had been led to expect.'

A third set of proofs was asked for and by March 12th 1971 Jeremy Prynne's patience was getting tested and he wrote to Crozier:

> I am writing to ask what on earth is supposed to be happening with the production of *Brass*. I have been assuming that the page proofs could be expected more or less as soon as the postal stoppage had been concluded, but I have had no news of any kind. There have been to my knowledge no revised proposals for the lettering for the cover, nor for the cover material, nor for the layout of the title-page. These delays are most unsatisfactory and I trust that you will do all you can to get prompt action from the press. It would be quite unacceptable for the final production of the finished book to be delayed after the end of May and I hope this can be clearly understood. I know that there have been difficulties; but one's patience is not indefinitely elastic.

As well as problems with the proofs the choice of colour and texture for the cover was proving to be a problem. The printers sent through various examples of cover paper which Prynne found 'dull and pasty with a boring surface texture' and as he put it to Crozier on March 22nd:

> If we really can't get a fully saturated colour effect then we must cut our losses and go for something darker, tending towards deep plum. But whatever we do we cannot go in for further delays....

In reference to the proof of the lettering for the cover Prynne had 'fancied something chunkier and more block-like in effect but I at least am prepared to compromise with this rather than persist with this letraset search. But as I said in my letter "the outline of the imprint" must be "as sharp as possible"... the whole business is exhausting but I suppose that the moment one relaxes one's efforts the situation falls to pieces.' That said, problems with proofing continued and Prynne wrote directly to the printers on March 26th:

> Thank you for your letter of 18th March, concerning *Brass*. I have since received the proofs which you dispatched to me, and

I have corrected a set of these and returned them to Mr Crozier. I am afraid there are quite a few places where corrections to the second marked proof previously returned to you have not been dealt with, so that these have had to be corrected again on the third marked proof which will be reaching you in the next few days. I have explained these in some detail in a letter to Mr Crozier, and I must say that I am more than a little disappointed at the lack of care taken with making these carefully marked and self-evidently necessary corrections. I hope very much indeed that all these remaining difficulties can be resolved with as little further delay as possible.

Crozier took a trip down to Salisbury in early April to go over the paste-up to corrected proofs with a Mr Berry and found a situation that would not have been out of place in the opening pages of Balzac's *Les Illusions Perdues*:

Now that I've seen his establishment I can see how the various contretemps occurred: Berry does most of the press work himself, on a very large flat-bed press, & they're not in the habit of locking up the type & arranging the pages until they get the type onto the press for machining. This means in fact that they're not in the habit of producing what we understand by page-proofs. It's a great risk on their part, but presumably appears less chancy when they're dealing with prose...As regards binding, I've arranged for them to use the heaviest Bokhara board on its own, with a flap at the edges of 4", & with 4 pp of endpapers in a grey paper.

Brass was finally published in December 1971 and there were immediate complaints about the way the whole procedure had been dealt with. Crozier and Prynne both pointed to the glaring errors that had appeared and the notes and letters they provided pointed to important things about their procedures as both publisher and poet. In a letter of 12th December Crozier made it clear that 'my purpose in operating Ferry Press, which might be seen in some quarters as a distraction from my professional and writing activities, is to provide a service to a neglected section of the writing community: to make texts available and to do so as immediately as possible to the moment of their composition.' Prynne's notes which he put together on 6th January 1972 addressed the whole idea of the particular layout of a poem, perhaps echoing the Creeley-Olson statement that 'Form is never more than an extension of content':

> Because the text was poetry it would of course raise specially acute problems of good design and layout sense. My arrangement of a text on the page does not follow obviously regular margins or spacing, but every aspect of spatial arrangement is deliberate and an essential part of the poem's meaning. In most kinds of prose one could argue that provided the words and punctuation are set accurately, and the paragraphing followed, literal fidelity is guaranteed. But in setting poetry, and particularly the kind which I write, all the spacing between words and lines, indenting and carrying down, the whole visual set of the word on the page, is part of the literal meaning of the text. Failure to get this right would be as much a printer's error as dropping a word or using a wrong font.

Prynne's last comment in his eleven notes highlights the errors made in printing 'The Five Hindrances':

> Type of the wrong font had still been used in the title of 'The Five Hindrances' and the spaces after each full stop not corrected to be consistent with practice everywhere else.

He also noted that page 35, the second page of 'A New Tax on the Counter-Earth' 'was grossly mis-positioned on the page, the text wildly off centre', before concluding that the publication of *Brass* 'was not a successful instance of professional fine printing'.

Given all this one would be forgiven for feeling that one was reading a different poem titled 'The Five Hindrances' in that now rare collectors' item, the first edition of *Brass*, and the poem only appeared correctly in Anthony Barnett's edition of Prynne's poems published by the press he began with Fiona Allardyce some eleven years later. It is worth quoting here from the letter which Prynne sent to Barnett in May 1982 after that Agneau 2 *Poems* had appeared:

> I have been looking at the book today and taking stock of my feelings about it; and I want to tell you how deeply satisfied and well pleased I am with how it has come out. I hope you have fully grasped how honourable I think it is, for this book not to be or seem merely a commercial product but to represent the work and involvement of someone who wanted to do it, so that it thus bears the badge of that origin. To be typeset by a poet has been for this book a most privileged destiny and more especially so since I have as you know a high regard for your own writing and the serious persistence of your work. I did initially have, as you will remember, anxieties about our ability to come right through with this project and not to find the unavoidable wear and tear an irksome burden. But we have all done it, in good time and with a fine result. I am profoundly grateful not only for your patient exertion but for your support and meticulous interest; I have been very glad to work together like this, and I thank you for it.

The letter continued to address a comment which was to be passed on to Fiona Allardyce concluding with the statement

> I am writing to her to tell her of my warm personal pleasure that she has been so much involved in this effort, and I hope that she will by no means take this as mere formality. I sometimes disavow much regard for the fate which befalls my work; but it is wonderful nonetheless to meet a personal support which proves itself steady and which rests on judgement as much as on generosity. And so, in fact, I thank you both. I had hardly expected to be so fortunate.

Anthony Barnett replied to Prynne's letter by pointing out that

> Since spending some days with the finished book I was struck by the feeling (that was absent while working on the book)

that it is very easy for an editor or publisher to lose sight of the author's view of his own work and in some measure to take it over through his own view of the work, and I began to wonder if my own intentions with regard to your work had overtaken what you might best wish for it yourself; even if that is not so here it is food for thought and clearly a danger as much when there is a wish for care as when there is none.

This story of publication would not be complete without reference to a letter Prynne sent to Barnett just after the Bloodaxe third edition of *Poems* appeared in early 2015:

> Studying the new, thus in relation to the previous, I have come to re-observe, very strikingly, that this book is still the one that you and I designed, all those years ago, to discover its object-character as a poetical compendium, from all those assorted typescripts which were our compost heap at the time. I recall most vividly your heroic struggle with that electronic typewriter, so *moderne* and yet so primitive, and your conjuration of a page format that would allow these poems to work in their own space while drawing identity from the companionship of the whole.

The letter goes on to refer to the 'life of the margins in relation to text assemblage' and 'a kind of latent humming sonority page by page, which is certainly of your own doing':

> The surviving constancy of these features, their coherence and fidelity to the text, are still most striking and notable. I know that we had many detailed discussions and experiments between us; but I also knew then and recognise now that it was your device that you discovered by profound reading and that you interpreted into the objective presence of the ensemble. The figure in the carpet! The ghost in the machine! Aurora borealis barely visible in the night sky! I was grateful then, for this exceptional care, and I am grateful now, and many readers have unknowingly absorbed the benefit of this inheritance.

Introduction for *The White Stones* (NYRB Edition, 2016)

Peter Gizzi

Very few books of poetry published in England in the 20th century have the aura of J.H. Prynne's *The White Stones*. The essential beauty of Prynne's work is a quality of mind. I vividly remember reading it for the first time in 1986 and being struck by its gorgeous surface structure and energetic belief system: it is a bright element, even psychedelic at times. Hard to believe that such a book would need an introduction, a book that has been passed from poet to poet for decades. It has long been, and remains, a touchstone.

The poems of *The White Stones* were written between 1964 and 1968. This was a period of great activity for Prynne, a time of many and new correspondences with British and American poets, and the inaugurations of various journals, most notably the Cambridge-based *The English Intelligencer,* edited by the poets Andrew Crozier and Peter Riley. Prynne was a central contributor of poems, essays, and letters to *The English Intelligencer,* where the majority of the poems in *The White Stones* were first published. Thirty-six issues appeared between 1966 and 1968, serving as a laboratory for an extended group of poets purposefully creating an English counter-tradition. A year before the publication of *The White Stones* in 1969, Prynne published *Kitchen Poems* and *Day Light Songs,* the latter included in this new volume, as is the 1969 essay/prose poem 'A Note on Metal'.

Now, almost 50 years on, there is a large body of discourse about Prynne's work, but as soon as one tries to pin down the original signal of these poems it gets slippery. They refuse to be categorised: If they're Marxist, they're also heterodox; if they're romantic, they're also analytic; if they're scientific, they're also magical. And while Prynne's method shares cardinal features with Charles Olson's projective verse, the romantic philosophical inflection is closer to William Wordsworth, Friedrich Hölderlin, and late Wallace Stevens. When I first encountered

Prynne's work, I felt that there was a braiding, like a double helix, of the Pound/Olson tradition with the Romantic/Stevens tradition, of high romanticism with physical, investigative, trans-historical inquiry.

In the course of the '60s Prynne developed deep and important friendships with some of the New American Poets, most notably Olson and Edward Dorn. In fact, after a voluminous correspondence with Olson, Prynne was responsible for preparing and editing the holographic manuscript of Olson's *Maximus IV,V,VI*. No mean task. There is an edition of the Prynne/Olson letters forthcoming from the University of New Mexico Press, which will further illuminate this important correspondence between these two brilliant and original men.

For this reason, it is worth rehearsing the elegant system that Olson proposed for an emancipatory poetics in his now venerable but still deeply relevant essay 'Projective Verse'. As Olson had it:

> …The two halves are:
> the HEAD, by way of the EAR, to the SYLLABLE
> the HEART, by way of the BREATH, to the LINE

Olson further elucidates: "I am dogmatic, that the head shows in the syllable. The dance of the intellect…" and goes on to say, "And the threshing floor for the dance? Is it anything but the LINE?" The line in *The White Stones* works both at the line break and in the clausal phrases that keep the machine humming and dancing from one idea to the next, one subject to the next, while constantly opening the horizon of meaning that each poem proposes. The work is full of necessary and productive restlessness in the service of discovery, you can feel the breath driving the poem. The contracted and sometimes crabbed grammar creates rhythm, but the percussive quality of the diction creates something very physical. The ending of the poem 'Song in Sight of the World' is a clear example of the syncopation produced from the technique of line and comma working together to both further and interrupt meaning:

> The light will do all this, to
> love is the last resort, you
> must know, I will tell

>   you, this, love, is
>   the world.

There is a feeling in this book that a language is coming to the speaker of the poem in the very act of composition—that is, in real time. For example in 'First Notes on Daylight' we find:

>   Patience is truly my device, as we wait
>   for the past to happen, which is to come into
>   the open. As I expect it to, daily...

These poems are faceted like crystal to daylight, or as Prynne would have it: "the striations are part of the heart's / desire." In many of the poems, this massing of clauses and perspectives creates an effect whereby any given singularity of personhood is defined and perhaps generated by a multiplicity of larger structural forces. In the magisterial poem 'The Glacial Question, Unsolved', the temporal structure is the geologic time and weather of the British Isles:

>   The falling movement, the light clouds
>   blowing in from the ice of Norfolk
>   thrust. As the dew recedes from the grass
>   towards noon the line of recession
>   slips back. We know where the north
>   is, the ice is an evening whiteness.
>   We know this, we are what it leaves:
>   the Pleistocene is our current sense, and
>   what in sentiment we are, we
>   are, the coast, a line or sequence, the
>   cut back down, to the shore.

In 'Thoughts on The Esterházy Court Uniform', one of the most romantically charged poems in this volume, we encounter an interiority, a private meditation on the costuming of the court in which Joseph Haydn composed; we feel the pressure of composition and aesthetics within a ritualized social structure:

I walk on up the hill, in the warm
sun and we do not return, the place is
entirely musical. No person can live there
& what is similar is the deeper resource, the
now hidden purpose. I refer directly to my
own need, since to advance in the now fresh &
sprouting world must take on some musical
sense. Literally, the grace & hesitation of
modal descent, the rhyme unbearable, the
coming down through the prepared delay and
once again we are there, beholding the
complete elation of our end.

A metamorphic language is at play in these poems, where the voice is more observational than sentimental: Naming is the prerogative for knowing. In Prynne's conception, both court systems and glaciers are players in a larger formation, they endure now in their afterlife as a lyric poem.

There is a utopian energy in *The White Stones* continually wheeling outward, which is why this work will never become a nostalgic object: It is constantly *happening*. Its readers will find binding narratives, science, economics, romantic love, history, prehistory organically deployed throughout the book's soundscape. To dramatize this multiplicity, to make it real and active on the page is one of the standing achievements of *The White Stones,* the ambition of a voice enunciating scale.

This book retains a deep glamour by means of its undeniable beauty and phenomenal architecture, its intellect, its vocabularies, and its singular way to song.

To a Reader

David Caddy

I was recently asked about my work as editor of *Tears in the Fence* and where my editorial predilections arose. I cited three sites of importance in shaping my desire to make the journal a challenging read. In chronological order the first was that flowering of literary magazines in the British Poetry Revival from 1960-1975, especially such journals as the *Grosseteste Review*, edited by Tim Longville and John Riley, *Curtains*, edited by Paul Buck, *Poetry Information*, edited by Peter Hodgkiss, *The Wivenhoe Park Review* (subsequently, *The Park*), edited by Andrew Crozier, *Alembic*, edited by Ken Edwards, Peter Barry and Robert Hampson, and above all, *Poetry Review*, edited by Eric Mottram between 1971 and 1977. I came to know Mottram through Bill Griffiths and Bob Cobbing, whose Writers Forum publications and readings were part of my pre-University poetry experiences, and he struck me a most serious editor at pains to read the totality of the poetic experiment during that period and to accord each area equal measure. Under his editorship, *Poetry Review* covered as wide a field of English, American and European poetry as possible and was not daunted by inflated reputations. He was acutely aware of the importance of the period and set about interviewing poets and bringing them together. I thought that Mottram was particularly good at seeing cultural and historical connections between poets and had little truck with overt labelling of poets. They are, he once said, raising a glass of red wine, not all deviants.

The second inspiration was *Horizon: A Review of Literature and Art* edited by Cyril Connolly from 1940–1949 and in particular, Sonia Brownell, the Venus from Euston Road, later Sonia Orwell. It was Sonia Brownell who read the submissions and made notes for Connolly on shortlisted material, and her eclectic taste which steered the magazine after Stephen Spender's departure in 1941. Although it is Connolly who delineated the difference between eclectic and dogmatic journals, it was Brownell who made the practice work. Her interests included French literature, philosophy and art, as well as American, South American and English literature, as is evident in Vol XII, No. 70, from October 1945. This issue heavily features André Malraux, Marcel Duchamp, as well as the first publication of 'Fern Hill' and 'A Refusal To Mourn The Death By Fire, Of A Child In London' by Dylan Thomas and other poems by George Barker and Geoffrey Grigson. Brownell read and filtered submissions daily. This work requires both close and broad reading at speed and essentially steers the ship. Brownell's internationalism and imaginative integrity is in stark contrast to the kind of 'little England' approach that dominated in subsequent decades. Brownell subsequently ran the Paris-based, *Art and Literature: An International Review*, with John Ashbery, Anne Dunn and Rodrigo Moynihan in the Sixties.

My third source of thinking came from the critical and creative writing of J.H. Prynne, who was first introduced to me by Kevin Nolan in a graduate reading group at Essex University in 1977. Our small informal poetry and criticism group was the setting for discussion of the imbalance between the poetry of Prynne, Olson and others, and the kind of critical thinking that was fashionable at that time. *Tears in the Fence* has always encouraged wide and close reading and a range of critical and creative approaches. J.H. Prynne's 'Tips on Practical Criticism', an introductory document for English students at Gonville and Caius, helped focus my thinking on how a literary magazine should present a more challenging reading experience. I decided to move away from a relatively cohesive approach involving themes and sub-themes to a more demanding jagged edge one with a clash of comparative items through juxtaposition. This moved the magazine more thoroughly away from the dogmatic towards the eclectic in the manner of Mottram's *Poetry Review* or Barney Rosset's *Evergreen Review*. Before and during this transition I addressed issues and problems around the nature of close critical reading in my 'Afterword' column. The column arose as a more formalised way of covering a wide range of new writing, criticism and biography in the manner of Cyril Connolly's short notices at the end of *Horizon*, and focusing upon the process of critical reading. This was supported by Sarah Hopkins' column, 'Cabin Noise', which covered a range of practical reading support projects in non-academic ways. As one correspondent wrote, 'You seem to be advocating a poetry that does something with language and still has relevance for the world that we live in. A fascinating challenge.' Prynne's notes on practical criticism, his lectures and monographs on Wordsworth, emphatical language, Shakespeare's *Sonnets*, and so on come with a range of comparative and secondary extracts from relevant contextual matter. He juxtaposes materials which maybe in contradiction to one another in order to aid elucidation and understanding. This approach finds its echo in my placement of stylistic near-opposites in the magazine. As John Wilkinson observed the magazine is rare in that it places the name of the author at the end of the poem or review rather than the beginning. This is an attempt to lessen prejudice and to encourage a relatively blind reading. Additionally I deliberately seek quirky pieces that help foster resistance to a more stable dogmatic reading. Reading Prynne's essays on individual poems, such as Wordsworth's 'The Solitary Reaper', helped give me a better grasp of stylistic pitch and meaning effects.

J. H. Prynne's lasting contribution to our lives is surely that he taught a great many of us to become better readers and seers in terms of being able to focus upon a range of matter, both historical and in the here and now. Rather like Cézanne, who heightened our sense of the visual, Prynne has elevated our sense of the poetic, of language and its ordering, leading to a deeper perceptual focus and momentary apprehension of where we are today.

'To take the whole condition of something':
On Prynne reading Olson

DAVID HERD

1

As it seems from this distance, when Jeremy Prynne lectured on Charles Olson's *Maximus IV, V, VI* at Simon Fraser University, on July 27 1971, his objective was, in a single utterance, to reorient readings of Olson's major poem. Transcribed by Tom McGauley, and first published in *Iron* magazine, the lecture is not quite so explicit as to declare this re-orienting intention.[1] What the lecture does declare, however, what it is perfectly clear about, is that its observations are grounded in ways of reading *Maximus* that were not conventional to the poem's reception. In drawing attention to these reading strategies, to Prynne's own references to the question of how one reads, of what, actually, is involved in reading, I want to make two straightforward claims. The first is that Prynne's lecture remains the most important single statement on the overarching meaning and structure of *Maximus* and that a good deal of critical trouble might have been saved if the lecture's implications had been more readily registered. The second claim is that when one thinks about the relation of Prynne to Olson, of the importance of the older to the younger writer, it is the *act* of reading to which one needs attend. What one gets, in other words, from Prynne's lecture, is a picture of what an active reading really consists of, a reading through which new dispositions are jarred into being.

The fact that, in lecturing, Prynne had an interest in the act of reading itself, in the materiality and agency of the readerly process, is made apparent at the beginning of the piece. As he reports,

> I said I would talk to you today about the second batch of Maximus, which I am glad to do, because my sense of the completion of that poem varies very strongly according to where I am, and this is a new place to be, so I have what seems to me a new poem with me, which it would be good to see if you could take some measure of.

As an opening statement this is straightforward enough: when one reads a major work in a new place, something about that unfamiliar setting can re-frame the reading. Straightforward at it is, however, this is not a statement whose implications should go unremarked, not least in the context of an Olsonian discourse. What Prynne raises, by drawing attention to the newness of his situation, is the question of relation. He has, by being in Vancouver, a significantly new relation to Olson's poem. The transposition is considerable. The setting of the Simon Fraser campus, on Burnaby Mountain, with its view of the Fitzsimmons mountain range to the north and the islanded B.C. coastline to the south and west, is unlike any setting one might encounter in the UK. It is, in particular, quite unlike Cambridge, to which Prynne refers, as he continues, as the place where Milton and Wordsworth, poets who also worked in epic structures, trained and read. What one has in the setting of the lecture, then, underscored by the sense of journey, half way round the northern hemisphere, is a new vantage.

The notion of the vantage, of the position from which one regards things, was, as Prynne well knew, important to Olson. Olson's word for it was 'view', the 'view' being (as he dedicated a series of seminars at Black Mountain College to explaining) the ineluctable frame of the individual's relation to the world.[2] Quite how one reads the status of the view in Olson is crucial to one's engagement with his writing as a whole, not least *Maximus*, which by one kind of account embeds a person's view in their locality the way William Carlos Williams embeds his principal poetic creation in the territory at Paterson Falls. Prynne's critical point from the outset of his lecture, however, is that the view can alter, that he is now reading *Maximus* from a different position on the planet and that with such a re-positioning what he is newly able to regard is the poem's defining axis.

With his opening statement, then, what Prynne brings to the fore is the material practice of reading, the circumstantiality of the act of attention by which a major work of literature is grasped. This is followed by a second statement in which, again straightforwardly, he situates the nature of his interpretive address. As he puts it:

> Some of you will no doubt already know this poem quite well; and to those I imagine I have little to say. I address myself to

those of you who either don't know it, or know it only very partially, because that seems to me to be the useful thing to do.

Here again, Prynne draws on Olson's theoretical idiom in order to turn his reading away from the conventions by which the poem's reception had come to be shaped. Whether a thing was useful, or not, was of the first importance to Olson, being the substance of the opening moment of 'Projective Verse': 'Verse now, 1950, if it is to go ahead, if it is to be of essential use, must, I take it, catch up and put into itself certain laws and possibilities of the breath.'[3] The 'useful thing' in the context of the lecture, as Prynne proposes it, in a room steeped in understanding of *Maximus* (accumulated by such resident scholars as Ralph Maud and through a poetic culture informed by such pivotal events as the 1963 Vancouver conference) was to address his reading beyond the existing critical discourse.

How actually he set about that, how he sought to jar a new relation to the poem into view, Prynne makes plain in the lecture's third statement of reading practice:

The other great poem of homecoming — there are two great poems of homecoming across the sea: the other, of course, is the wandering of Odysseus. What struck me last night, as I was re-reading the whole of *Maximus* right through just to see what it felt like, was how extraordinary it is that Pound should conduct his homecoming epic right the other way round, so that the moment of that particular resonant vibrant curved voyage of coming home should appear right at the start of the Cantos.

Embedded here, between references to the homecomings of Homer and Pound, is a simple but rather breathtaking statement about Prynne's preparation for his address: that the night before he had read 'the whole of Maximus right through just to see what it felt like'. Such a statement would have been variously challenging. At the level of duration it represents a challenge in that for some people present, and for some of Olson's most influential readers, it was the work of a life, not the work of a single sitting, to engage *Maximus*. Not that Prynne would have meant to imply that the poem didn't call for, or benefit from, sustained scholarship. What he does mean to propose, however, is that the poem could be otherwise engaged; that it was possible to read it, actively to apprehend it, in such a way that its structure as a whole, as opposed to the series of its parts, became the aspect one had in mind. What Prynne presents in his lecture on *Maximus*, in other words, is an image of reading at its most deliberate, framed by a dynamic sense of circumstance and charged by an act of will. To read in this sense, so the lecture implies, is to be fully intellectually engaged, is to become capable through a deliberate act of mind of extended cognition.

The reason for dwelling on Prynne's explicit reflections on and extensions of the readerly act is to show that it was through just such materially deliberate strategies that his conception of Olson was formed. One sees this in the lecture itself, in which a singular sense of the ambition and achievement of *Maximus* comes startlingly and strikingly into view. One sees it also in the scope and the trajectory of Prynne's own body of work, to which an early re-orientation of and to Olson was necessary. That trajectory out of Olson can be sketched in four moments: the conceptualisation of Olson in the lecture itself; the achievement of a new and distinctive poetic idiom through an engagement of Olson in *The White Stones*; the subsequent radical transformation of such a discourse as represented by, for example, the much later volume *Unanswering Rational Shore*; and finally, briefly, a return to the fundamental lessons in reading that Prynne's engagement with Olson continues to afford. Where the discussion comes to rest is on the expectation that a poetry such as Prynne's is built on: that there is a kind of reading, a kind of readerly act, through which the sense we have of our view point is significantly changed.

2

It is impossible to gauge from this distance the degree to which, with the changed materiality of his re-reading of *Maximus*, Prynne's conceptualisation of the poem altered. It is clear from *The White Stones*, as will be observed, that he had long-since been engaged in a deliberate turning of the terms of Olson's poem, both the terms it actively proposed and the terms it brought into view. What one can suppose, perhaps, is that in the event of the lecture itself, with its reframed reading, a particularly clear and purposeful distillation of his thinking on the poem became possible. The form that distillation takes is a weighing of the terms *Maximus* both invokes and ought not to invoke; a series of assessments in which possible terms are tried out for their usefulness, the key terms being: lyric, localism, cosmos, coast, planet, curve, epic, and home.

The terms that Prynne is most keen to separate out from the discussion are 'lyric' and 'localism', terms linked in his consideration by an attention to the part (as opposed to the whole). As he remarks early on, 'If we come to this poem of Olson's, we are in the condition of something which is not lyric.' The point of that 'not lyric' is to open up the discursive space in which he, and his audience, might adequately get the measure of the work. It is an important negation because, as Prynne appreciates, the poem frequently presents qualities that can be taken as lyric. He quotes a passage from 'The Twist', as an example of the 'gracious behavior of the lyric occasion'.

the flowers break off

but the anther,
the filament of now, the mass
drives on,

the whole of it
coming,
to this pin-point
to turn

in this day's sun,
in this veracity
there, the waters the several of them the roads
here, a blackberry blossom

It is a representative passage in many ways, settling on 'a blackberry blossom', and Prynne might have quoted many other moments to establish his point. For instance 'Letter 27 [withheld]', with the explicitly lyrical manner of its opening address:

I come back to the geography of it,
the land falling off to the left
where my father shot his scabby golf
and the rest of us played baseball
into the summer darkness until no flies
could be seen and we came home
to our various piazzas where the women
buzzed

Or as the poem continues:

An American
is a complex of occasions,
themselves a geometry
of spatial nature.

I have this sense,
that I am one

with my skin
Plus this—plus this:[4]

There is no question that the quality of the lyric is a quality of *Maximus*, that there are moments when the graciousness of such occasions is what one hears, and that in such hearing what one is being given is a series of parts: a 'blackberry blossom', the 'various piazzas', 'plus this—plus this'.

That, even so, for all the graciousness of its attention, *Maximus* is finally in the condition of 'not lyric', comes back to the geography of it. As Prynne writes, identifying lyric with locality:

Knowledge of the local and component parts of it, where each set is occupied by numerous instances, where there are more than one kind, is not first philosophy, though it may participate in that. So, if you have a condition of that order, then there is no lyric, because the lyric relies on the gracious condition of metaphor, and metaphor transfers the small into the large, and the one thing into the other; and the lyric is therefore not a condition of the whole, but a condition of the part.

There are three related questions here: the question of detail, the question of the poem's address, and the question of the view. To reiterate, one way to read *Maximus* is as a poem preoccupied with detail (a good deal of it supplied by Prynne himself through his work in the archives), as principally uttered via a mode of address we might call lyric, and framed by a view, or series of views, that are tied to the particularity of place. All of which is true of the poem, but is not, as Prynne insists, the poem's truth; the poem's truth being the relation to geography that, in the largest sense, Prynne takes to be its axis. As he writes:

> I know for myself that the primary structure of this poem is already complete. And complete in two major movements: the going out, the asking the great questions, the making of the great statements: and the coming back, the coming back across the sea, the coming back through the ocean, coming back to the shore, and then the shore fades into a condition of land, and the condition of land approximates to the condition of the planet.

Prynne's statement here builds on three earlier formulations. That:

> that condition of the cosmos brings about a condition also of myth as the structure of the language used, which allows for an extension into mythography, the writing of where one is.

That:

> The condition of coast now it seems to me is the condition of the relation between these two poems

That:

> We have the whole condition of that circular curve to the condition of space.

It is through these statements, through the combined trying out of terms, that Prynne arrives at the condition of 'not lyric'. What that condition constitutes, as he reads *Maximus* as articulating, is an apprehension of the quality of the planet as grasped at the moment lands meet sea; not the specific dynamics of Gloucester, but the condition of coast that those specifics are given to present. What the poem discloses, in other words, is as an appreciation of the planet as absolute and common ground. Or as Olson himself contends,

> As the people of the earth are now, Gloucester
> is heterogeneous, and so can know polis
> not as localism, not the mu-sick (the trick
> of corporations, newspapers, slick magazines, movie houses,
> the ships, even the wharves, absentee-owned[5]

Against which 'slaver' that 'would keep you off the sea, would keep you local,/ my Nova Scotians,/ Newfoundlanders,/ Sicilianos,/ Isolatos', what Olson points towards is 'the condition of the under-water, cut-water of anyone'.[6] What Prynne's lecture allows his audience to see in *Maximus*, in a single sweep, are the underlying structures that constitute the poem's ground. What he grasps is the poem's relation to the planet ('the geography of it' as 'Letter 27' proposes) and what he is capable of appreciating, by forcing his reading open, is the way, via the many, that Olson sets out to present the whole. The question the lecture leaves unanswered is how, if at all, Olson's poem reconciles the occurrences of lyric utterance with its sense of the whole condition, how, or whether, it is able to voice in such a way that such a sense of the whole, rather than the part, might be the basis for speech. The question the lecture leaves unresolved, in other words, is how the condition itself—the condition of 'not lyric', of mythography, of coast, of curve, of home—might be understood to be the basis of utterance. Which means that the key term is condition itself, the question being how language might take cognizance of its ground; how it might be articulated in such a way that its condition is voiced.

3

This question of how language voices its condition is one of the questions, perhaps the main question, Prynne addressed himself to in *The White Stones*. As in the lecture, what that process significantly amounted to was a trying out of terms, and what that trying out sometimes consisted of was a turning round of what Olson seemed to propose. One such turning is 'First Notes on Daylight', which it will be helpful to quote in its entirety:

Patience is truly my device, as we wait
for the past to happen, which is to come into
the open. As I expect it to, daily & the question is really what *size* we're in, how much of
it is the measure, at any one time. Patience is
the sum of my inertia, by which the base-line
lays itself out to the touch
    like the flower in
    heaven, each pebble
    graded in ochre. How
to extend, anyway to decline the rhetoric
of *occasion*, by which the sequence back
from some end is clearly predictive. We
owe that in theory to the history of person
as an entire condition of landscape–*that*
kind of extension, for a start. The open
fields we cross, we carry ourselves by ritual
observance, even sleeping in the library.
    The laggard, that is,
    whose patience
    is the protective
    shield, of the true
    limit to *size*.
"The ceremonial use of the things described",
the *cinar* trees or the white-metal mirror, forms
of patience, oh yes, and each time I even
move, the strophic muscular patter is *use*, in
no other sense. The common world, how far we
go, the practical limits of daylight. And as I
even think of the base-line the vibration is
strong, the whole sequence of person as his
own history is no *more* than ceremonial

> the concentration
> of intersect: dis-
> covery back to
> the way over, the
> entire crossing an open fabric, which we wear
> stand on or carry in the hand. That this could
> really be so & of use is my present politics,
> burning like smoke, before the setting of fire.[7]

In drawing attention to 'First Notes on Daylight', in the general context of *The White Stones*, I am not suggesting that the poem is either, precisely, representative of that volume or that it is the book's strongest piece. It is, to be sure, a remarkably measured poetic statement, but because it is in the manner of statement, a thinking through of poetics, it does not have the aesthetic reach of, say, 'The Glacial Question, Unsolved' or 'Thoughts on the Esterházy Court Uniform'. That it is not representative, on the other hand, owes to the variousness of Prynne's volume, a set of poems that take formal difference to be one of their principles of inquiry. How the poem does figure, in relation to its context, is (as with the lecture) as a kind of distillation of recurring terms. Recursion (etymologically the movement 'again back') is a key procedure at this moment in Prynne's trajectory, with the linguistic return being one of the ways Prynne captures what, in the lecture, he would call the condition of the curve. And the point is that the terms that surface in 'First Notes on Daylight' are axiomatic to the volume's inquiry, the terms on which the burden of its meaning largely rests.

As Alex Latter has pointed out, one context within which 'First Notes on Daylight' operated was the exchange of views that informed the thinking behind *The English Intelligencer*, Prynne's poem being, in part at least, a response to Peter Riley's 'Working Notes'.[8] By the same token, the context for *The English Intelligencer* was very much Olson's poetic agenda, one question for the journal being how the American poet's terms might be put to different, or further use. If Prynne's poem is answering Riley, then, it is also deliberately answering, or rather, very deliberately reading Olson, the Olson poem in question being 'Letter 27 [withheld]'. As Olson's poem has it:

It is the imposing
of all those antecedent predecessions, the precessions
of me, the generation of those facts
which are my words, it is coming

from all that I no longer am,
yet am, the slow westward motion of

more than I am

There is no strict personal order
for my inheritance.

No Greek will be able
to discriminate my body.

An American

is a complex of occasions,

themselves a geometry

of spatial nature.

To which Prynne responds:

How
to extend, anyway to decline the rhetoric
of *occasion*, by which the sequence back
from some end is clearly predictive. We
owe that in theory to the history of person
as an entire condition of landscape—*that*
kind of extension, for a start.

In so far as Prynne is in dialogue with Riley, what he is in dialogue about is Olson, whose 'archaeologist of morning' stands behind the title phrase 'First Notes on Morning', and whose 'antecedent predecessions' (a phrase taken from the philosopher A.N. Whitehead) are clearly echoed in Prynne's 'sequence back' that is 'clearly predictive'. What's at issue, however, as Prynne makes explicit, is the 'rhetoric/ of *occasion*', the same rhetoric that he wanted to wrestle Olson away from in the lecture, against which, as the poem proceeds to say, what he wants to explore instead is the 'condition of landscape'.

To underline, what is at issue here is not that Prynne is engaged with Olson, but rather the deliberateness of the reading that constitutes that engagement. In the poem, as in the lecture, Prynne subjects Olson to a most concerted re-assessment, such that terms that are both present in, and important to, Olson's lexicon are, in Prynne's handling of them, shown to be at odds. The 'rhetoric/ of occasion' is to be 'declined'; the 'condition of landscape' is to be explored. Prynne's wariness toward the 'rhetoric of occasion' has already been largely articulated in relation to the lecture: that it implies both the standpoint and the sense of individuation characteristic of the lyric. How 'First Notes on Daylight' develops the question is, as the poem puts it in its opening line, in terms of 'patience', 'patience,' being 'truly my device, as we wait/ for the past to happen, which is to come into/ the open'. It is in the quality of 'patience', and a poetry of patience, that the limitations of a 'rhetoric of occasion' are exposed. What the idea of the occasion suggests, as 'Letter 27' indicates, is that poetry's relation to time can be achieved through particular moments, moments when meaning might be made acutely present. Which is fine, perhaps, for the poet whose basic medium is the event, as in the case of Frank O'Hara, say, but it is not fine for the poet whose medium is the geological *durée*: the geography of it, as Olson calls it, or the 'geometry/ of spatial nature'. As the title of Prynne's poem implies, we can read it as something like an annotation, a note in the margin of the older poet's 'morning' work. And what the note says, rigorously, is that one aspect of the poem's rhetoric is at odds with its deeper preoccupations, that what we need is not a poetic of the occasion, but one that registers its condition.

The question is, what might such a poetic of condition amount to; how, in the poem, might one arrive at a form of language in which an understanding of our condition—of curve, landscape, planet, home—constitutes the basis of utterance. This is, needless to say, a difficult question to answer; the glacial question is, after all, unsolved. It is possible, however, to indicate some respects in which, in *The White Stones*, Prynne sets out to meet that task. Reading itself is fundamental, as in the reading that constitutes research, such as is recorded in the notes to 'Aristeas, in Seven Years' or 'The Glacial Question, Unsolved'. Research is hardly in itself sufficient, however. Really what matters is the relation the utterance of the poem, its voice, has to that content, which is less a question of research, whatever period or condition that content might come out of, and more a question of vantage within the work. Such a question of vantage, or view, in *The White Stones* is by no means simply a matter of pronoun, since the speaking position is as often characterized by a voicing 'I' as by a voicing 'we'. What matters, rather, is that the poem achieves continuity: that its utterance carries continuity between things, parts, and, more demandingly, that the position of utterance is in some sense continuous with the condition the poem sets out to present. It is in this sense that what Prynne calls, in the lecture, the condition of the curve, is important, the condition of the curve being precisely continuity, a sense of always coming back. What is required, then, if it is possible to imagine it, is a language that curves, in which the continuity of turning, as opposed to a separated stance, becomes the base-line language effect.

Roughly speaking, that's what *The White Stones*, breathtakingly, might be said to achieve. How the poems achieve it is partly to do with pace, to do with the patience of the utterance, so that what one finds always, as one reads, is one element of the poem becoming another. In this sense *The White Stones* could not be less like an open field poem, because its elements—one hesitates to speak of parts—could not be so dispersed. Consonant with such an emphasis on patience, and its attendant pace, is the fact that what one is dealing with in the poems of this volume is, characteristically, the single statement. Which is not to make a grammatical point, but rather a point about mood, that a poem like 'If There is a Stationmaster at Stamford S.D. Hardly So' achieves an articulation that cannot easily be broken into. 'First Notes on Daylight' is similarly so, the utterance being all of a piece, so that if one is to quote it then really one has to quote it whole. And then, crucially, there is the question of recursion, of the terms to which the poem returns, so that semantically the writing is always coming back round. All of which generates the impression that, at very least, the poetry has gained the measure of the condition of language, where condition is both the full extent (the word in 'Notes on Daylight' is 'size'), and also the limitation of the ground on which we stand; and where the vantage point is such that, in so far as it is possible, the poetry is looking not 'towards' or 'onto' but 'from'.

Whether this could really be so, whether, that is, the poetry hasn't simply—though simply is hardly the adverb—achieved a linguistic illusion, however remarkable, is the question with which 'First Notes on Daylight' ends:

> That this could
> really be so & of use is my present politics,
> burning like smoke, before the setting of fire.

That this could really be so, that it could the case that a poetry could articulate our condition, and that, more so, that such an articulation could be of use, is, as the poet puts it, his present politics. What that means, how such an articulation could constitute a politics, and how in certain respects it still should, is the issue I want to return to in the final section. Before arriving at that sense, though, it is important to consider how Prynne's trajectory out of Olson developed, how the rigorous reading to which he subjected the older poet's lexicon entailed a future resource.

4

On the face it, at the level of the title, there is a continuity between Prynne's 2001 pamphlet, *Unanswering Rational Shore*, published by Object Permanence, and his lecture on Olson, both works apparently being concerned with what the lecture calls, 'the condition of the coast':

> Coast: I mean that ambiguous delicate line between the land and the sea, with its prime sexual ambiguity that Whitman recognised with such delicacy…. That condition of coast now it seems to me is the condition of the relation between these two poems, these two sets of poem, the first *Maximus* and the second *Maximus*, except that the first *Maximus* is the sea, the second *Maximus* is the land. You come right round in that way.

There is a structural analogy to be drawn. The 14 poems of *Unanswering Rational Shore* are cut in two, the blank white central strip of the page standing between the two sets of 7 lines, this formal cut and balancing being anticipated by the sequence's epigraph

> lo mismo
> lo mismo[9]

being the Spanish for same, the same both sides. It is reasonable enough to assume, therefore, that the condition of the shore is, in some sense, the condition of the relation of the recurring two parts of the poems. That, however, is where the analogy stalls, or rather, where the earlier term is reassessed. So that whereas with the condition of the coast we have 'that ambiguous delicate line between', with *Unanswering Rational Shore* we have a border that is deeply unresponsive, the pun on the final word underlining the point. Unanswering. Rational. Sure.

The differences between the investigation of the condition of the coast that informs both the lecture on *Maximus* and *The Whites Stones*, and the condition of the shore that constitutes the later volume, are radical. Where, in the earlier iteration, the 'line between' amounted to a form of continuity, an expression of difference that emphasized the earth's curve, in the later volume the difference is a breach, a break in transmission, the language of the sequence presenting not return but arrest and rupture. Likewise, if the underlying border condition is differently conceived, so too is the base-line relation of the utterance to its condition. If singularity and return are the ways, in syntax, the mood of *The White Stones* captures its sense of linguistic horizon, the formulations of *Unanswering Rational Shore* are jammed into unresponsive relation. There is little listening going on within the poem itself—though the poet and the reader are required to listen hard, to the way the parts of contemporary language rebut and repel. That's the current condition, the volume seems to suggest, the act of linguistic repulsion, and perhaps, if we consider Prynne's sequence to be a re-reading, or development of, his earlier presentation of the shoreline, it always was. The condition of the coast, in other words, now seems fondly imagined by the lecture and in the poems of *The White Stones*, implying a continuity at the level of the planet whereas at the level of politics there is, and always was, breach.

Which initial commentary on *Unanswering Rational Shore*, one has consciously to observe, is very much in the spirit of a *reading*. What I mean by that is that whereas in early Prynne, for all that the vantage is brought into question, it is possible to equate such a notion of the view or vantage with the ambition of the poem. If we can't quite get there cognitively we can appreciate that the horizon of the condition is where the poem seeks to stand. In later Prynne, of which *Unanswering Rational Shore* is exemplary, there is not such a sense of vantage, but a sense rather that the language of the poem, though hardly unshaped or unmediated, is being presented for use. There is a presiding sense of the present condition that we need to get at as we read the sequence, but getting it is to be achieved by the *act* of reading, the process of arriving at the *reading* being the process by which cognition of the condition is achieved. As the present reading gets it, then, as I catch and relate the phrases that recur across the surface of the writing, what I hear, explicitly, is a strong sense of appeal. In the first half of the first poem, for instance, following the disturbing opening image of damage ('Profuse reclaim from a scrape or belt') a form of appeal is issued in the opening sentence: 'Appellate at dictum at/ its debit resonance fixing prolusion, optic rage/ performs even dots right now.'[10] That repeated 'at', we might notice, is aggressive, 'at … at', addressing, or even attacking, rather than answering or paying heed. To which, in response, we get the appeal of the sequence's final clause:

> hot justice pleading for penalty
> in a rigged-up camp of love, courtship plays requited
> and branded so faintly at implicit final appeal.[11]

Here again the preposition is 'at', and so if justice is at work it is not in the form of a hearing, in the literal sense, but in the form of an assault, 'branded so faintly at implicit final appeal'.

Whose appeal? Who is branded? This is not straightforward to determine, nor must it necessarily be the object of a reading to arrive at such a determination. There is, however, a register, supplementing the explicit recourse to appeals that starts to bring a personage into view. That register is caught, in part, in the issuing of a claim in poem 9, where: 'Overstock digit perverse/ deployment adds a pungent new flavour, stepping/ forward to claim the spoilage'.[12] One catches the register also in the prevailing sense of a hostile linguistic environment, as 'Flush undergrowth/ makes itself felt, to weaponise space uttermost/ in dialect, absence decrees its neatened locations'.[13] Exactly how much the reader should invest in such phrasing is very much the question, but it is worth hearing the equation here: that it is absence that decrees that a location remains neat; that a location's neatness is achieved by keeping things, or people, out. And then one might notice, in arriving at this sense of the sequence's conditioning discourse, that the basic relation to the planet is rendered profoundly precarious. Thus, whereas in the lecture on *Maximus* what Prynne finally arrived at was a sense of planet as home, here, instead:

> On the track the news radiates like a planet auction,
> for the best rates hard to chew. If it seems too good,
> sucker, the pap is surely toxic, unless the glad
> hand goes your way, soft as velvet.[14]

The planet auction, it seems possible to infer, consists in the difference between sucking up toxicity or experiencing gladness soft as velvet; the relation to the environment being, in the worst possible sense, utterly contingent.

The personage who emerges out of this discourse—unanswering as it is, rational, and sure—the discourse of aggressively managed appeals, unheard, claims, hostile linguistic environments and global precarity, is perhaps named for us in poem 3, the personage for whom the shore is most urgent as a condition:

> The floor plan
> provides more for those who float there, get migrant
> and cross before the garland, breaking open its fall.[15]

There are three things to say about the appearance of the word 'migrant' here, whether as noun in the context of a contracted imperative ('get [the] migrant'), or as adjective in the sense of becoming, as in getting migrant. The first thing to say, by way of acknowledgement, is that just because the word 'migrant' makes an appearance in the poem does not entail that the word, or the personage, is central. The so-called 'migrant' is central now, for sure, in 2016, but it might be a little anachronistic

—just a little—to imply such centrality in a work of 2001. Perhaps. The second thing to say, however, is that in registering the presence of the migrant ('those who float there') in *Unanswering Rational Shore*, I am by no means the first person to propose their centrality to its discourse. As Michael Grant very eloquently put it, 'It is a poetry of exile, of wandering... The wanderer's country, the dwelling place of the nomad, is not a place of truth, but in abandonment of place altogether.'[16] But the third thing to say is that the migrant is hardly new to this discourse, that he or she was there from the beginning: from Olson's fundamental conception of westward movement; to his opening statement in the Rosa Mundi poem that 'Migration in fact (which is probably/ as constant in history/ as any one thing'; to the movement of Prynne's 'Aristeas, in Seven Years', where 'that they did migrate and the spirit excursion/ was no more than the need and will of the/ flesh'.[17] The migrant was always there, in other words, entirely integral to the 'condition of the curve'. The tragedy (the tragedy that calls for re-assessment) is that now, in the early part of the Twenty-First Century, he or she has been rendered quite so visible; the same, the same, as the epigraph humanly has it, but confronted by linguistic and physical refusal: *Unanswering Rational Shore*.

5

This discussion opened with an image of Prynne reading, and it is to the lessons of that image that I want briefly to return by way of conclusion. Like the fact of migration, the highly deliberate act of reading was present at the beginning of the lineage Prynne chose to develop. Thus Olson read Melville with sufficient rigour as to make him into the writer he needed for *Call Me Ishmael*. Similarly, in reading Olson, Prynne scrutinised the older poet so closely as to establish a tension between his framing rhetorics: between the rhetoric of lyric and view and part; and the rhetoric of geography and spatial geometry and coast. There is a third term in Olson (who liked to work in triads), one that Prynne does not opt to pick up and in which one could argue that something like a bridging is achieved. The term is *polis*, a term which for Olson constituted the frame and arena of disparate viewpoints, and a concept which, if we contemplate its function as social framework, provides a way of recognizing human movement between cultures and across the planet as well as the relation between already constitutionally connected individuals. Olson had a term, in other words, which operated between lyric position and epic scale, and by which vantage could be considered as more than the frame of the individual part. What Prynne grasped in Olson instead, or rather what he used him to articulate, was the necessity of registering the whole condition. It was a crucial move in modern poetics, one that allows one to get, actually to get in language, that we are continuous, that we are, really, in the condition of the curve. The problem is that such an understanding of the condition is not currently of use, or is as far as ever from being used, and so we what have is not the delicate line of the coast but the brutally unresponsive border. Prynne, that is, of necessity, subjects his own terms to scrutiny, and where we find ourselves is at a cruel, weaponised divide: *Unanswering Rational Shore.*

NOTES

[1] Jeremy Prynne, 'Lecture on Maximus IV, V, VI', Simon Fraser University, July 27, 1971, transcribed by Tom McGauley, *Iron*, October 1971; reprinted in Minutes of the Charles Olson Society #28, April 1999; http://charlesolson.org/Files/Prynnelecture1.htm and http://charlesolson.org/Files/Prynnelecture2.htm (accessed 11.1.2016). All quotations from the lecture are taken from these sites; no page numbers given.

[2] Olson's seminars took place in the summer of 1956 and were subsequently published as *The Special View of History*, Oyez, 1970

[3] Charles Olson, 'Projective Verse', in *Collected Prose*, ed. Robert Creeley & Benjamin Friedlander, University of California Press, 1997, 240

[4] Charles Olson, *The Maximus Poems*, ed. George F. Butterick, University of California Press, 184-5

[5] ibid, 14

[6] ibid, 15

[7] J.H.Prynne, *Poems*, Bloodaxe Books, 2005, 69.

[8] Alex Latter, *Late Modernism and The English Intelligencer: On The Poetics of Community*, Bloomsbury, 2015, 72-3.

[9] Prynne, *Poems*, 517.

[10] ibid., 519.

[11] ibid., 533.

[12] ibid., 528.

[13] ibid., 521.

[14] ibid., 524.

[15] ibid., 521.

[16] Michael Grant, '"Buxtehude in kedgeree"': on J.H.Prynne's *Unanswering Rational Shore*', http://michaelgrant3.blogspot.co.uk/2008/10/on-jh-prynne.html; accessed 11.1.2016.

[17] Olson, *Maximus*, 479; Prynne, *Poems*, 92.

'For the for you / and these to hold': Receiving J.H. Prynne's *Poems*

Joseph Persad

The occasion of a new edition of J.H. Prynne's collected poems provides a new stage for presenting the meaning of the poems within. The repeated exclusion of Prynne's first volume *Force of Circumstance and Other Poems* is one example of how republication is used to reimagine the extant body of work, heightening the sense that there is some kinship across the works deemed fit to stand together as *Poems*. The most recent edition of Prynne's *Poems* made slight but decisive changes in presentation. Where past editions were dedicated to deceased friends Bernard Dubourg, Prynne's French translator, and the poet Edward Dorn, the *Poems* are now inscribed "For the Future", and where paintings had provided the previous *Poems* with cover images, there is now a photograph of "native crystalline sulphur", its colour pleasingly in keeping with the established yellow and black colour scheme.[1] These changes both motivate, and are motivated by, the specific character of Prynne's most recent work, and the kind of labour it compels from a reader. To see this, it is useful to have a sense of the responses elicited by the different kind of performances undertaken by previously collected editions of the poems.

In 1982, Allardyce, Barnett put out the first collected edition of J.H. Prynne's poems. That book's blurb took aim at "early critical response to J.H. Prynne's work" for having failed to recognise that "the difficult" mentioned in the collection's first lines was only important in so far as it related to "the ardent 'matter' and the accompanying breadth of imaginative and political reference".[2] This advice was as pertinent to some of Prynne's enthusiasts as it was his opponents. The blurb ends with a quote from the poet Douglas Oliver, taken from the closing sentence of a reading of Prynne's 'Of Movement Towards a Natural Place' published in *Grosseteste Review*: "As the tight music of these stanzas trembles and shines…". Despite spending the majority of that reading giving serious consideration to the idea that the poem in question is 'about' something, namely a technical investigation of the processes belonging to the 'mental instant' that makes something qualitatively different from the past and the future, it is ultimately the 'tight music' of the poem that Oliver offers as the portal to the poem's meaning. The quote chosen for the blurb of Prynne's 1982 *Poems*, then, offers a counter-proposal to its insistence on paying attention to the poems' wide ambit of imaginative and political reference. It playfully uses a quote that itself uses the language of the poems: "Only at the rim does the day tremble and shine".[3] Oliver's ellipsis is coy, knowing this allusive conclusion to be essentially unspeakable, an effacement of criticism delivered as criticism, passing the task of interpretation back onto the poem itself.[4] It is the mention of 'music' that stops this play from collapsing into the kind of fetishisation of non-comprehension or sheer textuality that both Oliver and the rest of the blurb warn against, as musicality is able, at least in some of its aspects, to operate on a fundamentally different set of concerns to questions of comprehensibility.[5]

Oliver's measured inclusion of a cue from a poem as a way to guide the critical mind, tacitly approved by the 1982 *Poems*' blurb, has since decayed into a trope, as Timothy Thornton has identified in a frustrated review of *Acrylic Tips*: "[i]t seems uncommon to read an analysis of a poem or sequence by J.H. Prynne which does not at some point subside into a pyrotechnic but not always illuminating description of the poem's behaviour, using a barrage of select quotations from it, as if they guarantee the most incontrovertible account by coming from within".[6] Thornton's observation is spurred on by a recognition of his own practice in the review up to that point. He is wary of "something unappetisingly reductive about this approach [...] involving a diminishing circularity".[7] Even as it seems to some extent justified by the poems, this approach appears to fall short as criticism. As an alternative to such 'diminishing circularity', Thornton settles his reading of *Acrylic Tips* by saying: "The threats which issue from its heady pulp, which seems to traumatize itself further and with more vigour the more you read it, are that any new beginning is doomed to fail, and that its haemorrhage and infarction are not local and temporary, but are universal, permanent, contagious, and indiscriminate."[8] Claims to universality or permanence are also difficult to reckon with, imposing limitations on the ability to maintain any sense of particularity, although 'heady pulp' is true to the contents of *Acrylic Tips* in more ways than Thornton acknowledges. As well as the fleshy damage strewn throughout the poems, I read threads of narratives indebted to post-apocalyptic science fiction. If they can be read with an imaginative eye for Latinate syntax, surreal flourishes, and strings of nouns piled together to function as adjectives, again and again the later sequences offer up coherent and extensive streaks of stories, all of which seems to be encouraged by their carefully punctuated sentences. As sequences develop these streaks appear to be introduced and put back into play according to a faculty for identifying correspondences analogous to a totalising worldview that remains nonetheless deeply sceptical of the suppression of particularity.

Acrylic Tips begins:

> Assuming banishment for lost time back across nullity
>   in speck-through marking worthless eyelash, strict
> blast of sand eggplant prone, tampered dune how fast
>   the grievance solitary; krook pathways risen up
>
>
> To wheel and turn about spandrels high over submission
>   flexed to burnish and chomp get hungry for intimate
> newsy entrances.

Perhaps guided by a play on Browning's 'Childe Roland to the Dark Tower Came', I feel no strain in picturing a ruined landscape here, buffeted by sand, maybe engineered by survivors to support eggplant crops for sustenance. There is a lone figure walking, as if banished from their past life. Arbitrary fragments of the society that preceded the destruction seem to have survived, either as cosmetic eyelashes or ruined architectures, decadently forged pathways and portals around the now ruined city. Of course this is not all that is going on in these lines, but increased attention to the narratives operative throughout Prynne's poetry, as well as Prynne's own interest in narratives, seems integral to an enjoyment and deeper understanding of the poems' operative functions, as well as their engagement with broader poetic traditions.[9] Beyond poetic fiction, Andrea Brady has powerfully read the "politically interpolated topoi" threaded through *Acrylic Tips*, witnessing genetic mutations and the intertwining of American foreign and domestic policies.[10] At least part of the complexity of Prynne's poetic thinking stems from the simultaneous pressures of a commitment to poetic fiction and a sense of lived injustice. The blurb to the original *Poems* referred to this as a 'breadth of imaginative and political reference'.

One obvious aspect of *Acrylic Tips* that cannot be described as 'heady pulp' is the quality of the paper on which it is printed. Prynne's own riffs on poetry's material status, as in *Not-You*'s oblique recognition that the book's readers are "causing the forest / to fail softly by watching leaves turn", find a deeper corollary in the continued counterpoint that poetic form provides to the content encountered.[11] In *Acrylic Tips*, a single reading, or cursory glance through, will confirm that, however haemorrhaged the subject matter, the whole is confined to 10 poems each of 6 four-line stanzas, arranged into a conventional but elegant spacing on the page, with perhaps slightly longer line-lengths than might otherwise be expected. Such an appearance of conventionality at the level of form is fairly typical of Prynne's sequences from *For the Monogram* up to *Streak¬¬¬Willing¬¬¬Entourage¬¬¬¬Artesian*. Any sensation of formal arbitrariness comes up against the forms' real potential for signification, as line-endings, breaks between stanzas, beginnings, middles, or endings cause the poems' contents to tremble and shine. The variation of formal schemes from sequence to sequence focuses this emotive artifice to engender different ambiences, imposing a different kind of stillness on the operations of the poems. The various stillnesses come to form a contradictory dynamic with the energetic concern of the poems' content.

In individual book form, removed from subsequent collection, the poems' formal stillness can be elided in a sense of occasion. *Kazoo Dreamboats or, On What There Is* originally had a dedication that, unusually, was excised when it was included in *Poems*: "For the Jinling patriots".[12] The reference is obscure, perhaps referring to a community related to the Nanjing group of poets whose work Prynne had featured in *Parataxis 7*, but at least signposts that the poem is embedded in some part of the social world. Elsewhere, the publication of *Kazoo Dreamboats* was marked by the 2011 occupation of the Lady Mitchell Hall at the University of Cambridge, in protest against the government's dismantling of higher education. Copies of *Kazoo Dreamboats* were available at the occupation, and Prynne read from the poem for the occupiers. This was recorded, and is available via the Archive of the Now. It is a powerful recording, beginning with an introduction from Prynne that places the poem within an explicit context of resistance and solidarity. The reading includes an airing of the first half of Cui Jian's 'Yi Wu Suoyou' at the moment where *Kazoo Dreamboats* incorporates its English title: "for I had nothing at all".[13] Prynne's introduction to his reading explains that Cui Jian was one of the first practitioners of Chinese rock music, oppressed by Chinese authorities fearful of his influence over huge numbers of Chinese fans, with 'Yi Wu Suoyou' ultimately taken up as an anthem for the Chinese youth and activist movement involved in the protests of the late 1980s. Its performance at the occupation worked to establish a network of historical resonance, most obviously between the occupying students and the Chinese student movement that found resolve and purpose in the song.

The appearance of music in the recording has the additional effect of throwing the poetry into relief, a redemptive solo from a reeded instrument shining out in the performance's context as an intimation of the revolutionary energies the song was able to harness and guide, perhaps intended for recuperation in the hands of the occupiers. The sentence that immediately followed this solo in performance is sobering: "Fluting awash previous sure to find on the margin affront no big thing offset intercepted for fluid introits".[14] This is a model for the possibility of the present meaningfully engaging with the past. It is as if the reed solo had washed up from a distant shore, our contemporary awareness suggesting that its historical pertinence was no more than a kind of bluster. The sentence plays on liquidity; triggered by 'awash' there is the heard presence of a 'shore', and 'fluting' dissolves into 'fluid introits'. These 'introits' have a readily apparent etymological sense that suggests entrance passageways for water to flow through, as if the flute ended up on the shore a channel for lapping waves. Of course, there is also a liturgical sense, with wild fluting 'intercepted' to become the ritualized music of a church service. 'Intercepted' stems any suggestion that the fluting was predestined to lose its original import. It implies an active agency doing the intercepting that is also operative in 'no big thing', where the casual turn of phrase works in a similar manner to Adorno's use of English lifestyle jargon in *Minima Moralia*, evoking a contemptible figure whose very turns of phrase become the concealed site of a violent repression.[15] The suggestion is not, then, that a document of revolutionary energy is always already doomed to dissipate into the stillness of form, but rather that there are forces keen to give the sense that that is the case.

Maintaining an awareness of the vital energies of an artefact received from the past is figured throughout *Kazoo Dreamboats* as paying real attention to the continued existence of contradictions. While the reading at the Lady Mitchell Hall did not include the poem's rhapsodic vision of Mao's essay 'On Contradiction', it began by attending to that which is "nowhere near contradicted nor in show trials of adversary forensic lubricants", the blunt fact of "weapon system aggression" and its feverish exclusion from the well-oiled machines of public law courts and spectacle, and went through to the poem's conclusion, the site of its foundational contradiction.[16] The poem ends with a transition "from particulate vapour to consign into bedrock".[17] Following a quotation from Richard Bradley's archaeological work on monumental burial sites, this finite process of transformation is guided by the claim that the poem will continue to be "this song", "toiling and spinning", in counter-point to the presumed stasis of bedrock, evoking the earth rolling around its diurnal course.[18] Prynne first quotes from Bradley fairly early on in *Kazoo Dreamboats*, the issue of closure quickly becoming germane to the poem through Prynne's subsequent analysis of the quote: "'Monuments refer to a past but they are often directed to a future', to be made open is to know of its closure by way of being made, the way of derived difference semi-permeable by fate looked out for, not now viewed".[19] The complex temporality of a monument, aiming to inform as well as guide, becomes a way of figuring the ambitions of the poem. In an encounter with a monument, the onlooker necessarily becomes aware of their difference to the object, sensing either its material or formal qualities as something distinct to themselves and their time. In Shelley's 'Ozymandias', this encounter is ironic and sobering, the monument evidently having misjudged its relation to the future. Prynne is attentive to the possibility that feeling removed from the world of the monument might in fact lead to the sensation of a "fate looked out for, not now viewed", a future-oriented sense of kinship between the time of now and the time of the monument's creation, born from the recognition that the monument strove to remove itself from its time, and resisting a sense of universal demise that is otherwise all too easily apprehended.[20]

The monument under Bradley's archaeological investigation was the recumbent stone circle at Tomnaverie. A recumbent stone circle's most prominent feature is a long horizontally placed stone constituting one chunk of the circle's circumference, flanked by a portal formed of two tall and vertically upright stones. Bradley explains that the recumbent stone circle at Tomnaverie came about through a multi-staged process of construction "extended over a significant period of time" at a location "precisely aligned on the moon just once every eighteen and a half years".[21] Stratigraphic analysis suggested that the core of the monument was at first a cremation pyre on the summit of the hill. A large cairn was subsequently built around the pyre. Finally, this cairn was enlarged and a recumbent stone circle was constructed around it. As the cremation pyre transformed into the portal blocked by the recumbent stone, Bradley describes the relationships of the place to its surroundings on earth and in space as receiving "monumental expression". While the pyre had served to link deceased ancestors to the sky and the distant mountains through the ascension of smoke, the sense of closure provided by the installation of the large and weighty recumbent stone preventing easy passage through the surrounding portal indicated that "[t]he monument was closed to the living and only the light of the moon could cross the recumbent stone to illuminate the dead".[22] Still, "[e]very generation, the moon returned to its original position in the night sky".[23] This is a monument that looks forward with the present as it memorialises the lived life, punctuated by ritual, that went into its construction.

Prynne has on occasion been sceptical of the degree to which the creation and orientation of Neolithic monuments was predicated upon scientific knowledge, saying of Stonehenge and Avebury: "[t]hey never thought they would work. Oh, never. I mean, they were chance shots. Like, sooner or later it must come round again, and it must come round again because it was wanted: and if it was wanted, it would come".[24] It is significant then that *Kazoo Dreamboats, or On What There Is*, closes with an expression of the desire "[t]o be this". The monumental expression of Prynne's poetry cannot be guaranteed, although the conditions of longing for its possibility are carefully prepared for. An earlier poem by Prynne was already thinking of this:

If you set your mind to it, the words
tell you the first levels are free ones,
only the end is fixed by its need
to be freely led up to. And for me
all levels are held but the last,
the parting shot I don't dream of
but see every day. [25]

The placement of the recumbent stone is a fixed end that retroactively makes all the moments in its construction appear preordained to arrive at one point. Prynne's work is compelled by the possibility of maintaining a semblance of autonomous freedom, of alternative possibilities, within every moment that precedes the final statement of construction, even as the actual creation of a monument establishes a fixity and purpose capable of withstanding the kinds of fluidity that 'Yi Wu Suoyou' seemed victim to, something solid that will not melt into air. This would be the 'fixed' monument that is nonetheless 'freely led up to'. Embedded in *Poems*, *Kazoo Dreamboats*' evocative use of Bradley and monumentality comes to speak for the volume as a whole. The elision of 'For the Jinling Patriots' shifts focus away from the poem's connection to any historical place, time, and community, as the *Poems*' dedication 'For the Future' highlights the monumental aspirations put forward in *Kazoo Dreamboats* and latent in the poetry as a whole.

Importantly, *Poems*' 'parting shot' is not *Kazoo Dreamboats*. Prynne's subsequent collection *Al-Dente* enhances the creation of a monument by being filled with addresses to the reader, while its final poem, 'For Tom' ensures the collected poems maintain a trace of the personal affection commemorated in past dedications. Critics of Prynne's later work have identified an almost hatefully antagonistic attitude towards the subjectivity of their reader, with Joe Luna identifying a "kind of ugly imperative" in *Biting the Air*, "a poem which is constantly telling us to *do* things".[26] Keston Sutherland has expanded on this, suggesting that these imperatives, which are "demonstratively forever unable to be performed" are deployed in order to demonstrate "the impotence of the subject to be where truth is", locating truth instead "only at the extremes of language where the subject has been exceeded and is no longer required".[27] *Al-Dente* resists this approach to readerly subjectivity, its few poems all offering themselves up repeatedly: "all yet yours", "Yours / in readiness, "all your / own", "is yours". One of the few imperatives of the collection is a simple plea repeated as if a refrain in 'Subsequence': "share your own".[28] While *Kazoo Dreamboats* fixes the end of the monument's construction, *Al-Dente* recognises that this monument must be met. The sequence is at pains to present itself as an object to be encountered and responded to. Its tendency towards hesitant, stuttering repetition becomes a mark of considered vulnerability, a dialectic of insistence and changing opinion most present in 'Morning's mannered equivocations: these are poems "[f]or the for you / and these to hold, to on".[29] The offerings to the reader are in turn matched by a sense of plentiful abundance and loyalty: "brim over plainly moreover", "fill to all loyal found".[30] Readerly subjectivity comes to be a vital force for the poems and their futurity, and the poems want to show themselves as a source of trust and encouragement for their reader. The subject is required and welcomed, as only then can the monument be felt to exceed itself. None of this devalues the profoundly negative sense of despair that is put to work elsewhere in Prynne's poetic work. Such despair is allowed to enter monumental time, to be made historical, as the enduring heat and pressures of geological process are made bearably visible in crystals, just like the one that now adorns the cover of Prynne's *Poems*.

NOTES

[1] J. H. Prynne, *Poems* (Hexham, 2015) p.4 and p.5

[2] J. H. Prynne, *Poems* (Edinburgh & London, 1982). The lines referred to are from 'The Numbers': "The whole thing it is, the difficult matter: to shrink the confines / down."

[3] *Poems*, p.223

[4] It is perhaps demonstrative of a more general readerly attitude of the time to note that the same issue of *Grosseteste Review* that includes Oliver's reading also has a review of Prynne's *Down Where Changed* by Anthony Barnett that is almost entirely constituted of quotes from that book interwoven into a prose argument: a dedication to the effacement of criticism delivered as criticism.

[5] Prynne's later work on historical phonology would take seriously the potential relevance of musical concerns as they relate specifically to poetry, cf. e.g. *Stars, Tigers and the Shape of Words*; The William Matthews Lectures, 1992 (London, 1993) and 'Mental Ears and Poetic Work', *Chicago Review*, Vol. 55 No. 1 (Winter 2010), 126-57

[6] *Hix Eros* 4 84

[7] ibid.

[8] 84-85

[9] One example of such interest is made clear in a letter Prynne wrote to a translator of the epic of *Gilgamesh*, printed as 'Letter to Dr Andrew George, c/o Penguin Books' in *Quid*, 5 (August 2000): 2-7. The significance of the *Gilgamesh* narrative to Prynne's poetic thinking was in turn drawn out by Justin Katko in 'Sex – *Triodes* – Gilgamesh', *Hix Eros* 4, 43-49. Prynne's engagement with narrative poetry would bear fruitful comparison with the contemporaneous practice of Edward Dorn, Alice Notley and Douglas Oliver.

[10] Andrea Brady, 'No Turning Back: *Acrylic Tips*' in *Quid* 17 (June 2006), 80-83, 80

[11] *Poems*, p.407

[12] *Kazoo Dreamboats* (Cambridge, 2011), p.3

[13] *Poems*, p.656 . On the *Archive of the Now* recording, the music starts around 17:30, available via <http://www.archiveofthenow.org/

[14] *Poems*, p.656

[15] cf. e.g. the use of 'relax and take it easy' in Theodor Adorno, *Minima Moralia*, trans Dennis Redmond in Marxists Internet Archive, <https://www.marxists.org/reference/archive/adorno/1951/mm/ch03.htm>

[16] *Poems*, p.654

[17] *Poems*, p.661

[18] ibid

[19] *Poems*, p.644

[20] Prynne's thinking can perhaps be seen as a development of Wordsworth's view in his 'Essay Upon Epitaphs', where epitaphs inscribed on monuments are said to arise from and inculcate "an intimation or assurance within us, that some part of our nature is imperishable" (William Wordsworth, *Poetical Works*, ed. Thomas Hutchinson, rev Ernest de Sélincourt (London, 1936), p.729).

[21] Richard Bradley, 'The Land, the Sky and the Scottish Stone Circle' in Chris Scarne (ed.), *Monuments and Landscape in Atlantic Europe; Perception and Society during the Neolithic and Early Bronze* Age (London, 2002), p.136

[22] ibid.

[23] ibid, p.137

[24] J. H. Prynne, 'Lectures on *Maximus IV, V, VI* (Vancouver, 1971), available online at <http://charlesolson.org/Files/Prynnelecture2.htm>

[25] J. H. Prynne, 'Bolt' in *Poems*, p. 274

[26] Joe Luna *Hix Eros* 4, 88

[27] Keston Sutherland *Hix Eros* 4, 141

[28] *Poems*, p.670

[29] *Poems*, p.667

[30] *Poems*, p.671

Hearing Light

Iain Sinclair

'A picture is not a window'
—*J.H. Prynne*

For a few years poetry seemed to be the heart of it. And *Mr Prynne*—as black letters announced at the foot of his college staircase—was the heart of the heart, the nucleus. Those books were the news that stayed news. Before becoming something else, something more. Slender originals now take their inevitable position in the digital market place as rare and desirable objects with a significant price tag. Hard evidence of a better time. Or that is the pitch.

Nothing I've stumbled across in later days has persuaded me that any work coming out of these islands has more bite and burn than the independent poetry published and performed between, very roughly, 1968 and 1979. Of course the story rolls on; different streams, fresh internet fields. But the glaze of sentiment for that awakening, for *Kitchen Poems*, *The White Stones*, *Brass*, *Into the Day*, still dazzles and provokes. The liquid screen is not a pond to which we can return for reflections of younger, slimmer, brighter selves. The dedication to the 2015 edition of Prynne's *Poems* reads: 'For the Future'. And that was always, as the politicians and boosters say, the direction of travel. Moving briskly forward, while waiting for the past to happen again, and happen better. The integrity of the original curve is respected but it doesn't run out. There is barely even a pause. The poet chooses to publish in mirror image of accepted practice: from established, decently staid firm to hip mainstream (a captured independent about to be captured once more by bigger pirates); through alert and visible small press to self-perpetuated cottage industry.

Coming to Cambridge in 1971, with Christopher Bamford, a friend and collaborator from Dublin, to spend an afternoon with Jeremy Prynne, set up the decade. We had found our own way to Olson, Dorn, Creeley, looking west, but this conversation recalibrated those perceptions and nudged what was required, by way of close listening, to another place. I'd missed the fertile exchanges of *The English Intelligencer* years, and missed, therefore, raw exposure to the expected poets, Tom Raworth, Lee Harwood, Andrew Crozier, John Riley, Peter Riley, John James, Barry MacSweeney, Chris Torrance, but also early notice of those unexpected participants, J.G. Ballard and Jeff Nuttall.

Prynne dropped in one night on his way through Hackney in his Morris Traveller (or was it a bigger station-wagon?). He indulged a doubtless interminable 8mm flicker-film deluge, before revealing that he had *met* Stan Brakhage; visited him, probably corresponded. On his desk, when I returned, through those muffling double doors, to the rooms in Caius, I seem to remember, although I might be conflating several discrete occasions, twin piles of paper; the Rosetta Stone scratchings of Stephen Hawking and Charles Olson, in the process of being finessed, edited in some mysterious way by the only person capable of running with both. In my unreliable scenario, typescript heaps are shuffled and interwoven to reveal impossible cosmic truths. Black hole singularities burn through the stapled sheets Prynne gave me, around that time; the transcript of his lecture, 'On Maximus IV, V & VI', at Simon Fraser University. 'The curvature of the universe is love. I mean, you can know that; I mean, you can feel it; I mean it's just unmistakable. Some people can get it just like that from the night sky, for other people, I suppose, it takes a little longer.'

Or a whole lot longer. Or forever. But the letters, the generous response to fugitive publications, helped. There were no tooth-rotting confectionaries on offer; as Prynne confessed, he was not given 'to handing out fudge at parties'. But the crystalline pattern of those phrases in that black calligraphy? Braille hot-needled onto the eyeballs. The challenge was floated for as long as we believed it. And now, when the Prynne archive is assembled for inspection, we'll discover the full scope of the engagement with a range of British (American and European) poets. Intimate readings, where invited, for locals; proper arguments offered as if to peers. And help with grant applications, court summonses, academic business.

Letters shadowed production, as self-published chapbooks and pamphlets swam through the postal service. I see that Prynne was prepared to follow the pitch from first typescript to finished object, registering slight shifts as they happened, sometimes as a consequence of his critique. Until the point was achieved, in my case with *Lud Heat*, where I felt protective of an unruly text that, in its prose sections, was writing itself faster than I could adequately transcribe it, and the ears were stoppered against useful dissent. The book could be wrong, ethically or culturally, in its own way, as it stepped outside the fire-circle purity of what the best poetry of that era was attempting. And achieving.

By the close of the Seventies, with the dawn of Thatcherism, it was time to strike the tent. I'd written myself into an endgame and started to locate the psychopathology Chris Petit identified, in another context, as vacillating between paranoia and inertia. (Or, when he was feeling more upbeat, between drift and fracture.) I took to the road as a used-book dealer with a stall in Camden Passage, Islington, and occasional catalogues as my only form of publication. Nothing visible appeared between 1979 and 1987. But the itch was still there, to make a new start, putting aside reflex tricks I thought I'd learned, and working with fragments, offprints of a journal never kept. Here was the pride of the electively disenfranchised. I distributed three minimalist booklets, as unwelcome gifts, to a diminishing group of correspondents. The second of these, *Flesh Eggs & Scalp Metal*, a dyslexic desktop wafer, in an edition of twelve numbered copies, opened with an epigram from the Irish runaway, Francis Stuart: 'Everything is verboten... that isn't obligatory.'

Dates, locations and quotes track my random movements in pursuit of rumoured book shoals. Records of overnight lodgings, rarities snacked before they were sold, cinematic enthusiasms of the moment: Buñuel, Framlingham, Fassbinder, Glastonbury, Penzance, Sax Rohmer. And Cambridge. On 9 August 1983, I found myself kneeling beside the Cam. A short walk after some fruitless search or forgotten event. I was stopped in my tracks by the recognition of the home address found on a letter from Jeremy Prynne. My impressionistic sketching was nothing in itself, but it reminded me of paths not taken. And rivers still unswum.

A FEW HUNDRED YARDS FROM
THE DWELLING OF MR PRYNNE

...under slow flume,
        a net of pubic mosses

The Fort Saint George in England

sculls sweating fossil evidence
    of discontinued futures

Ecxcelsior!

so honour the moment: dip hand
        in moving water

This isn't what I wrote. Or published. Or revised in 2006. But that's how it comes through in February 2016. The original chapbook, wrappered in greaseproof paper, is a grey fossil from the river. A handmade paste-on label with the woodcut of a 'Plague costume as worn at the Marseilles outbreak of 1720'. And a final note addressed to the book-hustler Gerry X. 'This is what I meant, when you asked about usury. This isn't it. Your hands stay clean...' Gerry sold his inscribed copy and it finished in some American vault. He's mute now in a South London hospice.

I made the transaction with Jeremy Prynne, and received, on 10th December 1983, a copy of his own self-curated book, *The Oval Window.* A very unequal exchange, Gerry: my road-kill splatter-fragments for this intense, mediated and mesmerising *sequence.* 'The enclosed transgression goes back indeed into the border of darkness,' Prynne reported on his complimentary slip.

I was taken at once by the cover. Prynne's productions were, by habit, austere in the classical French style. Even the author's name out front could feel like a transgression. *Kitchen Poems* (1968) had that Olsonian North Sea oil-exploration chart. *Aristeas* (1968) reproduces a 14th-century drawing from the Topkapi Saray Library in Istanbul. *The White Stones* (1969) had a geometric design, based on stones somebody claimed to have seen in the poet's possession. *The Oval Window,* a gathering I connected with *The White Stones*, on no firm evidence, was the first one with a photographic design, full page, around front and back covers. Maybe that link was with a sense of place, or my partiality for stones and winter landscapes and 'the smell of diesel oil' on the road to the mountains.

So *The Oval Window* opened at the right time, in the lull of the lost years, between drift and fracture, with the promise of the hole in the jigsaw of the dry stone wall (much more enticing than the figure in Henry James's carpet). No mortar. No fudge handed out at literary parties. These northern barriers—keeping sheep in or out—are concerned with structural integrity, compressed forces, the interlocking of found or cut stones. I might be giving the image too much weight? The title and author's name, free-floating in the white window, could vanish in the blink of an eye. Because whatever that spoiled rectangle, the gap in the stones, presents, it isn't an oval window. 'A view is a window/ on the real data.' And the real data is all inside, in blocks and slates and bifurcating falls of native water.

At home, at night, I was fired by the play of this book and the diagnostic chart it feinted to offer. It was the usual story—failing faster, failing better—of trying to experience the rapid slide of words, without understand or breaking them down into questions that could be answered. Physiologically, something happened. Phrases, in sound and below sense, lodged. 'The internal view/ assumes an infinite linear address space.' Commentators were taken with that shocking news-clip in quotation marks: 'her mouth was sealed up by the burns'. I flickered, with a comforting sense of encountering the same morsel, again and again, in different places. Yes, there was structural integrity and compression, but there was also the kick, the twist, the submerged quotation, before the argument is brought back to its fixed terms: *window, view, fire, sea, snow*. And NCR cashpoint. And huddling against the force of wind at a listening post that is 'not quite a cabin'. Resting in a huddle against the dry stone wall. 'You listen out by the oval window, as/ calm waves flow onwards to the horizon.'

I was re-making the book, pebble by pebble, from a coherent structure: from its achieved tension to broken eggshells on the table (more like the nest of white stones). I had missed the major key, but there was no particular hurry; *The Oval Window* was staying close at hand. And there is always an energy specific to the first printing, to the way the poet chose to set up and distribute the book. It's quite a different thing when it reappears as part of the collected *Poems* in 1999. A collection that is *not* dedicated to 'the Future' but to the memory of Bernard Dubourg, Prynne's French translator. When the life-poems are brought together, there is gain, cumulative glints and glances on a much broader front; but the performance is less intimate. The original has the excitement and challenge of a letter thrust into the hand.

Then came a day when I met Prynne for lunch in Cambridge and walked across from his college to an Italian place, close to the market. The meat of our encounter was a narrative laid out somewhere close to the act of composition for *The Oval Window.* I was engrossed with following an account of, first, urgency; then, resolution. Quest achieved. The Cambridge poet's position in the hierarchy, the status of scholarship, the doors that sung open for a member of an old college in an old university, registered. Phone calls were made. Complicated arrangements brokered in the blink of an eye. It was like Jack London telling Thomas Cook to book him a passage into the lower depths of the East End. But Prynne was travelling north, far north, to some empty quarter; an urgent expedition involving overnight sleepers, and permissions, in triplicate, to invade secret state land that didn't show up on regular Ordnance Survey maps.

I was so hooked by this tale, with its traces of John Buchan and Hitchcock, that I barely noticed, if it really happened, the flash of the gold card that took care of our meal. I should have paid closer attention to the poems. 'Making excuses for the money numbers ahead.' 'Unofficial window on Treasury policy.' 'Wired up/ from the NCR cashpoint.' Credit is still a major runway into the territory. Why not? Use what there is. Use the tools available to you.

The afternoon resolves, the time available for this post-prandial exchange, through quiet paths and privileged ways into a private garden. Fellows' Garden? I couldn't be sure. A bench that must have been waiting for a conclusion to this story that would never come. I did recognise the pink outline of a house belonging to Caius, decorated internally by Serge Chermayeff, who collaborated on the De La Warr Pavilion in Bexhill. I'd been there, once, for a summer wedding reception on the lawn. The house was famous for its firework parties. The original design was by Raymond McGrath for Mansfield Forbes. When Sir Nikolaus Pevsner inspected the later division, under commission from Caius, into two distinctive houses, he remarked: 'What a tragedy!'

Journey's end for Prynne's *Oval Window* adventure involved a free pass through a series of manned gates: three of them, as in all the best myths. And then he was there, at the place where he had to be. Left alone in the weather. To get the job done. *Where? What job?* As soon as I was back in London, I took down my copy of the book from the shelf. 'Back indeed into the border of darkness.' I couldn't relate what I was reading to what I'd just been told. The word patterns fizzed and sparked, as before, warning me off, drawing me on. 'The sod roof almost gone.'

So now we find ourselves swept up in another complicated journey, part done, part in the future, documented fiction, a triangulation between three tricky to access mounds: Whitechapel, Oxford, Cambridge. The darkest singularity with which I've been involved, a book constructed around the inevitability of its own dissolution. The extract from *Radon Daughters* to which I was drawn back from time to time came in Book Two, Chapter Twelve. Another riverside setting, not unlike the Cambridge moment beside the Cam, but emerging from the heady pleasures of an early morning stroll through the Botanic Gardens in Oxford.

> 'Now the willows on the river are hazy like mist/ and the end is hazy like the meaning.' Helen, an unopened booklet resting in her lap, has arranged herself at a particular spot, not previously known, where lightly-weathered steps descend into the water. Unmoving, she appreciates the cool of the morning, the filtered bleach of light. She is here, waiting and not waiting, studiously disengaged...
>
> The slight weight of the card-covered book is, relatively, no weight at all. Face down (a dry stone wall, black intervals). So that, were she to prise the thing open, she would have to read from the back, come early on the poem with the river and the willows. ('Willow branches dip.') But the point, here, is *not* to read; to carry, appreciate the potential of just such an object. It does not insist, not yet. She picks it up, runs her hands over the monochrome cover, looks away... Helen's book

is complemented by a fresh white skirt. The poems rest across the raised declivities of her bare legs. Crisp cotton folds. The dampness of the grass soaks her dusty feet: light gold sandals.

'Calm is all nature as a resting wheel.' Breath is thought. On the far bank, branches heavy with leaf decline towards the turbid surface of the rivulet; dull reflections throw back an alternate woodland, shivering in the sluggish drift. Helen hoists an ankle across her thigh, slips off the sandal, stretches out her foot, smooth and high-arched, places it, hesitant, in the water...

She wrapped the booklet in her towel. 'Denial... always leads to political errors, of an/ essentially Trotskyist order.'

I barely remember how it felt to have the space to write this kind of book, but I do remember the willows, the river and the morning. *The Oval Window* was never there, as an object, until I invented the episode at my Hackney desk. I picked up on the Wordsworth quote about 'Calm is all nature' from a sonnet written when he was sixteen. But the 'wheel' was also a reminder of 'Lull's Device', a set of Zodiac wheels used for divination. (Not too promising in the cast made for this present text: 'Panic, Wrath, Blindness'.) And the symbol that carried me out of the trap of *Downriver*. 'Long enough to unspool twelve parallel wheels of fate, twelve concurrent dreams... Now there is a quality of yolky golden light revolving in a benign cartwheel... A spinning nimbus of maize and bees and song. A bowling hoop of sticky radiance: wasps, wax, feathers, corndust... across the estuary towards the cancelled land.'

This wheel owes more to Prynne than to Wordsworth and it isn't 'resting'. It's busy, a flaming fire-hoop to burn down a fortress of wooden stakes. Echoes are nothing more than echoes, the mush of acoustic footsteps hissing around the motorway fringe. Or the terrifying chatter of the dead a smacked-out junkie heard coming down the tracks, when he swam to the surface of consciousness after his latest binge, in an elevated railway cabin, out near Willesden Junction.

> The blur spot on both sides gives out
> a low, intense hum, sharp-folded as
> if to a feral rafter;
>
>   the field is determined

by the *exit window*, the lens rim or stop
which, imaged into image space, subtends
the smallest angle at the centre.

I knew that I hadn't listened with sharp enough ears to that low
hum, the voices in play. But even my trust in image was misplaced.
I wasn't a close reader of the frame. After the story on the bench in
the private garden, I should have picked up on the dry stone wall as a
shelter. 'It is not quite a cabin… the sod roof almost gone.'

Years later, after some Cambridge reading, drinks in Prynne's room,
another poet pointed out the Ordnance Survey map with the relevant
location. The base point was as firm and as floating as the reflection of
the mountain in Wordsworth's lake. There were cadres of interpreters,
now, like an Enigma rattle from Bletchley Park, sifting over the wheels of
text, eviscerating etymological dictionaries, teasing out Shakespearean
appropriations. *Richard II, All's Well that Ends Well?* Echoes, echoes.
Echo's Bones: 'mocked by a tissue that may not serve'. They are teaching
themselves Mandarin in the noble ambition to authenticate experience.
Like those charming literalists labouring through one of Charles Olson's
projective reading lists. While missing, entirely, their own footing on
the path through a thorn hedge.

Dumb to the end (mouth sealed up by burns), I recognised, too
late, the thing that was right in front of me, the book's title: that the
'oval window' was a technical term (among its other aspects). A part
of the ear. 'By ear, he sd./ But that which matters, that which insists,
that which will last…' BY EAR. 'An oval opening at the head of the
cochlea, connecting the middle and inner ear, through which sound
vibrations of the stapes are transmitted.' And the scholars present
medical charts, cross-section slices, in their Prynne dissertations.
External auditory canals that look just like the map of Gloucester on
the cover of the Jargon/Corinth edition of *The Maximus Poems*: inner
and outer harbour, Blynman Canal. There are skin-embedded, hidden
instruments by which we orientate ourselves, once we have travelled to
the place where we need to be.

I had my own problems with readings of *Radon Daughters*, also a
technical term. In garbled introductions and casual listings, the book
appeared as *Radon's Daughters*, as if it should be displayed as a romance
of the Celtic type, something to be butchered by David Lean with a

sleepwalking Robert Mitchum in priest's drag. Like a soap opera *Lear*. Instead of an attempt to signal the book's interest in the decay products of radon gas, gamma radiation, subterranean X-rays, and addiction to bad magnetism. This was, in its heavy-handed fashion, my most Prynne-influenced title. Sisters from Bristol took the name—from their own researches? from the book?—for their gimmick as musicians, performers. Now the terminology has also decayed, to the less seductive, but more politically correct 'Radon Progeny'. 'The solid radon progeny are deposited on the soil and water below, entering into the food chain and hence the bodies of birds, animals, fish and insects.' Premonitions of Olympic enclosures in the Lower Lea Valley. Fouled water table. Right title, wrong book.

Prynne's productions, arriving at irregular intervals as part of a sustained but fractured conversation, or acquired from the shallows of the antiquarian trade, were transfusions of spirit. And goads to reach out, further and faster. 'The years/ jostle and burn up.' The books informed, at some level or another, the harder pieces I attempted. In this game, there are no retakes. The story told on the bench in that garden was, it strikes me, a detonation in slow-motion. Like the climax of *Zabriskie Point* without the desert clarity. I'm almost ready for it now. Focus is softer but sound waves are still travelling down the tunnel. There are no resting wheels, but a few ditches and perimeter fences alongside English roads. 'This window is the perilymph of the vestibule.' A vestibule not yet entered. As Prynne said to me, in a latter sent on 6 April 1990: 'You have to see past what you see first, the featureless screen of empty distraction is the necessary pre-condition for striking the anvil.' And isn't the incus an anvil-shaped bone of the middle ear, a receiver of vibrations? Hearing light in its waxy passage. The satisfaction of waking to the challenge of another day, another cup of green tea with set-aside books piled, defensively, beside the bed. 'The smaller crises are equally intense,' Prynne warned, 'half-hidden and burning within their momentary frame-holds.'

Contributors

Masahiko Abe is an Associate Professor in English at the University of Tokyo. He did his BA and MA at the University of Tokyo and PhD at Cambridge University. His recent publications include *Politeness and English Literature: Examing the Kindness of the Narrator* (2015) and *Talking Like Children Helps: Strategy of Infantilism in Japanese Literature* (2015).

Anthony Barnett is the author of *Poems &* (2012), *Translations* (2012), *Antonyms Anew: Barbs & Loves* (2016), *UnNatural Music: John Lennon & Yoko Ono in Cambridge 1969* (2016), and co-editor of *Snow lit rev*, all Allardyce Book ABP.

Ian Brinton's recent publications include translations of Ponge (Oystercatcher), two volumes of translations of Yves Bonnefoy (Oystercatcher), editions of Andrew Crozier's work: *'Free Verse as Formal Restraint'* and *Thrills and Frills*, (Shearsman Books), an *Andrew Crozier Reader* (Carcanet Press); *An Intuition of the Particular, the Poetry of Peter Hughes*; *A Manner of Utterance, the poetry of J.H. Prynne* (both from Shearsman Books), and *Contemporary Poetry since 1990* (Cambridge University Press). He co-edits *Tears in the Fence* and *SNOW* and is on the committee setting up the new archive of Contemporary Poetry at Cambridge University Library.

David Caddy is a poet, essayist, and critic. He lives in rural Dorset from where he has edited the international literary journal *Tears in the Fence* since 1984. His most recent books are *Cycling After Thomas And The English* (Spout Hill Press 2013), recreating the poet Edward Thomas' 1913 cycle ride from Clapham Common to Salisbury; a book of poetry essays, *So Here We Are* (Shearsman Books, 2012) and *The Bunny Poems* (Shearsman, 2011).

Elaine Feinstein has lived as a poet, novelist and biographer for more than fifty years. Her versions of the Russian poet Marina Tsvetaeva was a *New York Times* Book of the Year and have remained in print since 1971. Her most recent book of poems is *Portraits* (Carcanet Press, 2015).

Ian Friend was born in Eastbourne, East Sussex, and attended art schools in Eastbourne, Exeter, Birmingham and London, completing postgraduate studies at the Slade School of Fine Art, University College, London. After living and working in London until 1985, he left for Melbourne, Australia to take up a teaching position and residency at the Victorian College of the Arts. He has lived and worked in Melbourne, Ballarat, Launceston and Brisbane during the past 30 years. He has worked and exhibited solely as an artist for the past 5 years and recently moved to Ipswich, 40 kms west of Brisbane to continue making art and breeding several different species of native fish in the large pond at the back of the property.

Harry Gilonis is a poet, editor, publisher, and occasionally critic. A long interest in the poetics of (mis)translation has included amongst its product *North Hills*, a project of 'faithless' re-castings of classical Chinese poetry. Selections have appeared in chapbooks and as a full-length book, *eye-blink*, from Veer Books; there was also a spin-off talk on revolutionary Chinese poetics, presented at the May 2012 London 'Poetry and Revolution' conference (and reprinted in a recent issue of *Tripwire* from Oakland, CA). His most recent publication highlights poetry of <u>successful</u> revolution, by Mayakovsky and others: *For British Workers*, out from Barque Press.

Peter Gizzi's most recent books include *In Defense of Nothing: Selected Poems* (2014), *Threshold Songs* (2011) and *The Outernationale* (2007). A new book, *Archeophonics,* is forthcoming this fall. He is currently the Judith E. Wilson Visiting Fellow in Poetry at Cambridge University.

Michael Grant was an undergraduate at Caius between 1959 and 1962, where he studied English under the guidance of, amongst others, Donald Davie and Jeremy Prynne. He subsequently taught English at the University of Kent, before, in the early 1980s, moving into Film. His publications include *T. S. Eliot: The Critical Heritage* (1982), as well as studies of the films of David Cronenberg, Lucio Fulci and Stanley Kubrick. He has also published poetry, the most recent volumes being *The White Theatre* and *Cinderella's Ashtray*, from vErisimillitUdE. He and Ian Brinton have collaborated on translations of Yves Bonnefoy published by Oystercatcher Press.

John Hall is a poet, essayist and recently (mostly) retired teacher. There have been two complementary selections of his poems (*Else Here* and *Keepsache*, both <u>etruscan books</u>), two volumes of essays (Shearsman Books) and a number of exhibitions of or including his visual texts. Most of his teaching was at Dartington College of Arts, where the arts were easily seen as entangled with each other and as needing each other's thought. In recent years he has enjoyed collaborating with others (Emily Critchley, Lee Harwood, Peter Hughes, Simon Murray, Ian Tyson).

Matthew Hall holds a PhD from the University of Western Australia, and presently teaches in Melbourne, where he lives with his family. He has published extensively on British late-modern poetry and poetics, including a recent monograph *On Violence in the Work of J.H. Prynne* (Cambridge Scholars Publishing, 2015). His fifth collection of poems, *False Fruits*, will be released in 2015. Hall is the Feature Editor at *Cordite Poetry Review* and is in the process of writing a critical monograph on Indigenous Australian poet Lionel Fogarty.

Michael Haslam was born in Bolton in 1947, spent the years 1965-68 at Cambridge University, and settled in a handloom weaver's cottage above Myth-olmroyd, West Yorkshire, in 1970, where he's been trying to concoct a sort of linguistic music from the disparate mental tones of Lancashire, Cambridge, and Yorkshire.

239

David Herd is Professor of Modern Literature at the University of Kent. His collections of poetry include *All Just* (Carcanet, 2012), *Outwith* (Bookthug, 2012) and *Through* (Carcanet 2016). He is the author of *John Ashbery and American Poetry and Enthusiast! Essays on Modern American Literature*, and the editor of *Contemporary Olson*. His recent writings on the politics of movement have appeared in *Los Angeles Review of Books*, *PN Review*, *Parallax* and *Almost Island*.

Peter Hughes' recent poetry has been published by Shearsman Books, Reality Street Editions and Equipage.

John James resides in Cambridge and Puisserguier, Languedoc. His recent publications include (2014) *Songs In Midwinter For Franco* (Equipage, 2015) *Sabots* (Oystercatcher Press) and 'The Green Ray' in *No Prizes Issue 4*, Winter 2015-16, ed. Ian Heames. The text 'Affection' in the present volume first appeared in *Shearsman 97 & 98*, Winter 2013/ 2014, ed. Kelvin Corcoran.

Peter Larkin was for many years Philosophy & Literature Librarian at Warwick University and is now an Associate Fellow. As a poet he works in the area of innovative ecological writing with a special interest in woodlands and plantations. His poetry also attempts to explore the idea of scarcity in its phenomenological aspects. His collections of poetry include *Terrain Seed Scarcity* (Salt, 2001), *Lessways Least Scarce Among* (Shearsman Books, 2012), and *Give Forest Its Next Portent* (Shearsman, 2014). He contributed to *The Ground Aslant: an Anthology of Radical Landscape Poetry*, ed. Harriet Tarlo (Shearsman, 2011) and published a book of academic essays, *Wordsworth & Coleridge: Promising Losses* in 2012. *City Trappings (Housing Heath or Wood)*, a poetic investigation into the status of countryside contained within the Birmingham conurbation, is due out in 2016.

D.S. Marriott is the author of *The Bloods* (Shearsman Books, 2011) and *In Neuter*, (Equipage, 2013). He lives in Oakland, California.

Anthony Mellors is the author of *Late Modernist Poetics from Pound to Prynne* (Manchester University Press, 2005). Recent poetry includes *The Lewknor Turn* (Shearsman Books, 2013), *The Christmas Album* (vErIsImIlItUdE, 2015), and *Confessional Sonnets* (Aquifer, 2016).

Rod Mengham is the editor of Equipage, which has published J.H. Prynne's *Not-You* (1993), *Her Weasels Wild Returning* (1994), *For the Monogram* (1997) and *Biting the Air* (2003); he is also the author of several poetry publications, including *Chance of a Storm* (Carcanet, 2015).

Joseph Persad lives and works in London. His latest book of poems, *CONTENT or, Emblems in 2016* is available via Moot Press. He is the editor of Troposphere Editions, and their magazine *Sure Hope*.

Peter Riley was born into an environment of working people in the Manchester area in 1940 and now lives in retirement in Hebden Bridge, West Yorkshire, having previously lived in Cambridge for many years. He has been a teacher, bookseller, and several other things and is the author of some fifteen books of poetry, and two of prose concerning travel and music. His most recent books are *The Glacial Stairway* (Carcanet Press, 2011) and *Due North* (Shearsman Books, 2015), which is a book-length poem. He was awarded a Cholmondeley Prize in 2012 and *Due North* was shortlisted for both the Forward Prize for Best Collection, 2015, and the Roehampton Poetry Prize, 2016. He contributes reviews of new poetry to the website *The Fortnightly Review* regularly.

Gavin Selerie was born in London, where he still lives. His books include *Azimuth* (1984), *Roxy* (1996) and *Le Fanu's Ghost* (2006)—all long sequences with linked units. *Music's Duel: New and Selected Poems 1972-2008* was published by Shearsman Books in 2009. *Hariot Double*, a juxtaposition of jazz, science and other modes of discovery, has recently been issued by Five Seasons Press. He often collaborates with poet and graphic artist Alan Halsey, as in *Days of '49* (1999). Selerie's critical work includes studies of Charles Olson and Edward Dorn.

Iain Sinclair is preparing an endgame text called *The Last London*. Recent poems gathered as *Seeschlange* will be published by Equipage.

Simon Smith's last collection from Shearsman Books was *1178 W. Sunset Boulevard* in 2014. Since then *Salon Noir* (Equipage, 2016), *Navy* (vErIsImIllItUdE, 2016) and *Half a just like you* (Oystercatcher, 2015), a trilogy anchored in the landscape and politics of Ramsgate and Southern France have appeared. *More Flowers Than You Could Possibly Carry: Selected Poems 1989-2012*, edited by Barry Schwabsky, will appear in late 2016 from Shearsman Books. He lectures on Creative Writing at the University of Kent.

Michael Tencer lives in the City of New York. He maintains the bibliography of J.H. Prynne at http://prynnebibliography.org/ . His first book of poetry, a collaboration with Ken Fox, is *Frack the Deuteronomy* (Saskatchewan: Earthly City Productions, 2016).

Nigel Wheale's books include *Raw Skies* (Shearsman Books, 2005), *The Six Strides of Freyfaxi* (Oystercatcher, 2010), and *Writing and Society. Literacy, Print and Politics, Britain 1590–1660* (Routledge, 1999). He writes regularly for 'emag' (English and Media Centre) and *Fortnightly Review* (online).

John Wilkinson was an undergraduate at Jesus College, Cambridge from 1972-75 and a graduate student from 1975-79. A selected poems, *Schedule of Unrest*, was published by Salt in 2014, and a new collection, *Ghost Nets*, will be published by Omnidawn in 2016. He is a Professor in the Department of English at the University of Chicago.

Lightning Source UK Ltd.
Milton Keynes UK
UKOW02f0002200816

281079UK00003B/376/P